In Defence of Home Places

The Nature | History | Society series is devoted to the publication of high-quality scholarship in environmental history and allied fields. Its broad compass is signalled by its title: *nature* because it takes the natural world seriously; *history* because it aims to foster work that has temporal depth; and *society* because its essential concern is with the interface between nature and society, broadly conceived. The series is avowedly interdisciplinary and is open to the work of anthropologists, ecologists, historians, geographers, literary scholars, political scientists, sociologists, and others whose interests resonate with its mandate. It offers a timely outlet for lively, innovative, and well-written work on the interaction of people and nature through time in North America.

General Editor: Graeme Wynn, University of British Columbia

A list of titles in the series appears at the end of the book.

NATURE | HISTORY | SOCIETY
GENERAL EDITOR: GRAEME WYNN

In Defence
of Home Places

Environmental Activism
in Nova Scotia

MARK R. LEEMING

FOREWORD BY GRAEME WYNN

UBC Press • Vancouver • Toronto

26 25 24 23 22 21 20 19 18 17   5 4 3 2 1

Printed in Canada on FSC-certified ancient-forest-free paper
(100% post-consumer recycled) that is processed chlorine- and acid-free.

Library and Archives Canada Cataloguing in Publication

Leeming, Mark R., 1980-, author
    In defence of home places : environmental activism in Nova Scotia /
Mark R. Leeming.

(Nature, history, society)
Includes bibliographical references and index.
Issued in print and electronic formats.
ISBN 978-0-7748-3339-4 (hardcover). – ISBN 978-0-7748-3340-0 (pbk.). –
ISBN 978-0-7748-3341-7 (PDF). – ISBN 978-0-7748-3342-4 (EPUB). –
ISBN 978-0-7748-3343-1 (Kindle)

    1. Environmentalism – Nova Scotia – History – 20th century. 2. Nova Scotia
– Environmental conditions – History – 20th century. I. Title. II. Series: Nature,
history, society

GE199.C3L44 2017   333.720971609'045   C2017-900048-9
                                                      C2017-900049-7

Canadä

UBC Press gratefully acknowledges the financial support for our publishing program of the Government of Canada (through the Canada Book Fund), the Canada Council for the Arts, and the British Columbia Arts Council.

This book has been published with the help of a grant from the Canadian Federation for the Humanities and Social Sciences, through the Awards to Scholarly Publications Program, using funds provided by the Social Sciences and Humanities Research Council of Canada.

Printed and bound in Canada by Friesens
Set in Garamond by Artegraphica Design Co. Ltd.
Copy editor: Francis Chow
Cover designer: George Kirkpatrick
Cover image: *Spirit of the Deep Forest, Eigg Mountain – James River Wilderness Area* (detail), by Alice Reed

UBC Press
The University of British Columbia
2029 West Mall
Vancouver, BC V6T 1Z2
www.ubcpress.ca

Contents

Illustrations

Environmental Action and the Question of Scale

Graeme Wynn

IN 1972, WHEN RENÉ DUBOS urged people to think globally and act locally, he did more than coin the phrase that became the mantra of the environmental movement. By offering up a slogan that resonated with contemporary circumstances and tapped into a deep well of popular sentiment, he framed a strategy for environmental action and sowed the seeds of a paradox that continues to complicate understandings of environmentalism.[1]

Between Christmas Eve 1968 – when astronauts aboard Apollo 8 entered lunar orbit and photographed Earth rising above the moon – and early December 1972 – when the crew of Apollo 17 transmitted the breathtaking "Blue Marble" view of Earth back to Houston – new Earth-images reshaped perceptions of humankind's planetary home, and made it easier for people to "think globally." Breathtaking pictures of a colourful orb against a dark void seized the public imagination, and gave credence to the idea of "Spaceship Earth," a singular, self-contained, and finite crucible of all life.[2]

To those familiar with the absolute dependence of astronauts upon their capsule and its systems for reclaiming water, recycling air, and scrubbing carbon dioxide, the spaceship metaphor drove home the fragility and interconnectedness of earth systems. For devotees of wilderness, it seemed to buttress John Muir's observation that everything was "hitched to everything else in the Universe." Aldo Leopold's argument (in his land ethic essay) that individuals are "members of a community of interdependent parts" gained new resonance, reflected in the surging popularity of *A Sand County Almanac*. The metaphor also reinforced the message of Rachel Carson's

Silent Spring, about the interrelatedness of Nature's parts, and gave popular purchase to the arguments of such diverse books as Paul Ehrlich's *The Population Bomb* (1968) and Donnella Meadows and her co-authors' *The Limits to Growth* (1972). Indeed, the revealingly titled *Whole Earth Catalogue* – at its most popular during this four-year span – was so named because Stewart Brand, its founder, believed that the image of Earth from space would encourage people to recognize their shared destiny and adopt more environmentally sound modes of living. Thinking globally emphasized the importance of ecological entanglements, even as it minimized cultural differences and disparate histories.[3]

The injunction to act locally brought these entanglements home and encouraged a form of arithmetic calculus in which wise choices replicated across the intricate mosaic of earth-communities would cumulate to shape a better planetary future, and ecological degradation of the earth system would subtract from the quality of local life. At one level, then, Dubos's catchphrase seemed to substantiate the idea, given resonant expression by American essayist and novelist Scott Russell Sanders, that "we can live wisely in our chosen place only if we recognize its connections to the rest of the planet." At another, it gave power to the people by suggesting that planetary-scale concerns could be addressed at the grassroots level by individuals working alone or in small groups. At a third, it implied that local life and local politics would benefit from attention to global issues. There was much of value in all of this.[4]

But the call to local action had other, paradoxical ramifications as it chimed, in diverse ways, with growing contemporary sentiment. In one register, it reified those very differences in culture and history that thinking globally tended to erase, as it encouraged a heightened "sense of place." Expression of the importance and virtues of place attachment seemed to burst forth in these years, possibly as a backlash against pervasive modernist architecture and city planning and the increasingly peripatetic character of contemporary life. Indeed, the geographer Yi-fu Tuan claimed to have coined the word "topophilia" to refer to "the affective bond between people and place or setting" in a 1974 book that at least in part lamented the erosion of that bond.[5]

Certainly the idea that people and place were connected was in the air. In 1977, American environmental philosopher Paul Shepard suggested that it was impossible to know who you were if you did not know where you were. More pointedly, Wendell Berry attributed the mindless destruction of the American landscape to the nomadic character of the American experience, and Scott Russell Sanders proclaimed his desire to "become an inhabitant, one who knows and honors the land," as he lamented the "vagabond wind" that forever drove his restless compatriots to relocate. North of the forty-ninth parallel, journalist Robert Fulford and civic politician John Sewell teamed up on a pamphlet about Toronto with the title *A Sense of Time and Place.* Northrop Frye tracked a more academic but parallel path when he framed "Where is here?" as a fundamental Canadian question, and Neil Evernden did likewise when he concluded that individuals did not exist without context, which was to say as "a component of place, defined by place." Similarly, Canadian historians embraced local difference when they seized upon the concept of "limited identities" as a means to understand the country.[6]

In another sense, the advice to act locally sanctified immediate experience, and entrenched what Ursula Heise and others call an "ethic of proximity" that valued intimate, bodily, sensory engagements with nature over more abstract forms of understanding (that were surely important to thinking on a global scale). In this vein, Norwegian philosopher Arne Naess, founder and figurehead of the deep ecology movement, pronounced that "the nearer has priority over the more remote – in space, time, culture, species." Such sentiments bled easily into broader suspicions, increasingly evident in the 1960s and 1970s, of "things-at-a-distance," of the impersonal character of urban and industrial life, and of modernity in general, even as they supplied oxygen to back-to-the land movements, the counterculture, the embrace of Indigenous ecological wisdom, and enthusiasm for the organization of society on bioregionalist principles. Later they seemed to fit easily with "postmodern" critiques of totalizing grand narratives and claims for the importance of local and "situated" knowledge. In sum, time and circumstances turned a forward-looking, four-word coinage emphasizing the links between everyday actions and global environmental circumstances against itself, to buttress "a general critique of modern socio-political structures" and resuscitate a traditional "sense of place."[7]

Mark Leeming carries us into the heart of this complex, conflicted intellectual terrain with his detailed examination of two decades of environmental activism in Nova Scotia. His astutely yet provocatively titled book, *In Defence of Home Places,* encourages us to think anew about the ways in which the tensions between local and global (and indeed among local, regional, and national) scales, and between traditional and modern perspectives, all seemingly endemic to environmentalism, played out on Canadian ground from the 1960s to the 1980s. From the outset, Leeming makes clear that his story turns on the "recognition and consequences of ideological differences within the environmental movement of a modern country" (p. 3) and that he develops it by considering three major controversies – over nuclear power, the use of chemicals in forestry, and uranium mining – in a single province. He also adumbrates his conclusions in his first paragraph: environmentalists struggled among themselves to find common ground on each of these issues (and by implication the basic questions of their cause). This divided the movement into modernist and non-modernist camps that were readily identifiable, by 1985, as mainstream and fringe players in the continuing drama of local and provincial environmental politics.

Leeming's approach is intriguing. It is focused resolutely on a single province, and more particularly on specific struggles and struggle sites within it. The three issues at the centre of these struggles have been controversial in many jurisdictions and locales, but Nova Scotia is, of course, a place *sui generis*. Relatively small in area (55,284 square kilometres) and population (almost 790,000 in 1971 and 922,000 in 2011), it remained substantially rural through the third quarter of the twentieth century. For thirty years after 1956, successive censuses showed the urban fraction of the province's population fluctuating between 54 and 58 percent, while that of Canada as a whole climbed from 70 to 76 percent. Although Halifax expanded steadily after 1961, most of Nova Scotia has grappled with the consequences of slow economic growth. Fewer and fewer people under the age of eighteen, and increasing longevity, pushed the median age of the provincial population upward.

By the middle years of the twentieth century, when per capita incomes in the Atlantic region were less than two-thirds of the national average, the region had endured a long history of boom-and-bust engagements with resource and industrial development. Nineteenth-century forest and fishing economies were infamously volatile. Later in that century, the economic future of the Maritime provinces seemed bright. With year-round rail access to the interior of the continent and an established presence in seaborne commerce, Nova Scotia and New Brunswick prospered from the development of cotton mills and sugar refineries converting imported raw materials into consumer goods for citizens of the new Dominion.[8] Rich sources of coal and ready access to iron ore supplies also gave rise to a major steel industry, and encouraged celebration of "The Industrial Ascendancy of Nova Scotia" – evidenced, in the words of a 1913 promotional booklet, by the province's "1480 manufacturing establishments, paying out $11,000,000 yearly to 28,000 employees."[9] But prosperity, always unevenly distributed, exacted its toll, as it changed accustomed terms and conditions of labour, and it largely evaporated after 1918 when changing circumstances undercut the industrial base developed in the preceding four decades.[10]

Clearly a laggard rather than a leader in the growth of national manufacturing capacity since the 1920s (or a "have-not" province, in the parlance of Canada's post–Second World War efforts to combat regional disparities), Nova Scotia was the focus – along with its Atlantic provincial neighbours – of several economic development or regional economic expansion initiatives in the 1960s and subsequent decades.[11] Among these were the provincial government's Industrial Estates Limited (IEL), given a mandate in 1957 to build industrial parks and attract new investment, and the federal Department of Regional Economic Expansion (DREE), established in 1969. Reflecting a commitment to the idea that Atlantic Canadians should have opportunities to prosper in their home provinces, the DREE tailored its programs to encourage entrepreneurs and industrialists to locate new operations in centres designated as "growth poles" within the region.[12]

Bold as many of them were, these initiatives had mixed success. Some (such as the Come By Chance oil refinery in Newfoundland and the Bricklin car factory in Saint John, New Brunswick) were notoriously ill-fated.[13] Others such as resettlement schemes in Newfoundland and the Comprehensive Development Plan calling for a massive transformation of agriculture, the diversification of manufacturing, and the development of tourism in Prince Edward Island were disruptive of older ways and hugely controversial.[14] Yet gains were made, at least in the terms defined by governments: IEL brought Swedish forestry giant Stora Kopparberg to Cape Breton, Swedish car manufacturer Volvo to Dartmouth, and French tire manufacturer Michelin to Granton, Bridgeport, and Waterville in Nova Scotia. Redistribution payments and various forms of federal government intervention in the economy helped to bring per capita incomes in the region closer to national standards (they now stand at about four-fifths of the latter mark). By definition, however, efforts to modernize regional economies spell change for regional communities, and such transformations are rarely straightforward.

This, in a nutshell, is where Leeming's story begins. In his telling, government- and industry-led efforts to plant the seeds of a modern economy in areas well known and valued by long-term and essentially conservative rural residents were the catalysts of environmental activism in the province. Because these new development projects threatened to remake particular landscapes in one way or another, and because they also laid siege, more or less, to traditional lifestyles and livelihoods, they were

almost bound to spawn opposition. Following the pattern set in Pictou
County, after the provincial government lured a kraft pulp mill to
Abercrombie Point – creating conditions for Scott Paper to flourish, but
threatening the lobster fishery and killing Boat Harbour, into which the
mill discharged effluent – the sense of personal harm created by the damming of rivers, the pollution of the ocean, or the despoliation of local
ecologies was fanned time and again by industry denials and dismissive
government responses, to produce an upsurge of environmental activism
across the province. Feeling vulnerable in the face of change, Nova Scotia
activists found both economic and emotional reasons to rise in defence of
local places. Yet, it is important to recognize, neither they nor their views
were entirely parochial: television, radio, newspapers, books, immigrants,
and personal connections brought the wider tide of rising concern about
environmental issues into the province and the region. Many heard the
message of *Silent Spring;* CBC television alerted viewers across the network
to the perils of pollution with "The Air of Death," broadcast in October
1967; the environment ministers of the three Maritime provinces sponsored anti-litter and anti-pollution campaigns in the late 1960s and early
1970s; and the government of Prince Edward Island stepped back from
the Comprehensive Development Plan under the influence of ideas developed by E.F. Schumacher and George McRobie.[15]

Diffuse, scattered groups with a range of local environmental concerns
came together in the early 1970s when it appeared that the Nova Scotia
government was negotiating the development of a large nuclear power
generating plant in the far south of the province to supply markets in the
northeastern United States. Opposition aligned on several axes: nuclear
power was linked to nuclear war; Nova Scotians would bear the risks and
Americans reap the benefits; soft energy solutions were better than the
"hard [nuclear] energy path"; the capitalist consumer development that
nuclear generators would facilitate should be abandoned in favour of a
"conserver society"; the government was being less than clear and trans-
parent about its intentions. Tracing these debates in some detail, Leeming
finds that arguments for smaller-scale, non-nuclear solutions and local
economic autonomy were advanced most forcefully by citizens concerned
about the personal risks associated with living near proposed nuclear plants,
and that their commitments were scaled upward as small rural activist
groups joined forces. In time, opposition in Nova Scotia coalesced with
similar hostility to nuclear development in New Brunswick under the
banner of the Maritime Energy Coalition (deliberately named to echo the
acronym of the proposed regional nuclear power utility, the Maritime

Energy Corporation). But as political commitments to nuclear power development weakened after the Three Mile Island disaster in Pennsylvania,
opposition arguments also shifted. Safety concerns and the hope of developing economically viable alternative energy systems trumped calls to
remake society.

Carrying this story forward through convoluted battles over the environmental effects of insecticide and herbicide spraying and uranium mining
in the decade or so after 1976, Leeming discerns growing resistance to environmentalist pressures from government and industry, and increasing
fragmentation among environmental campaigners. To gain a broad understanding of the politics and protests of this period, one might usefully
think of the spraying and mining episodes as engagements in a war fought
on many fronts, by coalitions of interest deploying several units using
different forms of ordnance and operating at a range of scales.

Beleaguered environmentalists sought (if we might borrow and adapt a
phrase from an earlier environmental protest elsewhere) to "secure their
nook of Nova Scotia ground from rash assault."[16] "Industry" – an amorphous coalition of interests – and their allies in government generally stood
shoulder to shoulder in support of economic expansion, which focused
their calculus of concern on measures such as jobs and profits. Still, they
sometimes disagreed over how to proceed, as advisers and strategists (for
example, accountants and trained foresters) preferred different forms of
action. Both sides found backing, of one sort or another, from beyond the
provincial battle zone, and engaged in "deliberate, systematic attempt[s]
to shape perceptions, manipulate cognitions, and direct behavior" to garner
assistance and further their cause.[17]

Each side struggled over the question of where and how best to engage
the other. Company executives sometimes favoured threats, bluster, and
action. Some government officials (particularly at the federal level) believed
that environmentalists might be "turned" or brought to accede to government agendas by the promise of influence; others (particularly provincial
actors) wished no truck or trade with their opponents and preferred
confrontation or judicial and quasi-judicial fora (the courts and Royal
Commissions) to resolve differences. Initially, environmentalists were
inclined to deploy the weapons of the weak – protests, resistance, and
the power of public pressure – to sway popular opinion and influence
politicians.[18] Over time, however, some adopted the view that bureaucratic
minds (and policies) were more likely to be changed by collaboration than
by resistance. Later, for reasons that Leeming details and that included a
growing conviction that scientific argument would win the day and legal

precedent would secure the gains, environmental campaigners were drawn into the judicial arena.

Commission hearings and court proceedings are costly enterprises, and they are conducted according to formal rules of evidence and proof. They also clearly serve to legitimize the state, and tend in long-running cases such as the "herbicide trial" to sap the resources of participants.[19] Insofar as the decision to go to court over the spraying of 2,4-D and 2,4,5-T drew Nova Scotia environmentalists into "a battle with the international pesticide industry" (p. 86), it was a tactic fraught with difficulty; the environmentalists' need for financial support brought disparate groups together to raise money but it also diverted their energies from other actions. And insofar as the presiding judge in the trial eschewed the precautionary principle and insisted on a nigh-impossible standard of scientific proof of harm from the use of herbicide, it was a doomed strategy.

When a Royal Commission on Uranium Mining was established in 1981, with the conservative Judge Robert McCleave at its head, his commitment to an increasingly scientific and legalistic three-stage inquiry seemed designed to wear down environmental protest. As things turned out, vigorous anti-uranium presentations emphasizing the "dangers of radiation exposure, the impossibility of safe tailings disposal, and the inseparability of nuclear energy and nuclear weapons" (pp. 134–35) wore down the commissioner during the first stage of hearings; the inquiry was suspended, and did not report until 1985. Then the commissioner proposed a five-year moratorium on uranium mining, even as he repudiated the claims of the "perverse" leftists who had spoken so forcefully before him.

Yet this was a divisive, if not pyrrhic, victory for the environmental movement in Nova Scotia. When the 1985 report was endorsed by environmental groups whose members had remained on the margins through the first phase of the inquiry, avoiding entanglement in what they described in unguarded moments as "side shows" mounted by "sleazy fanatics," it became impossible to paper over a division that had been developing for years. Lamenting that colleagues who chose to participate in and endorse official systems of decision making were more wedded to the process than the cause, grassroots environmentalists disparaged them as politically naive, "establishment bound" people dependent on government and corporate funding. So the lines between rural place-oriented and urban ecomodernist groups deepened. The former hewed to the long-standing environmentalist conviction that "only political pressure from large numbers of citizens could overcome the established unity of political and industrial interests that the official system was designed to uphold" (p. 134). They believed that "playing the game" thwarted the growth of political consciousness by suggesting that problems were well in hand and capable of bureaucratic solution. The latter held "a modern conception of economic development and risk assessment that devalued the personal experience of place and of home, discounted the inequity of metropolitanism, and preserved the privilege of expertise" (p. 136). Through the rest of the century, Nova Scotia environmentalists remained divided between those inclined to marry deep ecological positions with social justice concerns and those who preferred bureaucratically oriented "market" solutions to environmental issues.

"Think globally, act locally." The stories that Mark Leeming details in the pages that follow both complicate this simple injunction and demonstrate that there is no straightforward history of environmentalism in Nova Scotia or, by extension, any place else on the globe. They remind us that, at base, environmentalism is a resistance movement. Broadly, it casts itself in opposition to the despoliation of particular places (be that despoliation the pollution of a lake, the destruction of a view, or the clearcutting of a forested hillslope); the misuse of common property resources such as air and water or endangered species (think of campaigns against acid rain and whaling); and the insatiable expansionary logic of late capitalism and its close ally and political instrument, the modern state.

Engagement on such diverse fronts encourages, even requires, widely different strategies. Blockades and demonstrations in particular places can stop logging trucks or prevent the quarrying of a hillside (at least temporarily); they can also bring local acts of environmental plunder to global attention (think Greenpeace and the anti-sealing campaign). Not all environmental concerns are "end-of-pipe" ills (where harm occurs in a specific locale) or consequences of specific actions; still, protests against pillage of the commons, or contesting the global-scale consequences of particular behaviours, can have value, and they invariably take place someplace (here the best example may be the demonstration organized by 350.org outside the White House in Washington, DC, to oppose construction of the Keystone XL pipeline because of its implications for global climate change). For all that, blockades and protests are not always possible or effective – as environmentalists in British Columbia discovered when logging moved into remote areas of the mid-coast, where the media coverage so essential to garnering attention and support for any opposition was limited by difficulties of access. In such circumstances, other strategies, including "market campaigns" aimed at reducing corporate profits and tarnishing reputations by persuading consumers not to purchase the product, are likely to make more sense and have greater impact.[20]

Faced with the challenges of opposition, environmentalists also divide, legitimately, on how best to achieve their ends. We can think of their choices schematically. At one end of a spectrum of possibilities lies rejection of capitalism and a trenchant, unflinching oppositional stance. At the other, there is acknowledgment of the enormous power of politics and the marketplace and the conviction that gains can be made by regulation or by nudging the market this way or that to ameliorate its environmental effects. Intermediate positions abound, and members of those groups at the centre of Leeming's narrative occupied several of them. Those whom he characterizes as ecomodernists arrayed themselves towards the political-market end of the spectrum, convinced of the value of working within the corridors of legislative power to facilitate negotiations among environmental, industry, and state interests to limit environmental harm through regulation. Others, Leeming's "non-modernists," who resisted both transformation of their lands and lives and threats to their person, found themselves more comfortable towards the other end of this scale.

But to categorize is to generalize, and it is as well to remember that such schematic descriptions usually shrink or eclipse the range of motivations and convictions that drive individual behaviour, even as they tend to limit recognition of the ways in which individual and group commitments shift with changing circumstances. To flesh out this complexity, let us consider briefly three important environmental activists who appear in Leeming's discussions of the Nova Scotia campaigns against nuclear power and uranium mining, encompassing the span of their activist careers beyond the issues dealt with in these pages. Judy Davis (1951–2010) and David Orton (1934–2011) were friends and fellow environmental crusaders with strong attachments to rural Nova Scotia. Davis, said her obituary, died of cancer and "a broken heart, the latter caused by witnessing the continued destruction of the ecology of the planet through human exploitation, economic greed and war."[21] Orton, who habitually signed off his correspondence with "For the Earth," also succumbed to cancer after a brief illness. Susan Holtz, an American who had recently arrived in the province in 1972, was a member of the Halifax Society of Friends (Quakers) monthly meeting and rose to prominence through her engagement with the nuclear power issue.

Judy Davis was a radical activist who "never stopped fighting for environmental and social justice." Born in Pictou County, she lived for almost thirty years in a small log house on a ten-acre plot five miles from the village of Tatamagouche in Colchester County, where she came to understand "the importance of being rooted 'in place' to become an Earth defender."

Through her commitment to helping those less fortunate, and her in-clination to direct action, she had what many judged to be "a major impact on environmental, social justice, feminist, and workers' struggles in Nova Scotia." She was not, though, a "solidarity with Latin America" type of person," but someone who was firmly committed to "the human and later non-human, community" of which she was a part. Most of her organizing was done at the local scale.[22]

David Orton was a voracious reader, a prolific writer, a "deep green" activist, and an important Canadian thinker who brought together en-vironmental ethics and social justice concerns. His roots took time to strike in Nova Scotia soil. Born in Britain, he emigrated to Canada in 1957 to avoid compulsory national military service, after an apprenticeship in the Portsmouth dockyard, a year in the Naval Architecture program at Durham University, and discharge from the Royal Army Educational Core after nine months of service. After taking a BA degree from Sir George Williams University in Montreal in 1963, Orton completed an MA in Sociology at the New School for Social Research in New York and was admitted to the PhD program there. In 1967, his dissertation unfinished, he returned to teach at Sir George Williams University. Active in the Movement for Socialist Liberation (in which Andre Gunder Frank, the left Latin American economist was involved) and the "Internationalists" (precursors of the Marxist-Leninist faction of the Communist Party of Canada), Orton ruffled the feathers of colleagues and administrators during a tumultuous time in the university.[23]

When university administrators chose not to renew Orton's teaching contract, he threw himself into political organizing, ran unsuccessfully for federal office, was arrested at a political rally in Toronto and imprisoned, and worked on the Montreal waterfront. In 1977, he moved with his family to a temporary job in a salmon cannery on Haida Gwaii, in British Columbia. There contact with the Haida, engagement with the emerging issues surrounding the protection of South Moresby Island, and a kayak trip into that area persuaded him to focus his organizing work on environ-mental issues rather than social justice politics. This he did for two years in Victoria, before moving to Halifax in 1979. In Nova Scotia, Orton engaged a number of environmental issues, not all of them obviously local. In the 1980s, he spoke out against acid rain, the Atlantic seal hunt, pulp-wood forestry practices, and uranium in well water, even as he penned a blistering indictment of Judge McCleave and the uranium inquiry on behalf of the Socialist Environmental Protection and Occupational Health Group in October 1982.[24] Two years later, he moved with his partner and infant daughter to a "130-acre hill farm at the end of a dirt road through a forest" in Pictou County, where wood was the only source of heat.[25] At much the same time, Orton became aware of Arne Naess's arguments for deep ecology, which convinced him of "the importance of moving beyond the human-centered values (anthropocentrism) of the anarchist, social democratic, communist, and socialist traditions."[26]

Through the rest of his days, Orton strove to meld his social justice and deep ecological commitments. Rejecting Naess's position that the peace, social justice, and ecology movements should remain separate even as they stood beneath a Green movement banner, Orton became a leading proponent of "Left Biocentrism." Articulating this position through collaboration and engagement with like-minded individuals on a website established in 1988, Orton adopted the view "that the Earth belongs to no one and should be a non-privatized Commons." In furtherance of this basic ecocentric commitment, he produced a remarkable series of reflections on both specific environmental conflicts and more general philosophical issues confronting environmentalists. Published on the "Green Web" and in a wide array of publications (including *Canadian Dimension,* to which he contributed twenty-seven articles, reviews, and comments between 1989 and 2009), this impressive oeuvre defies succinct summary.[27]

In broad terms, however, Orton's written contributions clearly put Earth first and "express solidarity with all life"; they also oppose economic growth and consumerism, advocate voluntary simplicity, and espouse a bioregional rather than a global or strictly local focus, even as they call for a global redistribution of wealth. Equally clear is Orton's insistence on the importance of an environmentalism independent of government or corporate support or influence. But theory and praxis are not always easily aligned. Owning property and insisting that the earth should be a commons was one contradiction that Orton addressed by pointing out that capitalist society offered few alternatives beyond the short-term option of using "private property 'laws' to buy one's own place ... [for those who would further] conservation and wildlife preservation." He also saw ownership of his land as a necessary concession for its stewardship, and thus realization of the goal of "being the change you want to see in others and the world." Similarly, Orton refused to join the government-funded Canadian Environmental Network (CEN) or any of its constituent organizations, although he shared concerns with, and worked alongside, many of those who did. In his view, CEN accepted and legitimized industrial capitalist society, just as the Green Party (towards which he inclined for want of an effective alternative) was ultimately "in the business of putting forward fudge and 'market' or soothing eco-capitalist positions, which do not call industrial capitalism into question or bring about the needed fundamental shift in societal consciousness."[28]

Orton recognized that many Nova Scotians involved in environmental issues were rural dwellers responding to "'not in my backyard' situations." Judy Davis, he observed, was always "prepared to take on those in her immediate environment who wanted to spray biocides on nearby forest lands, blow up beaver dams down her gravel road because of someone's "flooding" complaint, or run a snowmobile trail in front of her house." Although she developed, through her association with Orton and others a sense of "fit" with deep ecology, "this self-awareness came from her own life experiences ... [not] from reading philosophy books or some kind of intellectual conversion." She joined protests against racism in all parts of Nova Scotia and supported Aboriginal issues (including the Mohawk in the 1990 Oka dispute) across the country. Although she stood (unsuccessfully) as a candidate for federal and provincial Green parties in the first decade of the millennium, her métier lay in organizing events such as a funeral procession and memorial service for the trees and the non-human inhabitants of the softwood forest being turned to woodchips at Spiddle Hill in Colchester County, and in rallying crowds with her musicianship. Orton admired such efforts and joined several of them. But wedded as he was to deep ecology's fundamental claim "that major ecological problems cannot be resolved within the existing capitalist or socialist industrial economic system," he found these efforts insufficient because they lacked the staying power to produce regime change. Local action could not achieve the required socio-political revolution. Anxious for transformation, he was also and often scathing of those pragmatists who sought improvement by tinkering with the industrial capitalist system. Such approaches he regarded as misguided; those who pursued them were deluded "pollyannas."[29]

Susan Holtz was one of those with whom Orton crossed swords. Asked to provide guidance to the Halifax Friends meeting on the issue of nuclear power development in 1972, she concluded, as Leeming points out in Chapter 2, that it would be an unnecessary spur to wasteful consumption. Taking an intellectual rather than a categorically oppositional stance towards the nuclear challenge, she quickly forged a nationwide coalition of people and groups opposed to nuclear power that only belatedly developed connections with other campaigners in Nova Scotia. Reflecting emerging ideas about the desirability of developing a conserver society and adopting what American environmental scientist Amory Lovins termed a "soft energy path," Holtz and a cluster of like-minded associates joined Nova

Scotia's Ecology Action Centre and operated under that group's banner
from 1975 onward. There they worked assiduously to assess the risks of
nuclear power and promote research into alternative energy technologies.
By the end of the decade, much of this work was being funded by government contracts: in 1980–81, Holtz was working in conjunction with
sixteen Nova Scotia municipalities seeking efficiencies in energy management (funded by the Nova Scotia Department of Mines and Energy);
updating an earlier study of soft energy paths under a contract with the
federal Department of Energy, Mines and Resources (arranged by Friends
of the Earth); investigating legal issues surrounding "solar rights"; and
assessing the potential for energy generation from waste biomass (the latter
two contracts funded by the Law Foundation and the Technical University of Nova Scotia).[30] Holtz saw herself as a conciliator, someone who
could serve as a bridge between radical environmentalists and the decision
makers who held the levers of political and economic power.[31]

In that vein, and though staunchly opposed to uranium mining, she
agreed (as Leeming notes) to comment on draft guidelines for mining
exploration prepared by Jack Garnett, assistant deputy minister in the Department of Mines and Energy. When Garnett subsequently claimed that
his guidelines had the approval of environmental groups, Orton made
clear his opposition to Holtz's actions and resigned from the uranium
subcommittee of the Ecology Action Centre. Here, as more generally, he
had no time for "shallow ecologists" (Leeming's "moderns") who "worked
the system" and accepted its rewards without seriously threatening its
legitimacy.

In the end, Davis, Orton, and Holtz were all local activists to some
degree. They made environmental concerns in Nova Scotia, or particular
places within it, a major focus of their attention. But the scale, purpose,
and tenor of their environmental commitments varied, and they differed
over the means most likely to be effective in achieving the ends that they
desired. Davis perhaps best exemplifies the resolute defender of particular
places against specific threats. Holtz was no less antagonistic towards
nuclear power and uranium mining than others, and was taken aback by
Orton's trenchant criticism of her efforts to deflect energy development
away from the hard path it constituted, considering it a gratuitous attack
delivered in a "spiteful and unscrupulous" way (p. 114). Orton, for his part,
was increasingly critical of the industrial-capitalist system. Although he
was deeply attached to his 130 acres of Pictou County soil, he denied the
propriety of his ownership, and addressed himself (particularly through

the medium of the Green Web started in 1988) to the radical, thorough-going transformation of human-nature relations.

Together, these vignettes illustrate the conundrums facing late-twentieth- and early-twenty-first-century environmentalism. Acting locally has its merits but the calculus of addition rarely translates into global gains. Standing at barricades in defence of home places might save this patch of forest or that mountainside from exploitation, but such local victories cannot stay the juggernaut of economic development and win the battle. Confrontations at struggle sites translate into a war of attrition. Rebuffed here, industry moves on to pursue its goals there; environmentalists rally anew to blockade again; the battle runs its course through injunctions, arrests, and acrimony, as the case may be; then the cycle is repeated. Environmentalists rarely have the time, numbers, and resources to exhaust the companies' drive to continue. Combatting the growth imperatives of industrial-capitalist society requires other tactics. Time and again, environmentalists have divided – just as Holtz and Orton did – over what those tactics should be. Almost half a century ago, Greenpeace espoused non-violent environmental action and used both spectacular protest and market boycotts to protect particular species and specific places or ecologies; sometime Greenpeace member Paul Watson came to favour more direct action: "holding up protest signs, taking pictures and 'bearing witness' while whales are getting killed in front of you doesn't achieve anything at all," he said. Meanwhile, others elsewhere in Canada strove to establish regulations to improve air quality, water and waste management, land-use planning, natural resource extraction, and energy policy.[32]

Should environmentalists work within the industrial-capitalist system to limit and ameliorate exploitation and despoliation of the earth, or should they endeavour to overthrow that system entirely? Are these really alternatives? Although Susan Holtz and David Orton divided bitterly when she opted for the former course and he espoused the latter, one has to wonder whether these approaches are mutually exclusive. Might urgent short-term actions – whether they be peaceful demonstrations like that organized by Judy Davis on Spiddle Hill or dangerous clashes of whaling and protest vessels on the high seas engineered by the Sea Shepherd Society – help shift policy horizons and achieve long-term goals of regime change, by raising awareness of the issues and persuading more and more people of the need to act? Or are they likely to have the opposite effect, because conflict can be dysfunctional? Is it possible, in our current circumstances, to achieve the kind of dramatic regime change that Orton sought in time to address the environmental challenges we face? Or does our best hope lie in developing a pluralistic decision-making environment in which conflict is only part of a conversation that encompasses the possibility of working to change things from within? The questions remain – and they turn on the imponderable intersection of scale and process. Surely moving the environmental agenda forward is an art, in which public awareness, appropriate regulation, and improved technology are equal parts of the story.

In the second decade of the third millennium, many of our most pressing environmental problems have diffuse and difficult-to-address origins; although we may experience them "at home," they are generated at some remove, often by persons who (or organizations that) reject responsibility for them, as they stand beyond the reach of local action and territorially bound legal and political systems. In other, more formal words, many of these challenges are transgenerational products of "extraterritorial forces." Thinking about the consequences of this in relation to the problem of climate change, Harald Welzer echoes Michael Maniates's ironic, and iconic, formulation – "Plant a Tree, Buy a Bike, Save the World?" – in describing "individualist strategies" as tranquilizers that soothe anxiety but achieve little. He also finds little prospect of effective political responses at the international level, given the time it takes for political processes to run their course. So he argues for action at an intermediate scale, between the local and the global.[33]

All of this might prompt readers to wonder whether the strong place attachment that Leeming identifies among "non-modernists" remains as vital and as valuable to effective environmental commitment as once it was. If the increasing connectedness of modern-day societies is spawning relatively placeless cultures, then – it might seem logical to argue – the strong sense of place-emphasis that led people to act in defence of local nature in the 1970s may consign environmentalism to irrelevance in the twenty-first century. In this vein, Ursula Heise insists that modern-day environmentalism needs to move beyond efforts to recuperate "a sense of place," to "foster an understanding of how a wide variety of both natural and cultural places and processes are connected and shape each other around the world, and how human impact affects and changes this connectedness."[34]

Others have urged the importance of developing a "progressive" sense of place, one that is "not self-enclosing and defensive, but outward-looking," and adapted to the conditions of postmodernity, in which "space appears to shrink to a 'global village' of telecommunications and a 'spaceship earth' of economic and ecological interdependencies ... and time horizons shorten to the point where the present is all there is."[35] After all, even David Orton acknowledged that although "our place is back-to-the-land ... we also have a whole computer network based there, which means we can communicate around the world."[36]

Should we, then, abandon our idea of places "as areas with boundaries around" them, and imagine them, instead, "as articulated moments in networks of social relations and understandings," with most of those relations and understandings "constructed on a far larger scale than ... the place itself"? Geographer Doreen Massey has argued this case, which requires, in Tim Cresswell's words, a shift from thinking about "place vertically – as rooted in time immemorial – to thinking of it horizontally, as produced relationally through its connections."[37] In this recalibration, the forces of globalization have reframed places; they are no longer locales buffeted by remote forces or the locus of romanticized escapism, but dynamic settings shaped by new philosophies, new forms of engagement, and new synergies between ideas and action at local and global scales.

Leeming complicates this argument by demonstrating that the past was less foreign than such narratives imagine. "Local" communities have long been responding to the actions – be they factory closures or toxic spills – of global scale political-economic-financial powers. They have had to assume responsibility for problems they have not created, and they have grappled with the uneven distribution of power and influence. Leeming's home-place defenders thought globally and acted locally, even as they worked at national and global scales to maintain particular conceptions of their localities. Risk assessments differed, and some communities were divided by conflicting opinions about how best to deal with them; in others, local responses helped build trust, engagement, resilience, and power. Peoples' struggles to secure what they held dear were moulded by individuals deeply committed to particular settings and shaped by local circumstances, but they turned, in the end, on emergent global concerns about the environment. Although they invoked the past, they were oriented to the future. By detailing the often bitter struggle between "the place-loving soul" of the environmental movement on the one hand and "the temptations of a placeless modernity" on the other, *In Defence of Home Places* enriches our understanding of politics and society in Nova Scotia, provides a valuable exegesis of the tangle of relations that brought the state, industry, and environmental activists into conflict and collaboration, and illuminates the strength of local environmentalists' resistance to modernity's "strategy of conceptual encompassment" (pp. 149–50).

Acknowledgments

I WOULD LIKE TO express my appreciation and gratitude to Dr. Claire Campbell, for her good humour, patient guidance, and sound advice during the research that led to the publication of this book. I would also like to thank Drs. Robert Summerby-Murray, Jerry Bannister, Alan MacEachern, Dean Bavington, and John Reid, as well as the two anonymous reviewers, for their helpful criticism and friendly advice. Similarly, I want to declare my gratitude to Valerie Peck at the office of the Department of History at Dalhousie University and to Randy Schmidt, Ann Macklem, and Dr. Graeme Wynn at UBC Press. I also wish to acknowledge the support of Dalhousie University and the Social Sciences and Humanities Research Council of Canada. Finally, my wife, Kazue, deserves and has my deepest gratitude for her wholehearted support of my work. She is more responsible than she knows for my being able to complete this book, and it is dedicated to her.

Abbreviations

2,4-D	2,4-dichlorophenoxyacetic acid
2,4,5-T	2,4,5-trichlorophenoxyacetic acid
AECB	Atomic Energy Control Board
AECL	Atomic Energy of Canada Limited
APES	Association for the Preservation of the Eastern Shore
BBPCC	Bedford Basin Pollution Control Committee
Btk	*Bacillus thuringiensis kurstaki*
CANDU	Canadian Deuterium-Uranium reactor
CAP	Coalition Against Pesticides (Cape Breton)
CAPE	Citizen Action to Protect the Environment
CARE	Citizens Against a Radioactive Environment
CAUM	Citizens Against Uranium Mining
CBLAS	Cape Breton Landowners Against the Spray
CCCC	Concerned Citizens of Cumberland County
CCNR	Canadian Coalition for Nuclear Responsibility
CEAC	Canadian Environmental Advisory Council
CEN	Canadian Environmental Network
CEPA	Chaleur Environmental Protection Association
CFS	Canadian Forestry Service
COPE	Communities Organized to Protect the Environment
CSG	Conserver Society Group
DDT	dichlorodiphenyltrichloroethane
DLF	Department of Lands and Forests (Nova Scotia)

DOA	Department of Agriculture (Nova Scotia)
DOE	Department of Environment (Nova Scotia)
EAC	Ecology Action Centre
ECC	Environmental Control Council
EMR	Energy, Mines and Resources
ENGO	environmental non-governmental organization
FACT	Fundy Area Concern for Tomorrow
FOE	Friends of the Earth (Canada)
FON	Friends of Nature
HFN	Halifax Field Naturalists
HFS	Herbicide Fund Society
IEL	Industrial Estates Limited
JAG	Joint Action Group
KASE	Kings Association to Save the Environment
LIP	Local Initiatives Program
LWR	light-water reactor
MEC	Maritime Energy Coalition
MEC	Maritime Energy Corporation
MOVE	Movement for Citizens' Voice and Action
NBEPC	New Brunswick Electric Power Corporation
NIMBY	Not In My Back Yard
NPSG	Nuclear Power Study Group
NSBS	Nova Scotia Bird Society
NSEA	Nova Scotia Environment Alliance
NSEW	North Shore Environment Web
NSFI	Nova Scotia Forest Industries
NSLPC	Nova Scotia Light and Power Company
NSPC	Nova Scotia Power Corporation
NSPCC	Northumberland Strait Pollution Control Committee
NSRC	Nova Scotia Resources Council
NSRF	Nova Scotia Research Foundation
NSSA	Nova Scotia Salmon Association
OFY	Opportunities for Youth
OPEC	Organization of the Petroleum Exporting Countries
PAN	Pesticide Action Network
PCAC	Purcell's Cove Action Committee
PEP	People for Environmental Protection
RESCUE	Residents Enlisted to Save Communities from Uranium Exploration

SCC	Science Council of Canada
SEP	soft energy path
SEPOHG	Socialist Environmental Protection and Occupational Health Group
SKMS	Save Kelly's Mountain Society
SSEPA	South Shore Environmental Protection Association
TCDD	tetrachlorodibenzodioxin
VOW	Voice of Women for Peace

In Defence of Home Places

Introduction

In Defence of Home Places traces the origins and development of environmental activism in Nova Scotia from the 1960s through the 1980s. At the core, it is about the recognition and consequences of ideological differences within the environmental movement of a modern country. This book considers three major controversies that shaped the environmental movement through the late 1980s and into the present day: nuclear power, chemical forestry, and uranium mining. Time and again, environmental activists confronting these issues struggled to negotiate differences of opinion on the basic questions of environmentalism: the causes of environmental problems, the proper relationship of humanity to the non-human world, and the actions most likely to achieve that relationship. By 1985, Nova Scotian environmentalists riven by these differences had divided their movement into mainstream and fringe environmentalisms, with quite different answers to the major questions before them.

Nova Scotian environmental activists mirrored their counterparts in other modern societies in disagreeing fundamentally over the basic structures of those societies. "Ecological modernists" believed that (most) environmental problems were unintended and technologically remediable side-effects of otherwise desirable industrial processes, and were inclined to address them through collaboration with the state and industry. They did not question modern society's commitment to its fundamental principles, including large-scale industry, economic growth, and the acceptance of science as the sole legitimate form of knowledge. "Non-modernists," meanwhile, viewed environmental problems as the necessary and evil consequences of these same commitments. They favoured radical changes in economy and society. Recognizing that neither the state nor industry would willingly subvert the modernist project, they pursued the politics of confrontation rather than consultation. While these groups cooperated often in the early days of activism, by 1985 the ecological modernists had drifted into a position in which they found further cooperation difficult and occasionally impossible.

Thus the history of Nova Scotian environmental activism speaks also to the definition of environmentalism everywhere. One group of researchers has long favoured an exclusive definition, insisting for more than three decades that the "lifestyle" environmentalism of the affluent world in the 1960s – characterized by the pursuit of clean air, clean water, and outdoor recreation as luxury commodities – is a qualitatively new development in the social history of the Western world, uniquely deserving of the label "environmentalism." It is, they say, a product of demographic and economic changes following the Second World War, set apart from contemporary and antecedent movements by its proponents' unprecedented wealth and comfort; this they call "postmaterialism."[1] Others favour a more inclusive definition, ranking such lifestyle environmentalism alongside prior anti-industrial movements and contemporary environment-themed activism in the less wealthy world, all of them motivated by reactions against the undesirable effects of industry, capitalism, and the dominance of scientific thinking, which impose an unfavourable monetary "discount rate" on the sacred sites, home places, and other economically incommensurable values held by poorer people.[2] This book falls into the latter camp.

Non-modern argument was rarely articulated in theoretical terms, and not until the end of the 1970s, partly in reaction to the consolidation of an ecomodernist mainstream, but to recognize its presence at the heart of environmental activism is to acknowledge that all environmentalism is born of a reaction to late modernity, and the "political, social, and scientific consensus that has dominated the last two or three hundred years of public life." Broadly, modernity is associated with the three key tenets already mentioned, plus a progressive theory of history, nation-state polity, increased use of inanimate energy sources, and a social and intellectual "system of objectification" by which uniquely local or personal forms of knowledge are replaced by a more legitimate universal way of thinking and speaking.[3] Ecomodernist reformers operated within the modernist project; non-modern radicals generally contested it, in diverse and inconsistent fashion. Both responded to its ecological impact.

The commitments of both sorts of environmentalists rested on personal and emotional foundations. Personal vulnerability motivated *all* environmental activism. It most often found expression in defence of economic and affective ties to local places, as the intrusion of new industrial developments into rural settings spawned reaction. Individual and collective protests focused on the degradation of known and familiar villages, coves, hamlets, and landscapes, rather than on some distant prospect or "the environment" in the abstract. Some local activists eventually embraced global perspectives, but rarely at the cost of their personal and local attachments. Only a handful of modernist activists who found it politically inexpedient to acknowledge local and individual experience (an illegitimate source of knowledge, in the modernist world view) truly abandoned the defence of home places as a central point of reference for their actions. In sum, the idea of and attachment to home place here outweighed (though they never completely displaced) network formation, resource distribution, class, race, and gender as the driving forces of environmental action.

For all that individual world views mattered, Canadian political culture also shaped environmentalism in Nova Scotia in the 1970s and 1980s. Government influence, both federal and provincial, helped to drive modernist activists towards conciliatory politics, and by unwitting extension helped to solidify the radical critique. In doing so, it also reduced the political impact of the two strands of activism, which often achieved real political influence when working in combination. In the end, this is the story of several groups of agents – governmental factions, activist groups, and various industrialists – negotiating the politics of social movements with varying levels of success.

Environmentalists in Nova Scotia participated in a national and international political conversation about particular environmental hazards. The issues in question in Nova Scotia – especially nuclear power, chemical forestry, and uranium mining – were subjects of major controversy across the country and around the world, where others took careful note of events in the province and attempted to intervene in Nova Scotia to the advantage of whatever party they represented in Ottawa, Washington, Stockholm, or other locales.[4] Nova Scotians joined federal non-governmental groups such as the Canadian Coalition for Nuclear Responsibility (CCNR) and Friends of the Earth Canada (FOE), and they participated in consultative groups, including the Canadian Environmental Advisory Council (CEAC) and Canadian Environmental Network (CEN). But the substance of the national story, the real action, took place within provincial, not federal, arenas. The story of environmentalism in Nova Scotia is thus a particularly clear window into the story of the movement in Canada.

This study highlights the salience of activity at the provincial level in Canadian environmentalism, and illuminates how activism operated on the ground by attending to the intragovernmental squabbles, the industry/ government collusion, the small rural activist groups' interaction with their better-funded urban peers, the cooperation between First Nations activists and other environmentalists, and the collaborations with peace activists, conservationists, and various social justice advocates that shaped events. There is a tendency in national studies to focus on the major players, such as Greenpeace or Pollution Probe, or on the federal and provincial government agencies established in the 1970s to deal with environmental problems, but while these make important contributions to the story of environmentalism in Canada, relationships within provinces best define it. The environmental movement, in Nova Scotia and in most parts of Canada and the world, has been firmly rooted in, and found its motive force at, the local level. Relationships between larger mainstream groups and governments were shaped in large part by the smaller, usually rural groups whose stubborn defence of their home places led them to reject (at least in part) the conclusions that the other two offered about the causes of environmental problems, the role of humanity in nature, and the role of environmentalists in the political process.[5]

That there ever was a national Canadian environmental movement at all is a matter of some debate. Whereas groups across Canada often shared common challenges and opportunities through the constitutional division of powers that gave the provinces jurisdiction over natural resources, there was very little formal cooperation at the federal level among Canadian environmental activists until the late 1970s, and even that seemed often tangential to the most vital emerging concerns of provincial and local movements. There was simply far more coalition, cooperation, and common concern among groups within single provinces. For these reasons, this book speaks of a Canadian environmentalism made up of provincial movements rather than a single Canadian environmental movement, an important distinction.

Far from the simple leisure pursuit of an affluent urban society, environmentalism appears a far more complex social phenomenon in its Nova Scotian iteration. It was a reaction to the ecological impacts of federal/ provincial development schemes designed to alleviate regional economic disparity, and it frequently reshaped those plans when they conflicted with small communities' visions of a viable, desirable, and just economic future.

Environmentalism arose in Nova Scotia in response to an unusual congregation of environmental events of national and international significance but crucially local impact. In little more than a decade after 1970, the province witnessed Canada's largest marine oil spill, an attempt to organize a regional nuclear-powered electrical utility, the improbable defeat of a Swedish multinational's plan to spray insecticides on Cape Breton Island, an internationally infamous provincial Supreme Court ruling on herbicides, moves by a French company to begin uranium mining in the midst of agricultural settlement, and the beginning of a decades-long fight to clean up the Sydney tar ponds, legacy of the Sydney steel mills and still the most toxic site in the country. Throughout this book, there appear men and women like Murray Prest, a Halifax County mill owner and bitter opponent of large-scale industrial forestry. Prest's economic self-interest in preserving a smaller-scale sawn-lumber industry and his ecological arguments against clearcut chemical forestry seem at first to invite a distinction between values and interests, but his position actually expresses a commitment to a non-modern way of life in which the continuity and meaning of the human (and economic) community depended on a relationship with the forest in which small trees were left for later generations of woods workers, and the forest cover was left intact to preserve the various ecological amenities (food, clean water, and so on) that the community required. Prest was not concerned with the philosophical coherence of his position or with acquiring a label for it; he accepted capitalism, for example, but rejected large-scale industry, political and economic centralization, and the total commodification of the forest. This book is the story of men and women like Prest – diverse in their dissent, united in their defence of home places.

CHAPTER OVERVIEW

Tracing the origins of environmental awareness in Nova Scotia, Chapter 1, "At Home and Abroad," recounts a diverse set of relatively minor controversies before the early 1970s. From Boat Harbour to Mahone Bay to Chedabucto Bay, these early struggles established the lasting pattern of environmental activism in Nova Scotia as a movement primarily motivated by rural communities' reactions to the negative consequences of industrial modernity: the pollution, the centralization of power in the city, the increasing exploitation of the hinterland, and the threatened destruction of traditional economies. These initial actions make it clear that early environmental

FIGURE I Map of Nova Scotian counties and relevant sites. *Cartography by Eric Leinberger*

activists in the province held well-developed and diverse opinions on the nature of their movement. Some were the intellectual brothers of the technocratic nineteenth-century conservation movement, others were radically suspicious of government motives. They were a diverse group of people, with starkly different economic and geographic origins, as demonstrated by the map of relevant sites in Figure I; their number included fishermen, trappers, medical doctors, Mi'kmaq band chiefs, farmers, students, and more. All were aware of the currents of popular ecology in the world at large. Government attempts to manage political radicalism, not limited to environmentalism, helped to create environmental activist organizations such as the Ecology Action Centre (EAC) in Halifax. These groups showed a generalized concern for "the environment" and an early tendency to focus on public education rather than on political pressure. Meanwhile, outside of the city, activists grew increasingly effective at challenging and changing the course of development policies that drew new industrial projects into their communities. By the end of the 1960s, they were mustering scientific arguments to shape public opposition to destructive industries, eventually prompting the government in Halifax to issue its own regulations in an attempt to blunt the critique. In the early 1970s, the rural movement's growing political power culminated in the ignominious defeat of a federal/ provincial plan to create a new national park on the province's eastern shore, and as links among activists of all types and locations grew stronger, they began to take up more ambitious causes.

Chapter 2, "The Two MECs," tracks the development of anti-nuclear activism from 1972 through to the provincial government's decision in 1980 to abandon plans for a single Maritime electric utility. Beginning with a plan to build a large nuclear power plant on the south shore to generate electricity for export to the United States, the narrative tracks a series of external factors responsible for seismic changes in the Nova Scotian movement: the oil price shocks of the early 1970s that ignited debate about the need for nuclear generation in the Maritimes, the limits to growth theory that widely popularized the notion in 1972 that economic growth could not continue forever on a finite planet, and the Three Mile Island nuclear disaster in 1979, which revitalized anti-nuclear politics across many jurisdictions, including the Maritimes. This chapter points to the importance of political jurisdiction in shaping Canadian environmentalism, as the attempt to unite the energy agencies of Nova Scotia, New Brunswick, and Prince Edward Island produced an activist backlash that strengthened and drew together the movements in all three provinces but collapsed with the end of the regional utilities unification plan. In Nova Scotia, organization against nuclear energy brought the first long-lasting and multi-issue activist groups to wide public notice. It also led many activists to realize the possibility of making their appeals directly to government, remaining within the parameters of the existing modernist energy policy rather than continuing on a course of total rejection of large industrial electricity generation. A politically conservative (though still strongly reformist) group of religious peace activists who eventually formed the energy committee of the Halifax-based Ecology Action Centre were crucial and early actors in this shift towards modernism and government consultation, and remained central figures in the movement for many years thereafter. The sense of personal vulnerability of farming and fishing communities remained a key motivating factor and sustained the defence of home places as a theme in environmental argument, but it was joined by the less geographically fixed contributions of immigrant American Quakers. Another central theme of this and subsequent chapters, mistrust of the very secretive provincial government, was a source of disagreement between the more urban ecomodernist activists and their rural peers. Nevertheless, both remained committed to a vision of the movement as a grassroots coalition of local groups with a common, province-wide purpose, so far as anti-nuclear activism was concerned; in neither the nascent ecomodernist mainstream nor the non-modernist groups was the notoriously self-centred NIMBY (Not in My Back Yard) activist ever to be found.

In Chapter 3, "Power from the People," the focus shifts to a hard-fought battle over the use of chemical pesticides in forestry, beginning in 1976 with a famous (and successful) campaign to keep Nova Scotia from following New Brunswick's lead in spraying insecticides from the air in a futile bid to reduce the numbers of spruce budworm on Cape Breton Island. The events recounted in this chapter demonstrate the growing determination of government and industry to resist environmentalist pressure, and the equally strong determination of some activists to change the minds of their opponents in the bureaucracy without resorting to radical tactics or rhetoric. The collision of the two played out in the infamous (and unsuccessful) herbicide trial of 1983, with which the chapter ends. The importance of global trends is central to the narrative of this chapter, with both environmentalists and the forest industry reaching beyond the province's borders for resources in their conflict, as well as for new arenas in which to make use of their respective gains within the province. But the limits of international assistance are fully on display as well in the second half of the chapter, as international connections help the more modernist activists pursue their case in court, where non-modern arguments carried no weight. Several secondary themes rise to prominence here, such as the agency of the news media, the internal politics of the provincial bureaucracy (and its commitment to the preservation of its own power), the continuing vitality of the resource conservation movement, and the rhetorical power of jobs and immigration status to both the advantage and the detriment of activists.

From the air above to the stones below, Chapter 4, "Two Environmentalisms," examines a comparatively brief but intense campaign from 1981 to 1985 aimed at preventing uranium mining in the province. Most of the action discussed in this chapter occurred in and around the hearings of the Nova Scotia Royal Commission on Uranium Mining, during which activists finally acknowledged the full extent of their differences. This is a story of fragmentation – and the fracture in the movement was bitter – but the campaign to halt uranium mining was a surprising success, owing in large part to the persistence of the radicals, who continued fighting desperately to defend their homes. Links with peace and conservation groups are once again on display, along with the urban activists' greater tendency towards modernism and the global links of every set of actors. Among the central themes, the influence (and rejection) of metropolitanism ranks high as a factor in Canadian environmentalism, brought into focus by the vitality of rural activism in the Nova Scotian movement. Indeed, Canadian environmentalism as seen through the prism of the province's experience appears inextricably bound up with the discontents of metropolitanism, between regions of the country as well as between rural and urban locales within provinces. So, too, do the results of the activist schism reflect a national reality: the increased articulation and political consciousness of radical environmental critique, and the growing commitment of the ecomodernist mainstream to consultative processes. Government action around uranium mining in Nova Scotia also illustrates the extent to which judicial and quasi-judicial forms – courts and commissions – serve to reinforce the modernist mode of thought, as well as the extent to which pressure politics continued to win results.

Finally, Chapter 5, "Watermelons and Market Greens," offers a short overview of some major environmental controversies of the 1980s and demonstrates the persistence of the fissure in the province's environmental movement. Important to note is the ability of radical and mainstream activists to cooperate despite their differences, when involved in such issues as the threatened demolition of Kelly's Mountain for a granite quarry. Local grievance and defence of home places still drove environmental activism in the 1980s, as it does today, and the provincial and federal governments still encouraged ecomodernist positions. The provincial movement, however, settled into a new pattern in the 1980s, with radicalism centred geographically on the north and south shores and on Cape Breton Island, and with modernist environmentalism predominant in the city of Halifax and the central mainland.

The process by which the ill-defined activism of the late 1960s became the theoretically and politically articulate alternative environmentalisms of the 1980s, the narrative contained in these chapters, is not a decline-and-fall story. It is a story of intellectual growth and differentiation in a diverse movement. Environmental activists did err at times in pursuing modernist policies too stridently, but they also demonstrated the power of both strands of the movement to effect change in development policy by working, if not in close collaboration, at least on parallel tracks. If there is a lesson to be taken from these pages, it is not that environmentalism in Nova Scotia failed, but that it has always contained the elements of success, and at times has even managed to make them work.

I

At Home and Abroad
The Genesis of Environmentalism

Nova Scotians in the first half of the twentieth century were ambivalent about changes to the provincial landscape. The earliest large hydroelectric dams in the province were remote from settlement and not dramatically larger than the mill dams that had dotted the province's rivers since European settlement began. Even the creation of Lake Rossignol in Queens County by the Mersey Paper Company in the 1920s, which drowned ten natural lakes and over ten thousand acres of land, took place without significant objection.[1] By the end of the 1950s, however, the different biological impacts of small and large dams were better understood, and free-flowing rivers were better appreciated as refugia for Atlantic salmon.[2]

Just as more people were coming to appreciate the value and vulnerability of rivers, the Nova Scotia Light and Power Company (NSLPC) sought permission to dam the Gold River in Lunenburg County for hydroelectric power. The project would have flooded slightly more than two thousand acres from the village of Chester almost to the border of Kings County, creating two long flowage lakes where once there had been a single river channel and eight natural lakes. Worse, two sections of riverbed between dams and powerhouses would be left permanently dry. Had the power company's engineers set out to demonstrate their ability to utterly unmake a river, they could not have designed a better exhibition piece.

There was no question that NSLPC's plan would have ended salmon fishing on the river, and it drew immediate, vocal opposition from sport fishermen in the province, especially in the city of Halifax. In the face of such opposition, the Stanfield government created a Royal Commission in the summer of 1961 to recommend a solution. Led by Halifax lawyer Russell McInnes, the commission operated on a tight schedule. Nonetheless, McInnes promptly expanded the inquiry to investigate dams and fisheries on other rivers. Opponents of the project "consisted almost wholly of persons interested in sport fishing; particularly salmon fishing by rod," but they included, and had the support of, powerful members of the province's economic elite, including Frank Sobey, then head of the province's industrial development agency.[3] They were also supported by the federal Department of Fisheries, whose representative called it "a mistake [to] absolutely destroy salmon and other anadromous fish" on a biologically healthy river merely for "the cheapest possible power."[4]

With remarkable speed, McInnes issued a recommendation before the end of the year, condemning the project and endorsing the conservationist gospel. Since European settlement, he wrote, "the peoples and Governments of this province have used, abused, and for the most part indiscriminately destroyed its natural resources with a prodigality that would be incredible if it were not so patently and painfully obvious."[5] His recommendations included a stay on any and all hydroelectric works anywhere in the province until a long-term planning exercise could be completed and a sport fishermen's licensing system created to support a program of scientific conservation. Significantly, he also adhered to the classic conservationist's elevation of the common good over local preference: the "large majority" of residents near the Gold River had registered support for the project in the hope of new jobs, but McInnes insisted that such jobs would be few and that "the Gold River and every other natural resource and tourist attraction of this province belongs to the people of the province as a whole [and] it should not be available to satisfy the whims or desires of the persons living closest to it."[6] Public opinion carried a weight in his ruling that it did not carry in much conservationist writing – McInnes stopped short of insisting that only scientific experts could determine the common good, and he acknowledged the legitimacy of popular opposition, so long as all citizens of the province enjoyed equal influence – but apart from the threat of public disapproval implicit in the use of newspapers as a forum for elite dissent, genuine popular resistance played very little role in the fate of the Gold River. Unlike the narrowly institutional forest conservation of the provincial Department of Lands and Forests (DLF), however, river conservation in the 1960s reached out to average Nova Scotians with the message that industrial development could be dangerous, and could be stopped.

Among those heard by the McInnes Commission was a group of professional scientific conservationists outside of government who called themselves the Nova Scotia Resources Council (NSRC). Active since 1959, and dedicated to "ensuring the cultivation and the optimal use of the Province's resources [via] carefully considered land use and sound management of plant and animal life,"[7] this private association was no protest group; its representative at McInnes's inquiry was Harrison F. Lewis, retired chief of the Canadian Wildlife Service, and its recommendations to the commissioner (largely reproduced in his own recommendations to government) earned praise for their "reasonableness."[8] But the NSRC represented a trend in the province that saw natural history clubs seeking incorporation, hoping to push government to act on a conservation agenda.[9] Wildlife conservationists in Nova Scotia, whose legislative victories dating back to 1794's Act for the Preservation of Partridge and Blue-Winged Ducks were dismissed by Lewis as "a sop to an advanced minority and not meant to be taken seriously," were particularly keen to organize and willing to use the weight of membership numbers to achieve something more substantial.[10] The Nova Scotia Bird Society (NSBS), founded by Lewis, Robie Tufts, and other professionally interested naturalists, also witnessed rapid growth in its public membership over the following months.[11] Later, in response to the Gold River episode, yet another group of sportsmen and scientists formed the Nova Scotia Salmon Association (NSSA). Aware of a need to incorporate pollution abatement into habitat protection, these new conservation organizations were at once more than simple "wise use" conservationists and less than the radically skeptical environmentalists of the late 1960s and early 1970s. They also remained active and collaborated with various environmental groups in the 1970s and 1980s.

Opposition to the Gold River scheme was further bolstered by an unusual international preservation organization, the Friends of Nature (FON). The first FON group was created in Maine in 1954 by a young publisher and shipwright, Martin Rudy Haase, and a small number of associates. Their initial purpose was to preserve as recreational wilderness one small island (McGlathery) in Penobscot Bay, then under threat from a pulp and paper company. Success breeds confidence, however, and the group's attention soon turned to similarly threatened wilderness areas elsewhere. Unconcerned with the national loyalties that hemmed in so many other groups, FON set out to assist in the creation of wilderness parks in Costa Rica and Tasmania, with uncommon success. In 1967, Haase and his family relocated to Chester, Nova Scotia, in a bid to keep his two young sons out of the way of the seemingly interminable Vietnam

War, and FON came with him. More accurately, Haase was FON, and he found in Lunenburg County a new set of associates with whom to continue his wilderness advocacy, in two host nations.[12]

Despite their jaundiced view of America's military adventures and nuclear arsenal, FON was never a politically radical group. Its operations reflected the privileged milieu from which it came: letters and direct appeals to the political elite achieved virtually all of the group's victories. The personal intervention of President John F. Kennedy's adviser and head speechwriter, Ted Sorensen, for example, opened the door to the creation of the Cabo Blanco Nature Reserve in Costa Rica, on FON's advice. In that sense, there was little to differentiate FON from the earlier tradition of both conservation and preservation in North America, in which elite recreationists (hunters, hikers, and mountaineers) and elite technocrats (foresters, biologists, and engineers) pursued novel goals via traditional politics. In another sense, however, their philosophical position linked them much more closely to the new environmentalism of the 1960s. Haase's FON linked concerns about land and habitat to pollution, population, and lifestyle questions. In 1955, seven years before the publication of Rachel Carson's *Silent Spring*, FON began a campaign to encourage a permanent ban on DDT (dichlorodiphenyltrichloroethane) and similar pesticides, which transitioned into a fight against the US defoliation program in Vietnam (and, in the Cold War context, linked FON's anti-chemical work to its anti-nuclear advocacy). The group also frequently insisted that "people must voluntarily turn to a 'lower' standard of living commensurable with available renewable resources," and helped to popularize the ideas of the afforestation advocate Richard St. Barbe Baker and back-to-the-land gurus Helen and Scott Nearing.[13]

Defenders of the Gold River argued not only for a fishing river but for one of the last *healthy* salmon rivers in the province, and their successors in the NSSA, along with Rudy Haase at FON, were well aware of the expansion of clearcut pulpwood forestry in the province and the annual DDT spray program in neighbouring New Brunswick, as well as the fatal consequences of both practices for the insect and fish life of rivers.[14] If their political habits still generally directed them towards technical and scientific expertise and gentlemanly lobbying out of the public eye, there were also hints of a new awareness – in the NSBS's quest for membership numbers, and in the use of the press in defence of the Gold River – that public opinion might now support a reaction against the intrusion of industrial modernity into more and more remote corners of the land. There were even hints of the deeper challenge to come, questioning the need, the value, and the possibility of continued accelerating exploitation of nature. At the end of the 1960s, all of these disparate trends came together, far too quickly for single-issue conservation groups to keep up with, but those groups did not fade away or reject the new political reality. They continued to adapt and to forge alliances with their new and more radical peers, subtly moulding the future of the environmental movement in the province.

"Calamity Howlers": Estuarine Environmentalism

The Gold River episode was a portent of things to come. Threats to bodies of water signalled the beginning of new environmental concerns at the end of the 1960s. In this, as in so much else, Nova Scotia's experience reflected and amplified the pattern in the rest of North America and the world. The provincial government's quest for economic development had changed the face of the province, often for the worse, and the change was not evenly distributed. New industrial projects tended to cluster around harbours for a number of reasons, including ease of access, available workers, clean water supplies, and the availability of the ocean as a sink for industrial waste. By extension, the new activism of the era centred on the same locations, the majority of them rural, as local residents fearing for their traditional lifestyles and livelihoods under new land-use and water-use regimes found the traditional politics of dissent ineffective against polluters working hand-in-hand with government. Fed by direct observation of environmental ills and mistrust of government, as well as by a rising global environmental consciousness, new ideas and patterns of activist behaviour spread across the province from these estuarine enclaves. Environmentalists made increasing use of scientific research, not to convince politicians of their claims as their conservationist forebears had done, but to draw ever greater popular support to their campaigns of political pressure. And with the new style of environmental politics came a new and lasting pattern of participation, with a much greater presence of women, young people, Mi'kmaq, and working-class Nova Scotians.

One of the first instances of the new activism occurred in Pictou County. In 1965, when the provincial government finally enticed the Scott Paper Company to build its newest, state-of-the-art kraft pulp mill at Abercrombie Point, an unusual provision in the agreement had the province rather than the pulp company operating the mill's effluent treatment facility. Seizing on the natural lagoon of nearby Boat Harbour as a cheaper alternative to a purpose-built treatment plant, the Nova Scotia Water Resources Commission put up dams in the lagoon to divide settling and aeration ponds, walled it off from the sea, and constructed a pipeline under the East River of Pictou to carry to the new facility 25 million gallons each day of effluent water, dissolved and suspended bits of wood pulp, and various toxic leftovers from the kraft bleaching process. Economically at least, it was a success story; the Scott mill prospered. Boat Harbour, on the contrary, died. Once a popular site for swimming, boating, and fishing, its waters promptly turned black after the mill opened, as the oxygen demands of decomposing wood pulp left nothing to support life.[15]

Particularly keen to celebrate their sense of belonging to a particular place, and particularly ill treated during the creation of the facility, the Mi'kmaq of Pictou Landing were among the first to react to the environmental downside of development, though even at Pictou Landing they were not alone. From the perspective of the band's negotiators, the destruction of the harbour was not even supposed to have happened. They had been dispatched to meet with federal and provincial officials early in the province's talks with Scott, after the band indicated that it would not accept the conversion of their reserve's beautiful natural harbour into an industrial facility. In 1966, they were taken to a pulp mill in Saint John, New Brunswick, where water issued clear and clean from the outflow pipe, and were reassured that the same conditions would prevail in Pictou. With an offer of $60,000 as compensation for fishing rights on the table, and, according to Pictou delegate Louis Francis, a generous supply of alcohol as well, the band's team agreed to the government's terms. When effluent began flowing into Boat Harbour, they realized their mistake. The Saint John lagoons they had been shown were not even receiving effluent at the time of their visit, and $60,000 was a pittance next to the millions it would cost to build a truly state-of-the-art facility – $4 million for the most modest improvements at Boat Harbour proposed by the optimistic and quite conservative Rust Associates report in 1970.[16]

Members of the Pictou Landing Band had good reason to feel helpless in 1970. "I guess we're beaten," was Chief Raymond Francis's assessment, but they would not give up, and in their fight they had allies as well, willing as never before to challenge the authority of the state.[17] Though environmentalist coalition across the province was not yet common, local solidarity was, and non-Native residents of Pictou Landing felt nearly as deceived as the band. Since 1965 they too had been demanding answers from the water commission, and had received similar assurances that no pollution of water or air would result from the project. As the progressive degeneration of the harbour and its surroundings confirmed their fears, however, more and more residents turned to a local citizens' committee (eventually named the Northumberland Strait Pollution Control Committee, or NSPCC) to press for answers. Municipal councillor and NSPCC member Henry Ferguson wrote for the people of Pictou Landing in 1970:

> With the winds down the harbour we get air pollution from Scott Paper, then with the winds east we again get pollution, this time from Boat Harbour. The fumes are really terrible, almost unbearable. Then we get water pollution coming down the East River from leaks in the pipe across from the Scott Paper Co. to Pictou Landing. Then water pollution from Boat Harbour when the tide is coming up and runs along Lighthouse Beach and into Pictou Harbour.[18]

To that, he added swarms of mosquitoes and gnats, expropriation through flooding of harbourside land without notice and with minimal compensation, and threats to the Northumberland Strait lobster fishery. The last was particularly worrying in communities along the shore, where the Maritime Packers Division of National Sea Products reported a 26.7 percent drop in lobster landings in 1968 and a 42.2 percent drop in 1969.[19] In fact, the threat to the fishery became a major rallying point for activists.

Official response to public outrage at Pictou Landing was muted at best. Accustomed to working without heed to local opinion, E.L.L. Rowe, the chairman of the Water Resources Commission and a former chemical industry employee who had designed the leaking subriver pipeline and had promised minimal disruption to life around Boat Harbour, doubled down on his defence of the facility. He insisted that he personally found the smell of the rotting lagoon and the "rotten egg" hydrogen sulfide fumes from Scott's stacks inoffensive, and that the province could not make funds available for the solution of merely aesthetic problems. He also made it clear that mercury contamination of the mill effluent from the associated Canso Chemicals plant would have to be tolerated, as the development of the plant had "gone too far" and cost too much to be altered.[20] Other officials and politicians holding similar views attracted attention from time to time, including the agriculture minister, Harvey Veniot, who dismissed the affected locals with the oddly poetic epithet, "calamity howlers," or the fisheries experts at the Department of Fisheries in Ottawa who would only repeat that Boat Harbour's effluent had been tested and proven non-toxic to lobster larvae.[21] But it was Rowe who earned the greatest ill will as the man directly in charge of the facility, whose public pronouncements so often failed to hold up to scrutiny, and who had been more than usually candid about his priorities in the use of public funds. More inclined to talk about municipal sewage treatment than the effluent of privately owned industries, he played what Tom Murphy in the *Mysterious East* called "the little verbal game called 'Why-Don't-You-Talk-About-The-East-River-And-Shut-Up-About-Boat-Harbour.'"[22]

Local activists refused to be put off the issue. Unable to secure a hearing and unable to sue the province for nuisance without permission from the government, they turned fully to public opinion as a source of influence. And as a tool for generating public support, they turned to science, and thus to criticism of the facility as a threat to the local fishing economy. The NSPCC commissioned a report from Delaney and Associates that followed the brown film of Boat Harbour effluent twenty kilometres down the shore and calculated that about 185 tons of organic solids spilled into the sea from the harbour each day.[23] D.C. MacLellan at the Marine Studies Centre at McGill University found that the effluent resulted in an unusually high mortality among the plankton at the base of the Northumberland Strait food chain, and Dr. J.G. Ogden at Dalhousie University answered the federal fisheries experts by reminding them that, toxic or not, dark-brown effluent that blocked sunlight from reaching the sea floor would deprive lobster of both food and sheltering seaweeds. "A sheet of opaque glass put over the lawn is not toxic," he said, "but it will kill the grass. The effluent from Boat Harbour is as effective as a sheet of black plastic."[24] So armed with expert authority of their own, the NSPCC members pursued their environmental justice arguments in the press on behalf of the Mi'kmaq and Northumberland Strait fishermen deceived or ignored by the federal agencies designated to safeguard their interests. Nor were their aims narrowly or selfishly defined; one fisherman-activist told Tom Murphy that compensation for losses might not be welcome if it allowed the condition of the strait to continue deteriorating. "We want our environment cleaned up, rather than subsidies for a dirty environment," he said.[25] Dr. J.B. MacDonald, MD, one of the NSPCC's leaders, explained that he had come to the issue out of concern for his own summer home at Pictou Landing, but quickly discovered the medical risks of sulfur dioxide in the air and a stew of unknown chemicals in the harbour's water, as well as the injustice of secretive government deals drawn up without "explanation, justification, or revelation of alternatives" to the public.[26]

In the early 1970s, the NSPCC expanded its range of concerns to include the whole of industrial and municipal pollution affecting the Northumberland Strait, no longer content to entrust the solution of any such problem wholly to the Water Resources Commission or the Department of Fisheries.[27] "Regrettably," noted MacDonald, "one must be hurt to become an active and sustained anti-pollution fighter. This is not as it should be. Intelligent people should not see their environment, their homes, their country being destroyed and sit back placidly and take it."[28]

Boat Harbour was the most bitterly fought of the late 1960s battles, but it was far from the only one. At the same time that Dr. MacDonald was discovering the need for citizen activism, other groups were forming in the province after their own personal experiences with the dark side of development. In Halifax, residents on the shores of the Bedford Basin and Purcell's Cove learned much the same lessons derived from Pictou Landing's experience. Like Pictou, urban Halifax was no stranger to industry, but new developments in the 1960s brought an intensification that seemed to threaten residents' traditional recreational use of the harbour. A growing population in the Halifax area had the city government searching for a site for a sewage treatment system more advanced than the existing one.[29] At the same time, proposals for new industrial developments at previously unused locations, such as a container ship terminal at Navy Island in Wright's Cove on the Dartmouth side of the basin, came up frequently. As in Pictou, the reaction against environmental costs imposed from above came early in the planning process: both the Bedford Basin Pollution Control Committee (BBPCC) and the Purcell's Cove Action Committee (PCAC) began protesting in 1969 that the decision to dedicate greater and greater proportions of the basin's shore to industrial purposes, and the decision to flatten and infill thirty acres in the village and harbour at Purcell's Cove for a massive central sewage treatment plant, were both unjustifiably undemocratic and would subject locals to unanticipated and irreversible environmental dangers. Robert Martin's complaint about the level of public consultation at Purcell's Cove might have come from the pen of any of his peers on the basin or in Pictou County: Should citizens "wait until City Council has done all the thinking they expect to do before expressing their views? Are they to be given a chance to let off steam only after City Council has made its decision?"[30]

Residents of both communities demanded a say in development schemes before plans were finalized, but in Bedford they faced a potential multitude of future projects that could be addressed only with regular public input into the planning process. Accordingly, the BBPCC set to work compiling a major report, which it released in 1970, on the future of industrial and recreational development on the basin, making use of the lawyers, engineers, and planners among its members to argue against unrestrained industrial growth in the city planners' own terms.[31] There was no official response. If the somewhat less wealthy and professionally resourceful defenders of Purcell's Cove, fighting to stop a single project, could be publicly dismissed as ignorant of the inevitability of development, the BBPCC required a different tack on the part of the city and province: silence in public, while the ever-present and tight-fisted Mr. Rowe at the Water Resources Commission circulated among his colleagues a dismissive assessment of the activists as impractical "academic" people with a "lack of appreciation of priorities in the expenditure of public moneys," selfish, unscientific, and not to be taken seriously in their "public relations" exercise.[32]

In the face of such official intransigence, the genuine public relations efforts of Purcell's Cove met with greater success. The PCAC's hectoring methods, undeterred by the condescension of experts or the hostility of bureaucrats, eventually prompted the city council to promise that the cove would not be infilled, scuttling the previous odds-on favourite site and sending the search for a sewage plant location off on its own long and eventful history.[33] The BBPCC, conversely, barely stumbled into 1971 as an active organization, "embittered and in disarray" from its failed attempt to appeal to provincial and city planners.[34] Though certainly possessed of more economic power on average than the cove residents, the BBPCC had no great deal of political clout with which to force their perspective onto the planning agenda, no equivalent to the political power of massed public anger. Successful or not, the lessons learned by both groups echoed the experience in Pictou County, where the NSPCC's public pressure campaign finally resulted in some acknowledgment of the problem at Boat Harbour and some investment in improvements in 1972, though without any corresponding acknowledgment of the activists' role in bringing them about.[35] Government could be moved on single issues, it seemed, but only grudgingly and only under threat of political embarrassment, and not to the extent of giving up its control of development planning.

If Boat Harbour's ruination was not sufficient warning against the urge to "sit back placidly" and let the state's planners have their way, the Canso Strait industrial complex rang in the new decade in 1970 with an infamous debacle, the *Arrow* oil spill. The construction of the Canso Causeway linking Cape Breton to the mainland early in the 1950s turned Port Hawkesbury into a viable deep-water port, and provincial government encouragement brought to the area a pulp mill in 1962, a heavy-water plant in 1970, and an oil refinery in 1971. Port Hawkesbury was to be a "growth pole" for western Cape Breton and the eastern mainland, areas appearing in desperate need of an economic boost.[36] The urgency of industrial growth targets, however, left no room for the assessment of environmental risk, much less for the avoidance of it. Discontent with scantly regulated development existed, but the hundreds of jobs that came with the complex were welcome relief for many, and Dr. MacDonald's assessment held true: people had to be hurt before they could become active pollution fighters.[37]

At 9:30 a.m. on February 4, 1970, a Liberian-registered tanker carrying sixteen thousand tons of thick Venezuelan Bunker C oil struck Cerberus Rock in Chedabucto Bay on the approach to the Canso Strait. Damage to the ship was not great, but the captain was unable to free it from the rock. It languished for eight days, attracting barely any attention from Canadian authorities, before a salvage attempt on February 12 caused the hull to break in half, spilling part of its cargo into the sea and sending the stern to the bottom of the bay, still full of oil. Imperial Oil Limited, owner of the cargo, attempted with some success to burn off and disperse the spilled oil, but neither the company nor anyone else had any experience dealing with spilled oil in such cold waters. For a further eight days, Imperial tried in vain to contain the mess, before the federal government finally stepped in and appointed a three-man task force with instructions simply to "deal with" the oil.[38]

"Operation Oil," as the task force called its work, was a $3 million cleanup that managed to at least prevent a bad situation from becoming worse. Dr. Patrick McTaggart-Cowan, executive director of the Science Council of Canada, Dr. H. Sheffer, vice-chairman of the Defence Research Board, and Captain (N) M.A. Martin, deputy chief of staff at Maritime Command, presided over a three-pronged mission: remove the oil remaining inside the broken *Arrow*, collect as much as possible of the spilled oil at sea, and clean up more than 125 miles of coastline already painted black with crude. Each objective presented novel problems. The bow section of the tanker was largely emptied in the spill, but the oil remaining in the stern section, at rest at the bottom of frigid Chedabucto Bay, had thickened into an immovable mass due to the cold. At sea level, booms could no longer contain the froth of oil and water drifting about, but dispersant chemicals were deemed too toxic to be used in the bay's rich fishing grounds. And on shore, oil clung to rocky cliffs, sandy beaches, and drifts of sea ice, soon to melt and re-oil anything the task force managed to clean.

The three men in charge and the corps of military engineers and civilian researchers under their command had to invent new techniques for each situation; despite the mania for development at Port Hawkesbury and the predictably difficult environment of the Atlantic Ocean in winter, and despite recent high-profile oil spills in California and the English Channel, no one in the provincial or federal governments had ever prepared for the possibility of such a spill.[39]

The cleanup operation took roughly seven weeks. Navy divers managed to tap a new valve into the hull of the sunken stern and inject steam to warm up the congealed oil enough to pump much of it out into a waiting barge, the *Irving Whale*.[40] Their engineer counterparts worked simultaneously at a furious pace to design and build "slick lickers" to pick oil from the surface of the sea, and de-oiling washers to clean fouled fishing gear. On shore, everything from shovels to bulldozers was used to collect oil from the beaches. The task force expressed pride in its achievement; locals expressed frustration at a job half-done. A great deal of oil remained within the sunken hull, occasionally oozing out during stretches of warm water temperatures over subsequent years; as a result, small oil slicks still regularly gummed up beaches as far away as Sable Island. As for the oil-crusted cliffs along Chedabucto Bay, even McTaggart-Cowan had to admit that the oil on rock was "there to stay," and would eventually harden into something like asphalt.[41]

Perhaps surprisingly, the wreck of the *Arrow* did not provoke activist organization on the scale that Boat Harbour or the various developments of Halifax Harbour did, mainly because fishermen already had their own associations through which to urge on the cleanup, and the small number of other activists from communities around the bay seem to have found the issue too large and intractable to deal with. A group called Action Arrow existed briefly, and the author Silver Donald Cameron remembers joining a small group of people who sealed up the corpses of oiled seabirds in plastic bags and mailed them to Ottawa in protest, but in truth Operation Oil had done about as much as was technically possible at the time, and along the way the federal scientists and naval personnel involved had learned a great deal about how to handle oil spills in cold seas. The fate of the bay seems to have been treated less as a winnable fight and more as an object lesson in the consequences of waiting too long to start fighting. "The Gulf Refinery is still there," wrote the *Mysterious East*, "Cerberus Rock is still there. All over the world the big tankers are slipping off the ways into the water. Which one will give Chedabucto Bay its next coating?"[42] What the *Arrow* did for environmental activism in Nova Scotia was confirm the growing suspicion that government planners, the duly appointed experts, could not be trusted to pursue industrial development unsupervised by a concerned public.

The isolated adventures in environmental activism at Boat Harbour, Halifax Harbour, and Chedabucto Bay had a few common elements.[43] One was mistrust of government. Another was the very local focus of concern and the unity of purpose among the more and less wealthy residents of those local places, as well as the roughly equal participation of men and women.[44] The age of men's club conservationism, when sport fishermen from Halifax could save the Gold River with minimal public involvement, was clearly at an end. Finally, the truth of Dr. MacDonald's recipe for activism held in every case: either prospective or concrete, some actual personal environmental harm was required to inspire a pollution fighter and defender of home places. Nova Scotia's leap into industrialization by invitation (its participation in federal/provincial development schemes and its pursuit of foreign direct investment through the Stanfield government's own development agency, Industrial Estates Limited) brought a scale of industry previously unknown to rural corners of the province, and a corresponding surge in the number of affected individuals. Also, once active, no group ever entirely disappeared. The NSPCC carried on its struggle with Boat Harbour and other threats to the strait for years, as did the Pictou Landing First Nation. The dead bird mailing activists of Chedabucto Bay went on to lead a rural recycling campaign in Richmond County and open an environmental education centre in Port Hawkesbury.[45] Even the Bedford Basin and Purcell's Cove committees, both soon nominally defunct, contributed members and experience to successor organizations in the city. The pattern of politically populist and scientifically literate activism crossing lines of race, class, gender, age, and geography became the norm for Nova Scotian environmental activism and provided the basis of further organization in years to come.

ASPECTS OF A GLOBAL WHOLE

Personal experience of environmental harm is not in itself sufficient to explain the rise of environmentalism. The new spirit of activism also had roots in new ideas about the environment, the state, and democratic power that were anything but local. The previous decade had changed the political landscape of the world, especially in Europe and North America. Opposition to the state and industrial society fuelled New Left and civil rights movements that violently challenged the legitimacy of existing social and political systems. A generation of openly critical and rebellious young people joined forces with labourers and racial minorities to protest the Vietnam War, the nuclear bomb, the excesses of capitalism, and the marginalization of the politically weak.[46] Meanwhile, a countercultural movement within the greater uprising encouraged the articulation of alternative ways of living. It was in this context that an international environmental consciousness formed. Concerned people made connections among nuclear warfare, chemical pesticides, economic imperialism, and the inequity of capitalist industrialism and drew conclusions about the welfare of the most voiceless of all politically weak constituencies, the natural world. At the same time, the kind of quality-of-life concerns that had long vexed urban sanitary reformers – clean water, clean air, and the like – appeared to have reached a global scale.[47]

The expanding reach of the new activism owed something to the spread of colour television and the realization among network programmers that environmental disasters made good dramatic content. More important was the novel scale of real and potential environmental harm. Worldwide radioactive fallout from nuclear weapons tests, biologically mobile transborder chemical pollution as detailed in Rachel Carson's 1962 bestseller, *Silent Spring,* and the disastrous consequences of marine oil spills such as the infamous *Torrey Canyon* in 1967 were real, and televisual mass media only magnified their impact as shared experiences. A series of popular publications in the years following Carson's both fuelled and fed on the anxiety: Garret Hardin's "Tragedy of the Commons" (1968), Meadows and colleagues' *The Limits to Growth* (1972), and E.F. Schumacher's *Small Is Beautiful* (1973), to name but three popular titles, recounted the realities and offered a diagnosis of dangerously out-of-control modernity.[48]

All of these new ideas about environment, politics, and the value and possibility of perpetual economic growth were as current in Nova Scotia as elsewhere. They permeated popular culture and inspired any number of the small, local anti-pollution fights of the late 1960s. In the city of Halifax and along the eastern shore, the intellectual inheritance of US and Central Canadian environmentalism played an especially visible role in shaping the new movement, where a wave of US draft dodgers and back-to-the-land immigrants seeking rural ways of life brought their personal experiences to bear. Provincial and municipal leaders were also unintentionally helpful in fostering subversive notions in Nova Scotia in 1970, when in the pursuit of their own set of popular ideas about urban planning, they invited some radical thinkers from the United States, the

United Kingdom, and other parts of Canada to dissect the social problems of the city of Halifax.

The Progressive Conservative government of Premier G.I. Smith (1967–70) had great faith in central economic development planning, as had the Stanfield government before it, and relied extensively on its Cabinet Committee on Planning and Programs – a group of experts better known as the secretariat – to direct development spending. Like Premier Smith himself, the secretariat exercised power only briefly, but they were determined to shake up the structure of power in the Halifax region, where they believed political stagnation limited politicians' willingness to follow planners' advice. To that end, just before Smith's ouster, they organized a weeklong public consultation and investigation of the city by twelve world-class experts in everything from tourism and labour to public finance and the structure of government. They called it Encounter on the Urban Environment. The format was virtually unheard of, having been modelled on a singular event in Australia two years earlier, and few people outside of the secretariat seemed to understand what was intended. The Voluntary Planning Board, which provided funding, expected a major but more or less conventional development study. The city mayor, Allan O'Brien, wanted a list of policy proposals. What they got was a structured confrontation, the brainchild of the secretariat's Len Poetschke, in which the visiting experts called on all levels of private and public life in the city to explain and account for its problems.[49] Open microphones and open minds brought hundreds of speakers to the panel's daily hearings to expose the frustrations and social tensions of the city, while detailed television coverage took those hearings to the population at large. Nor did the panelists sit in silence; they queried, probed, and sometimes criticized those who came to speak. The churches in Halifax, they said, were out of touch, newspapers plodding and conservative, and citizens walking in the political darkness with their eyes closed. Discontent was plain to see, but Haligonians displayed a "reluctance to come to terms with the political process," according to Dr. Martin Rein of the United Kingdom's Centre for Environment Studies: all they had was "indignation without information, without tactics and so no strategy."[50]

Len Poetschke was no subversive, much less the rest of the secretariat. They hoped to harness the energy of public participation coming out of Encounter as "part of a planning process" in which government (planners) provided the "framework" for decisions, such as the necessity for industrial economic development or the central importance of the core business district of Halifax, and the people provided the political firepower with which to overcome bureaucratic inertia.[51] Boiled down to essentials, they hoped to manage and direct the power of public opinion the way a road planner directs the flow of traffic. But the secretariat's days were numbered once Gerald Regan's government took office in 1970 – the new premier had his own set of expert advisers. Last-ditch efforts by Poetschke and his colleague Fred Lenarson to create a citizens' arm for the Halifax-Dartmouth Municipal Area Planning Committee (MAPC) in the year following Encounter brought together a coalition of peace, environment, and social justice groups (eventually settling on the name Movement for Citizens' Voice and Action, or MOVE) that frustrated the planners' intentions by challenging MAPC's closed-door planning process. In this they were aided by Encounter panelist Reverend Lucius Walker, executive director of the Interreligious Foundation for Community Development in New York.[52] Walker's participation shows the degree to which Encounter and its consequences represented an accelerated version of trends happening in the rest of the industrial world, in which diverse activists and civil society leaders formed new coalitions and negotiated difficult relationships with politically powerful sponsors. The Nova Scotian version of the story also highlights the participation of environmental activists in those coalitions.

The events of Encounter week and the creation of the MOVE coalition changed the shape of environmental activism in the city, and eventually across the province. The experience of activists during the Purcell's Cove and Bedford Basin controversies, ongoing at the time, was much the same as the experience of the Africville Action Committee or the Heritage Trust, diverse groups united by their confrontations with the stone wall of government.[53] As the *4th Estate* newspaper put it, "our government, politicians, civil service, and government agencies are all somewhat paranoid. They won't answer questions. It is extraordinarily hard to find the real roots of power."[54] But complaints hadn't satisfied the Encounter panel. When a witness at one hearing mentioned a common front of area environmental groups (the "ECO" coalition) dedicated to public participation and education, panelist Edward Logue replied that such groups "merely preserve the survival" of the current political system (an adequate summary of the secretariat's hopes for MOVE); Dr. Rein reminded the audience that there was "no non-political way of effecting changes," and citizen participation without political action was "a grandiose way of preserving the status quo."[55] The critique hit home, and the members of the loose-knit, "amorphous and anonymous" ECO group, still little more than a mailing list put together at the end of 1969, recognized that even though their goal of public education was sound, they could "never be a force in political

terms [without] ... achieving form in the eyes of government."[56] In the
MOVE coalition they saw a chance to be something more, and as the
coalition took shape it therefore included representatives from the fast-
fading BBPCC, the PCAC, the Eastern Shore District Pollution Committee, the Cole Harbour Environmental Council, the Halifax Wildlife
Association, and a number of other environmentally concerned small
groups and individuals.[57] It also included, in the later stages, a new organization called the Ecology Action Centre (EAC).

The EAC, which would go on to have a hand in virtually every environmental controversy in the province for the rest of the century, was born
from a bit of experimental pedagogy at Dalhousie University, one of that
institution's own responses to the student unrest of the 1960s and demands
for more student autonomy. For a brief time, groups of eight or more
undergraduates with a faculty sponsor were allowed to design and conduct
their own courses. Few applied (do-it-yourself course design was never
really a high priority for student radicals), and fewer were approved, but
one group did earn approval in the 1970–71 year to run a course on
"Ecology and Action," and one of the students who led the effort, Brian
Gifford, made it his class project to create an organization in Halifax
dedicated to public environmental education (ironically, exactly the in-
sufficiently political goal the ECO group was talking itself out of at the
same time). The ecology course and the EAC that came out of it were
well aware of the difficulties faced by their activist peers in dealing with
the provincial and municipal governments: the Nova Scotia Resources
Council's Dr. Ogden, the PCAC's Alan Ruffman, and the BBPCC's John
Bentley each conducted classes for the group, and Gifford, in the process
of investigating the role his new association might play in the city, took
time to consult with Frank Fillmore, activist and editor of the radical paper
the *4th Estate*.[58] But the student group, unique among environmental
associations in the province, did not find its motivation in personal vulnerability to some specific harm or experience of environmental injustice. As
students, middle-class professionals in training, they came nearest of any
activist group in the province to the post-materialist definition of environmentalism. They took their inspiration solely from the generalized culture
of environmental concern in the industrialized world, and their organizational models from distant student peers like Pollution Probe, not nearby
groups familiar with the context of Nova Scotian politics. "Information
and education" rather than political action, said Brian Gifford, "are what
the Centre is all about."[59]

The earliest concerns of EAC activism were recycling projects, urban air quality, and urban planning: things for which the students could secure federal government funding. Doing so was vitally important. The first two years of the EAC's life, the period in which it established itself as a resource centre for the city, were funded through yet another response to sixties youth unrest, this time on the part of the Trudeau government: the Opportunities for Youth (OFY) and Local Initiatives Programs (LIP), which funnelled hundreds of thousands of dollars to youth groups across the country in the early 1970s. With OFY and LIP funding, the EAC was able to run a demonstration paper recycling project and keep a shifting set of five to eight student staff busy adapting a Pollution Probe environmental education kit for schoolteachers and compiling information kits on forestry, energy, and public transit.[60] Eventually, its persistence earned the group a reputation as a reliable source of information, and people in the city began to contact it for answers to pollution and resource-related questions.[61]

While EAC was, and remained for years, a very local student organization of small influence, its creation (as well as that of the MOVE coalition) demonstrates powerfully the currency of combined environmentalist and social justice ideas in Nova Scotia at the end of the 1960s. Federal spending provided the necessary support, but belief in the importance of the issues provided the people willing to take it up. The EAC did not often share the sense of urgency or political cynicism that drove groups born of single issues to oppose the provincial government's plans so completely. It did not agree with its own associate in Cape Breton, *Arrow* protest veteran Margo Lamont, for example, when she urged it to oppose the entire Canso Strait development plan.[62] But it did share with the rest a genuine concern over environmental harm, and a belief in the imminence of a resource supply crisis according to the projections laid down in the Limits to Growth theory.[63] It also held a firm commitment to public participation, to the point that it was willing to accuse the Regan government of "offending the doctrine of democracy itself" by leaving the mechanisms of citizen input out of its Environmental Protection Act in 1973.[64]

Urban activists, with their focus on education and principle, were joined in the quest for democracy in land-use planning by yet another group of issue-specific rural activists fighting a bitter campaign on the province's eastern shore in 1972 and 1973, a group whose new brand of environmental activism was clearly well informed by the worldwide movement. While almost every environmental controversy at the end of the 1960s and beginning of the 1970s in Nova Scotia centred on a harbour or a river, water woes were not alone in feeding the new activism of the era. Where once land conservation was the purview of fringe preservationists like the FON group, by the late 1960s provincial governments had once again hit on the idea of promoting tourism in the region through the designation of national parks.[65] The ideal and greatest victory of the US wilderness preservation movement was to the government in Halifax simply another form of economic engine with which to raise the province out of relative poverty. Unfortunately for the government, Nova Scotia's coast (to the government's eyes the obvious and only choice for a tourist landscape) offered no convenient unsettled patches. A park, as then understood, had to comprise a natural landscape without human habitation, other than the transient paying tourists. In order to create a park, people living on park lands would therefore have to be removed. That was exactly the plan proposed at the end of the decade for Ship Harbour National Park on the eastern shore, and exactly the occasion for Nova Scotians to demonstrate that the new environmentalism posed a much more radical political threat than its conservationist antecedent.[66]

Plans to create a new national park on the eastern shore existed as early as 1965, but the normal planning process and Premier Stanfield's preoccupation with the leap from provincial to federal politics delayed negotiations for years. By the time federal/provincial talks came to light in 1969, there were still multiple proposals on the table, all of which involved the removal of well over a hundred permanent and seasonal residents' homes between Musquidoboit and Sheet Harbour in Halifax County, and none of which involved inviting those residents to help determine the final shape of the park. Despite some initial resistance from locals who petitioned the federal government to avoid expropriations in the creation of the park, both Premier Regan and Halifax Eastern Shore Member of the Legislative Assembly Garnet Brown were eager to see the plan go ahead, and were little concerned with local sentiment. Negotiations continued behind closed doors, resulting in 1972 in a plan that would remove about 250 homes from newly designated federal lands.[67]

Reaction on the eastern shore was swift and angry. A group of residents came together, calling themselves the Committee to Prevent the Proposed Park (later the Association for the Preservation of the Eastern Shore, or APES), and from the summer of 1972 to the end of 1973 pursued an ever more insistent campaign. The APES comprised both lifelong residents and new arrivals to the province, though their opponents in government found it convenient to focus their criticism on one of the leaders, Gordon Hammond, who had been involved in the recent successful fight to halt construction of the Spadina Expressway in Toronto.[68] The focus on Hammond once more highlights the combination of local grievance and a widely shared culture of populist activism, as well as the determination of the provincial government to undermine and marginalize protest. Hammond became the favourite target of politicians determined to paint him as an outsider, a troublemaker, and "a welfare case who drives a car" (i.e., a possible criminal), and the whole of his organization as a "group of johnny-come-latelys, people on welfare, kooks, hardline Conservatives, and small children," selfishly preventing the development of the eastern shore.[69]

Unfortunately for Regan and Brown (as well as for federal minister of Indian Affairs and Northern Development Jean Chrétien), the kooks went from strength to strength. Four years earlier, they had gathered five hundred names on a petition sent to Chrétien's office; after the controversy broke in earnest in 1972, they gathered nearly three thousand names, carried out a letter-writing campaign to Province House, conducted two marches on the legislature, and won 90 percent support in a *Dartmouth Free Press* poll of the eastern shore.[70] Angered by Brown's talk of kooks and welfare cases, activists struck back, calling the premier (who had stealthily avoided one protest rally on his way to work at Province House) "Rear-Door Regan" and earning press coverage all the way to Toronto with their criticism of his "callous disregard for the existing population of the area, for their ancestors who cleared the land, built their houses and worked so hard that we might enjoy what we have today."[71] Others literally struck back, such as one of Brown's constituents, who launched a punch at the MLA a few days after the "kooks" comment, or threatened to do so on protest rally banners promising "THIS IS YOUR LAST PEACEFUL DEMONSTRA-TION" or in Hammond's slightly more subtle predictions of "civil unrest" if the plan should go ahead.[72] APES tactics included support for much more popular provincial park proposals and for a conception of parkland that included the "existing mutual harmony between man and nature," on the European model of national parks containing human settlements. Members also made time for a frank and factual deconstruction of the province's unsupported assumptions about the job-creating potential of a national park. They knew enough not to be trapped into top-down consultation processes as well, and turned the first of the public meetings held by a federal/provincial advisory committee into a debacle for the park planners, complete with threats of arson and armed resistance.[73]

This was not the only instance of opposition to national park development, but Regan was in a more difficult position than most premiers.[74]

APES activists often referred to an autocratic and bitterly resented eviction process at New Brunswick's Kouchibouguac National Park, and many Nova Scotians remembered with ill-will the expropriation of land for Cape Breton Highlands National Park. On top of that, Regan's government had acceded to a plan to reconfigure the Cape Breton park's boundary and allow the conversion of Cheticamp Lake into a hydroelectric reservoir.[75] With a provincial election expected in 1974, Regan wished to avoid charges of treating the electorate as "sheep that are driven from pasture to pasture," and to the consternation of both Brown and Chrétien, he reversed course abruptly in December to support a series of provincial parks in lieu of Ship Harbour National Park.[76] Regan tried to shift blame onto Chrétien's federal office, but the APES campaign was clearly instrumental in the triumph of grassroots environmentalism over the provincial government. Earlier decisions – to preserve the free flow of the Gold River or direct a million dollars or two towards cleanup programs at Boat Harbour, even the decision to cancel negotiations on a US investor's electricity generation scheme in 1973 (see Chapter 2) – scarcely dented the development bias of provincial policy. But the Ship Harbour project championed by the cabinet in Halifax was turned aside through popular political pressure, by average citizens who refused to accept the government's modernist assumptions, by people who were, in APES director Irene Edwards's words, "able to see beyond the 'riches' promised and hold onto a normal love and desire to keep that which is ours."[77]

Such attachment to place combined with a growing worldwide awareness of pollution and "the environment" to reframe ways of thinking about industrial society's intrusion into rural spaces. Buoyed by this new global politics, activists began in earnest (and in concert) to demand real influence on policy, and to question the promises and premises of modernity. And they began to work together.

ORGANIZATION AND REACTION

Cooperation among environmental groups in the province seemed far off at the end of the 1960s. Shared knowledge had resulted in very little shared action. Local groups conducted their campaigns mainly in isolation. All of this was changed by an intensely local event affecting a handful of farms in Annapolis County, an event that aligned with the mainspring of environmental anxiety in contemporary North America: the dangers of biocidal chemicals.[78] Tentative though its gestures towards unity may have been, the anti-herbicide campaign of 1970–72 epitomized a developing provincial environmentalism that compelled government reaction. The Gerald Regan government (1970–78) dealt with more unexpected environmental campaigns in its first four years in office than any other government in Halifax encountered in a similar period, while holding only minority control of the Legislature, and it took very little time for them to realize that environmentalism held the potential for real power and that they needed to channel activists in a more manageable direction and defuse campaigns like the anti-parks movement that threatened development objectives.

The trouble with herbicides began not with a celebratory announcement of some new industrial development but with the incremental expansion of an existing government program. The use of the herbicidal chemicals 2,4-D (2,4-dichlorophenoxyacetic acid) and 2,4,5-T (2,4,5-trichlorophenoxyacetic acid) on roadsides by the Department of Highways and at the behest of the Department of Agriculture (DOA) for the control of farm weeds began in the early 1960s and quickly expanded across the province.[79] Chemical weeding was fast, effective, and cheaper than manual clearing – everything the officials in charge could hope for – and the obvious choice when the DOA wished to remove farm weeds from its Crown farmland on the lower Belleisle Marsh in Annapolis County. So it was done, on the third and fourth of June 1969, by a Maritime Air Services plane hired to spray 2,4-D, 2,4,5-T, and Dicamba over the province's 580 acres. But the plane delivered both more and less than promised. Spraying in a strong breeze, the pilot spread his payload over thirteen or more nearby farms, damaging crops two miles from the marsh. The chemicals left grasses unharmed, as intended, but their drift onto vegetable crops was ruinous. It was also undeniable. Local farmers were quick to band together, forming a "disaster group" to press for action and winning a fast response from the DOA, which investigated and awarded about $30,000 in compensation to thirteen farmers, including Robyn Warren, whose 10 acres of cauliflower abutting the government land were utterly destroyed.[80]

An unfortunately common agriculture misadventure then turned into disaster. Believing the DOA's claims that the herbicides were safe for use on grazing land and were harmless to humans and animals, Warren continued to pasture his dairy herd on the marsh and thought little of the direct exposure of himself, his father, and his brother, working in the fields as the spray plane did its work upwind. In the winter of 1970, Warren's cows aborted pregnancies (fourteen times in sixteen months), bore stunted calves, and showed a remarkably high rate of twinning (most of them stillborn). The family, meanwhile, developed abnormal heartbeats and swollen thyroid glands, symptoms consistent with, but not conclusively traceable to, herbicide poisoning. Doctors advised them to stop consuming the produce of their own farm.[81]

Both the manufacturer and the DOA insisted that any herbicides on the ground would have been destroyed by soil bacteria within days. In 1970, Warren replanted his cauliflower and lost the crop, along with his lettuce, celery, and corn. All of them grew quickly to unusual size before withering away. Tissue samples sent to an independent lab returned positive for 2,4,5-T, 2,4-D, and Dicamba – impossible, according to the DOA, which began insisting that the spray plane carried no 2,4,5-T (though it admitted requesting all three chemicals). The department refused to test for 2,4,5-T itself because, as the deputy minister said, "2,4,5-T was not used. Therefore why test for it?"[82] But Warren did continue testing, at his own expense, and continued to receive results showing the chemical in significant quantities in both vegetables and cattle fetuses, well into 1971. The department still refused to acknowledge a link between its own spray and Warren's troubles, but began advising farmers that herbicides might last weeks, months, or longer in cool, salty soil such as that found in the Belleisle Marsh.[83]

Warren's mounting calamities attracted national attention. The *4th Estate* in Halifax and the regional magazine *Mysterious East* investigated, as did the Toronto *Globe and Mail* and the CBC's national Sunday magazine program.[84] By the time the *Mysterious East* reporter arrived in the middle of 1971, half of Warren's apple trees had died – not half of the orchard, but half of each tree, on the side from which the spray had drifted.[85] Doctors who treated the family knew they could never prove conclusively the cause of their ills, but the Medical Society of Nova Scotia had already called on the provincial government a year earlier to review the use of chemical herbicides in roadside and agricultural spray programs; Warren's case offered apparent confirmation of their fears.[86] Environmental activists used the Medical Society's announcement to push for a ban on the use of the offending chemicals. Rosemary Eaton of the Cole Harbour Environment Committee took a particular interest and a leadership role in the campaign after opposing the use of chemical herbicides on the CN railroad passing through the harbour.[87] Beset from all sides, Premier Regan acted to ease the pressure on his government, suspending chemical spraying by government agencies for a year and instructing the Nova Scotia Research Foundation (NSRF) to investigate safety of commonly used sprays. He even convinced CN to impose a moratorium on spraying, and spoke to reporters about chemical persistence, groundwater contamination, and destruction of wildlife.[88]

A year's suspension is little more than a scheduling adjustment, without some further success, and despite the novel common front on a single issue, the campaign against chemical pesticides lost momentum through a year of quiet research by the NSRF. Worse for the activists, despite the premier's use of environmentalist buzzwords, the investigation he initiated adhered religiously to what Bill Templeman in 1971 called the "legal logic" of the Warren case: proof of harm required that a causal chain, A to B to C to D, be traced backward to establish that only A and nothing else could have caused B, then C, then D. It was a standard of proof virtually impossible to meet within the dense web of ecological connections found on an average farm.[89] The NSRF found no evidence that chemical pesticides posed a risk. A year passed, and spraying resumed on roadsides, railways, and power line rights-of- way.

Still, the nascent anti-chemical coalition opened the eyes of the Regan government to the potential power of environmental activism and the need to do something to direct it away from conflict with government objectives. The subsequent serial shocks of pollution fighters, popular democrats, and park opponents ensured that the problem stayed at front of mind. Duplicity was one response. Even as the premier praised activists' concern for a healthy agricultural system, the DOA reacted "as if it were defending Moscow," compiling stacks of public relations material with which to defend and promote the use of herbicides.[90] And the Regan government began to develop an environmental program of its own. "It is essential that the image of a reform be established quickly," wrote the premier's head policy man, Michael J.L. Kirby, to his friend David Watts at the US Department of the Interior, "in order to indicate to the public that we are a reformed [sic] minded government and are serious about solving the problems of pollution."[91] Kirby insisted that the government must take command of the definition of "pollution," not only for the sake of the next election or to counteract the "scare propaganda which is so common today" but to preserve the policy-making prerogative of the provincial level of government.[92] Provincial governments faced a challenge to their jurisdiction over natural resources in the early 1970s, from the new federal Environmental Protection Service. Kirby was deeply anxious that the triple threat of electoral politics, environmentalists' demands, and federal interference could scuttle the already shaky ship of Liberal government.[93] Cost-conscious environmental skeptics in the bureaucracy were equally frightened that feckless, pandering politicians at two levels of government would trap the province into spending promises that it could not afford, or worse, that that federal government would seize jurisdiction and render the province's efforts at crafting industry-friendly regulations moot.[94]

The need to take control of environmental issues gave form to the Nova Scotia Environmental Protection Act. Legislative summaries that Kirby had acquired from his friend in the United States ("so that we can, quite frankly, steal some of them") sped the legislative process along and bolstered the "image of a reform."[95] Above all, however, the act had to co-opt at least a portion of environmental activists and, at the same time, restrict the definition of environmental problems to the kind of sewage-and-smoke-stacks treatment systems that the Smith government had been pursuing in the late 1960s.[96] Certainly it had to include nothing that might encourage doubts about the manageability of the problems created by modernist economic development or about its sustainability. Activists were invited to comment on draft legislation, and they did, but from the beginning the centrepiece of the act and its primary concession to popular environmentalism was the creation of an Environmental Control Council, including a large number of non-government members, to investigate environmental issues at public invitation and report back to the minister. As a replacement for the Smith government's Environmental Pollution Council, an internal government body widely criticized for its insularity and secrecy, the ECC was supposed to be public, "apolitical, and independent of government."[97] All this it achieved by being also entirely powerless, unable to even initiate hearings or release reports without the minister's permission. For a short time, however, the council was granted freedom to act, and it attracted the interest and participation of some of the more optimistic members of the activist community, Alan Ruffman of the PCAC and MOVE, for example, and Dr. Ogden of the NSRC.

The Regan government's attempt to take the reins of environmental politics met its first test in the early 1970s in Lunenburg County at the Anil Hardboard plant, at the peak of a classic estuarine campaign for the defence of a home place. The controversy in Lunenburg was near enough to Halifax to attract the attention of the EAC and MOVE coalition – another sign of the tendency towards cooperation – but it was almost entirely the work of another small group of affected locals, this time people in and around the village of East River. The leader of the effort, Robert Whiting, was a hunter and trapper living in East River in 1967, when the provincial government proudly announced the opening of a hardboard fabrication plant next to his home. Touted as a triumph of industrial development, the largest plant of its kind in the world, and the first direct North American investment by an Indian firm, the project came complete with promises that there would be no noise and no pollution of the East River or Mahone Bay.[98] It did not take long for Whiting and his neighbours to see that the reality was rather less than promised. The water of the East River ran red and brown after Anil began production, and the stain of dissolved and suspended wood particles spread well out into Mahone Bay. Salmon numbers in the river declined, and not long afterwards shellfishing was prohibited in the bay. Not until much later did the company admit the presence of phenol, formaldehyde, paraffins, and aluminum sulfate in its effluent, in addition to the load of organic matter.[99] Noise and light from round-the-clock operations vexed those living nearby, and a combination of ash and red dust reached somewhat further afield, while a rotting stench rose from the abandoned quarry converted into Anil's effluent treatment facility and from the swamp through which it discharged into the East River.[100]

Residents "grumbled among ourselves," according to one activist, until Whiting began to organize resistance. Having sold his home next to the plant, he could easily have left the problem behind. Instead he wrote reams of letters to the company, the media, and every level of government, and urged his neighbours to do the same. Allies came slowly: Al Chaddock, a newly arrived artist from Halifax, remembered that "when I first met Bob I thought he was crazy, like just about everyone else did at the time."[101]

Government attempts to quiet dissent eventually brought more allies to Whiting's side. In 1969, the highways minister, I.W. Akerley, who served as president of the National Council of Resource Ministers, had told reporters that the problem at Anil had been "cleaned up." At much the same time, E.L.L. Rowe had opined that with "a new industry like Anil establishing [itself], you have to bend over backwards."[102] Three years later, prior claims forgotten, Rowe and a new minister, Glen Bagnell, were celebrating a new cleanup plan and reassuring locals that the plant's effluent, still brown, "does not contain the harmful wood fibres."[103] But residents of East River had long since learned not to take anyone in government at their word. It took long and patient effort at recruitment and public pressure, but when the newly formed ECC decided to make East River's problematic development the subject of its first public hearing, Whiting's "small army" – now organized as the East River branch of the South Shore Environmental Protection Association (SSEPA), with the support of the FON in Chester – was ready for an official confrontation with Rowe and the management of Anil.[104]

The ECC's hearing, held in a school auditorium in Chester in December 1974, was a ringing success for the East River SSEPA and a demonstration of the power inherent in the combination of local grievance and scientific abstraction. Witnesses ranged from local schoolchildren speaking about the loss of their swimming and fishing areas, to artist Al Chaddock, who arrived carrying a thick slab of matted wood fibre pried from the floor of Mahone Bay, to Norman Dale of Dalhousie University's Institute for Environment Studies, who urged the council to examine sea life in the bay for objective evidence of the effluent's effect.[105] Three presiding council members, finally face to face with the problem, were forced to conclude that the Little East River was "grossly polluted" and to recommend a more comprehensive treatment and monitoring system.[106]

In Chester, the ECC appeared to be a viable forum for change, but after the Anil hearing, the council's freedom was reduced and its members soon complained that they were being ignored by the Department of Environment.[107] Their report on Anil failed to satisfy activists, who expressed disgust at the provincial government's plan to dilute the plant's effluent in the wider reaches of Mahone Bay, where it might not provoke broad public reaction. "It's not over yet," Whiting said, "it's no good to build a pipeline if they'll be sending the same stuff offshore."[108] There would never be another ECC event quite like the fiery confrontation in Chester, however.[109] By 1975, it had served its political purpose. The results of the ECC's first hearing had met government expectations, kept the focus on pollution abatement and away from development policy, and convinced some of the most vocal environmentalists to limit their attacks during a time of political weakness for the Liberal government.

CONCLUSION

An efflorescence of environmental activism at the end of the 1960s built, piecemeal, the conditions for a sustained movement, beginning mostly around polluted harbours such as Boat Harbour in Pictou County and Chedabucto Bay in Guysborough and Richmond Counties, and moving from there to other areas and issues. As that movement coalesced, governments, conservationists, pollution fighters, and political radicals each began attempting to mould the emerging environmentalism into something that conformed to their own respective interests. In the process of negotiating a place for environmental activism in the provincial polity, activists proved that they had the power to alter and sometimes entirely frustrate centrally dictated modernist development policy.

Through such means as the Environmental Protection Act and the ECC, the Regan government attempted with some success to mute and redirect radical environmental protest into channels more consistent with the "end of pipe" vision of environmental regulation. In this they were assisted by the fact that their rivals at the federal level were equally intent on preserving the planning prerogative of experts and administrators, and therefore offered no greater opportunities for more profound activist input. The traditional conservationism of the early twentieth century was vastly preferable, for government experts, to a populist non-modern activism that threatened to squeeze governments between an unavoidable obligation to be seen to do something about declining environmental quality and an unchangeable imperative to pursue prosperity through industrial development. Many no doubt hoped that environmental activism was a passing political fad, soon to fade into yet another regulatory commonplace managed by the appropriate experts, and that a few years of temporizing would suffice to negate the trap. Though they acknowledged environmentalism's growing political power in Nova Scotia, few in government appreciated the mutual reinforcement of environmentalist ideas and awareness of industrial blight, or the inevitable continued growth of the former in lockstep with the latter, as more and more rural residents found their homes and livelihoods jeopardized by developments that, from the planner's perspective, promised to be more profitable on balance.

APES's Irene Edwards accused the province's politicians in 1973 of being "in a state of shock," panicking and in search of scapegoats because they lacked "the ability to comprehend that these people ... could see beyond the rosy future painted for them."[110] About their panicked response she could not have been more right, but some in government realized that not all activists rejected the rosy future of modernism, that the link between environmental activism and the radical politics of local place defence might be mutable, and that government might find common ground with a segment of the movement willing to support the prerogatives of science and expertise. The triangular relationship between those perceptive few in power and the modernist and non-modernist sides of the growing environmental movement shaped environmental activism in Nova Scotia over the following decade.·

2

The Two MECs
Anti-Nuclear Environmentalism

THE TRIGGERING EVENT THAT brought Nova Scotia's scattered environmental activists together in a lasting way was a surprise to almost everyone. The first indication to the public that the new Regan government might be considering a nuclear project came in June 1972 by way of the Halifax *Chronicle-Herald.* Claiming to have information from a source inside government, the newspaper reported that the premier had met personally and in secret with representatives of a US company, Crossley Enterprises Limited, that wished to build a nuclear plant on tiny Stoddard Island, near the southwestern tip of the province.[1] Details remain scarce, because the project never moved past the informal proposal stage; however, the plan, as it emerged from further leaks and admissions over the rest of the summer and the following winter, was to build ten US-style light-water reactors (LWRs) on Stoddard Island and transmit the electricity generated there directly to New England via undersea cable. Had it been built, the complex would have been the largest generating station in the world, at twelve thousand megawatts, though some immediately doubted that the plan could ever work.[2]

Details about the Stoddard Island project were not available in the summer of 1972, but Nova Scotians were amply supplied with cautionary tales from the province's (and the country's) history of industrial development. Nuclear promotion was, after all, merely another step in a long line of industrial promotions in Nova Scotia, the secrecy of which (and the record of environmental damage) united environmentalists in opposition. After

the election of the Stanfield government in 1956, the province had negotiated secretly with a succession of multinational corporations to bring new
industries to Nova Scotia through an arm's-length Crown corporation
called Industrial Estates Limited (IEL). The notion that a well-chosen set
of incentives and subsidies could overcome the structural disadvantages
of the region within Confederation and reindustrialize its economy ne-
cessitated certain omissions and alterations in the province's industrial
regulations. Unionization was discouraged and transparency in negotiation
eschewed.[3] Environmental concerns were inevitably discounted as well in
IEL negotiations, and environmental activism tended to follow whenever
and wherever the ecological consequences of industrialization threatened
people's homes, farms, or businesses. There was a growing sense in the
province that IEL's secrecy effectively served as an environmental equivalent
to anti-union regulations, keeping any activist backlash from emerging
until it was too late.

Suspicion of IEL combined with a well-founded suspicion that the federal government would sacrifice even more of the public good in its quest
to promote nuclear technology. Atomic Energy of Canada Limited (AECL)
was twenty years old in 1972 and enjoyed an uncommon measure of support from the government of Canada. Originally, nuclear reactor technology had been the domain of the military, part of Canada's contribution
to the Second World War–era Manhattan Project, but over the previous
two decades the federal government had spent billions developing the
Canadian Deuterium-Uranium (CANDU) reactor system in hopes of
becoming a major world supplier of civilian nuclear technology. The high-
technology sectors of reactor design and construction, heavy-water production, and nuclear fuel fabrication drove Canadian ambition, but at every
link of the fuel chain there was a great deal of money to be made in the
business of nuclear energy. The results never did quite live up to the promise, though Canadian CANDU salesmen did at least manage to sell reactors
to India, Pakistan, Argentina, and South Korea.[4] Government enthusiasm
never waned, however. From the days of its infancy during the Second
World War, the Canadian nuclear industry was not so much supported
by government as it was a part of the government, and any challenge to
that relationship would have to be formidable indeed.[5]

Given the context, it was perhaps not wise for members of the Regan
government and the publicly owned Nova Scotia Power Corporation
(NSPC) to initially refuse comment on the leaked Stoddard Island plan
for several days. When the premier finally spoke, he offered only equivocal

denials that any earnest negotiations were afoot.[6] By then, it was too late. The opposition Progressive Conservatives had discovered the issue and happily forced Regan into fresh and ever less credible denials as more information came to light, repeatedly highlighting the government's reluctance to volunteer any facts on new developments.[7] The secrecy surrounding the project united those opposed to the Stoddard Island proposal. For every declaration of disinterest by the federal energy minister ("unless," he said, Canadian CANDU reactors could be used instead of American LWRs), there was a countervailing shock, as when Crossley Enterprises' Canadian holding company was revealed to have purchased Stoddard Island in 1971, or when the man who handled the acquisition, Halifax lawyer Ian MacKeigan, was appointed Nova Scotia's new chief justice in 1973.[8] Through a year of uncertainty, suspicion of the government's intentions was the link that bound environmentalists together.

Unsurprisingly, the earliest reactions from existing environmental nongovernmental organizations (ENGOs) focused on the issues of government secrecy and public participation. The Nova Scotia Resources Council (NSRC) was cautiously hopeful of a new attitude of openness to scientific advice on the part of government, embodied in the new Department of Environment and the proposed Environmental Control Council. No doubt any skepticism NSRC members harboured grew stronger after they drew the premier's ire by insisting on a public examination of the risks and benefits of nuclear power – conducted by the appropriate experts, of course – and by wondering aloud, in the case of former NSRC chairman Dr. Donald Dodds, how it squared with the provincial development plan to build light-water reactors in Nova Scotia even as the safety of their design was under investigation in the United States. As the journalist Ralph Surette later reported, the premier was incensed and "had no intention, he said, of scaring off investors by making public the terms of negotiations, no matter what the project was."[9]

Surprisingly even less critical in its public statements was the younger (in terms of both its members and the organization itself) and typically more radical Halifax-based MOVE coalition. The coalition had come together only in 1971 and was still struggling to negotiate funding from the federal government when it was called upon to state its position on nuclear power. The executive, while privately noting its own unanimous opposition to the project, decided to restrict its public statements to a call for open public negotiations.[10] Political calculation may have played a role in the decision, but it is just as likely that the nuclear question represented one of the first of many cases in which the coalition struggled to reconcile the views of its diverse membership with its leaders' desire to use the coalition's higher profile for specific causes. In their different ways, then, both the NSRC and MOVE were reluctant to antagonize the provincial and federal governments. Though they both declared an interest in educating the public about the dangers of nuclear energy, the real work of doing so fell to newer organizations.

Four Acadia University academics calling themselves the Nuclear Power Study Group (NPSG) filled the gap. From October 1972 to the following March, the NPSG produced six bluntly factual and scientifically grounded articles detailing the likely biological, toxicological, and economic effects ten nuclear reactors would have at Stoddard Island, as well as what kinds of effects could not be predicted ahead of time. Chief among the unknowns: what might happen as a result of discharging ten million gallons every minute of twenty-degree-warmer water into the ocean in the richest lobster fishing district in the province, from which a quarter of the annual catch was landed. Radiation dangers, accidents, and employment impacts were also unknowns. The NPSG's stated purpose was to "contribute to informed public discussion." As such, the group explicitly eschewed an "alarmist position," to the point that its writing sometimes drifted into textbook-style scientific exposition.[11] But the four academics were not averse to taking a stand. In summing up the series, they dispensed with scientific reserve long enough to observe that, in contemplating the US connection, including the burden of risks and the disposition of benefits, "the word 'exploitation' comes to mind."[12]

By early 1973, anti-nuclear ENGOs in Nova Scotia were establishing links with each other, and although the NPSG was not heard from again (likely due to Dr. John Brown's departure from Acadia), their essay series was reproduced in the press and by groups across the province who wanted to borrow the scientists' mantle of legitimacy and authority. One group that did so, and also provided some of its own research, was the fledgling Ecology Action Centre (EAC) at Dalhousie University in Halifax, a member of the MOVE coalition and sometime collaborator with the NSRC.[13] Though the EAC was dependent on government funding, its initial membership was, unlike MOVE, wholly environmentally focused and eager to expand beyond its initial preoccupation with urban issues of city planning and recycling. The centre's first publication on nuclear power, in December 1972, openly opposed the Stoddard Island project. Citing routine radiation exposure, accidental releases, thermal pollution, radon from uranium mine tailings, and the unsolved problem of nuclear waste storage, the document concluded that "the electricity, the profits, and even many of the jobs would go to Americans, while Nova Scotians would take the risks." After such a litany of complaints, its closing recommendation for open, public negotiations between Crossley Enterprises and the provincial government seemed comically redundant.[14] In its policy statements and grant proposals throughout 1973, the EAC repeated its emphasis on the injustice of Nova Scotia's assumption of nuclear risks for the benefit of the United States, but it also kept up its agitation for public participation and also showed a strong commitment to the limits to growth thesis. The centre warned that the province would eventually have to deal with its own energy shortage, and by the end of 1973, a year when the international politics of oil pricing bolstered the theory that there were hard ecological limits to the continuation of economic growth, its coordinator was advocating a policy of zero demand growth and zero energy exports.[15]

Another group that leaned on the NPSG's scientific ammunition organized over the winter of 1973. The new South Shore Environmental Protection Association (SSEPA), which would go on to play a central role in the province's environmental movement for a decade, targeted all three levels of government in an attempt to defeat the Stoddard Island proposal politically, rather than merely request public participation or work at public education. Following the lead of the Southwestern Nova Scotia Lobster Fishermen's Association (and sharing members with it), the SSEPA won unequivocal support from the Barrington and Yarmouth municipal councils, Progressive Conservative offshore resources critic and MP for South Shore Lloyd Crouse, and Liberal social services minister and Shelburne County MLA Harold Huskilson, by impressing upon them that, in the words of fishermen's association president Glen Devine, "this whole area [and its voters] depends entirely on fish."[16] Under the leadership of author and activist Hattie Perry, the SSEPA gained its greatest success in October 1973, when Premier Regan attended a public meeting in the tiny village of Barrington Passage, about ten kilometres from Stoddard Island, and found waiting for him hundreds of nearby residents who wanted only one thing. He gave it to them: a clear promise of public consultation on any proposed nuclear plant in Shelburne County, and another that no project would be approved that might harm the fishery.[17]

Political pressure had won a victory for the SSEPA. The assurances given at Barrington Passage, combined with the failure of the proponent to quickly address the suggestion of CANDU reactors from the federal Atomic Energy Control Board (AECB), seemed to spell the end of the Stoddard Island proposal by 1974. There was, however, no corresponding revival of trust in government and no dissolution of the groups that led the fight. If anything, the continued commitment of the Regan government to two badly functioning heavy-water plants built to supply the Canadian nuclear industry in the late 1960s at Glace Bay and Port Hawkesbury suggested a continued interest in nuclear technology.[18] Hattie Perry continued enthusiastically to lead SSEPA's opposition to nuclear development schemes through her writing, leaning on the NPSG's research and adding her own on alternative energy sources and the health effects of radiation. She drew on an international discussion of nuclear dangers but always returned to the threat posed to the local fishing economy and the lack of appreciable local benefit.[19] The SSEPA also showed its continuing concern over the threat of government secrecy at an ECC public hearing in Yarmouth a month after the Barrington Passage meeting, where, according to the ECC, "the people present cited the example of the apparent lack of an environmental assessment study for the Strait of Canso [refinery and shipping complex] as evidence that these kinds of projects and developments can and will go forward without public approval."[20]

NOT IN ANYBODY'S BACKYARD

Anti-nuclear activism in Nova Scotia was fully immersed in a worldwide movement of the same type. It attracted the attention of pacifist immigrants, especially Quakers, veterans of American anti-war protests who worked to draw attention to the links between nuclear war and nuclear power, and to introduce other Nova Scotians to a placeless international peace movement. Anti-nuclear protestors in Nova Scotia were also well aware of the actions of the Clamshell Alliance later in the 1970s in Maine, where activists resorted to civil disobedience to fight nuclear development. The strongest and earliest connections outside of the province, however, were with the anti-nuclear movement in New Brunswick, where protestors faced an energy project that enjoyed the full support of the AECB. New Brunswick's activists, like Nova Scotia's, found their strength in determined defence of local places and economies, especially rural places. As the two governments (and that of Prince Edward Island) planned new collaboration, these primarily rural activists demonstrated the emptiness of the parochial "NIMBY" (Not In My Back Yard) stereotype by reaching out to each other to form a common regional front.

Premier Regan's clearly reluctant climbdown over Stoddard Island and continued support for the heavy-water plants were not the only reasons to fear a resurgence of the nuclear idea in Nova Scotia. Even as word of the South Shore project spread in 1972, news broke of another nuclear plant proposal across the Bay of Fundy in New Brunswick, which would eventually become the Point Lepreau generating station.[21] The Nova Scotia Power Corporation's general manager immediately denied having any interest in the project, but with the failure of the Stoddard Island plan activists were wary of the provincial government's intentions. Within a year, Regan and the same NSPC official transformed wariness into alarm by promising to decide on whether to buy into New Brunswick's planned second reactor or to build one of their own instead, perhaps somewhere in northeastern Nova Scotia. The success of the Organization of the Petroleum Exporting Countries (OPEC) oil cartel in 1973 gave proponents of atomic technology a second chance to sell their wares to the public, and statements like "we have to get into nuclear power" from the provincial energy agency meant that activists in the two leading organizations had to remain ready to push back.[22]

Whereas the SSEPA transitioned more or less seamlessly to general anti-nuclear activism, the Ecology Action Centre had more trouble. The centre's student staff had better reason than most to appreciate the limits of finite resources in 1973: that was the last full year of federal government funding they would ever see. Across the country, student groups that had enjoyed the largesse of the federal Opportunities for Youth and Local Initiatives Programs during the heyday of student radicalism found the government's commitment to youth empowerment fading along with the threat of youth rebellion. Many groups simply melted away, as MOVE would soon do, but the EAC staff were determined to find the means to keep the organization running. Remarkably, they did, but the transformation from fully funded organization to registered charity – in a sense a liberation from the government purse – had the perverse effect of blunting the centre's radical spirit. With a newly formed board of directors drawn as much from the academic and business communities of Halifax as from the centre's older constituencies of student leaders and environmental activists, the EAC returned to the nuclear power issue in late 1974 at the request of the SSEPA and immediately fell into disagreement over what position to take. Some of the new directors insisted on hedging the centre's opposition to nuclear energy in case of social and economic need, while others argued that such ill-defined hurdles would vitiate any real opposition and urged a categorical rejection of nuclear power. A vote ended with a statement of opposition, but the centre chose to refocus on the less controversial issue of public participation as the central matter of energy policy going into 1975, rather than the limits to economic growth or environmental justice arguments that still preoccupied their South Shore peers.[23] The year ended with the centre's survival in doubt and its ability to function severely compromised, leaving a void in the Halifax activist scene that was promptly filled by a group of very different origins but very similar tendency to look first beyond the local context.

During the height of the Stoddard Island controversy, another gathering of Haligonians opposed to the scheme and to nuclear development in general had taken shape from elements of the Voice of Women for Peace (VOW) organization and the Halifax Friends Meeting (Quakers). Both groups had a long association with peace and social justice issues and, in the case of VOW, a history of connecting environmental and anti-nuclear activism, though their work had mainly been in opposition to nuclear weapons rather than nuclear energy. VOW was a national coalition of groups formed in 1960 to oppose Cold War nuclear brinkmanship. Its Halifax leaders, Peggy Hope-Simpson and Muriel Duckworth, pulled together a resourceful group of well-to-do Halifax women and quickly turned the local VOW into the most active branch in the country outside of Toronto, with a keen appreciation for related issues.[24] At the Halifax hearing of the federal Man and Resources program in 1972, the group displayed a keen appreciation of the link between peace, environmental justice, and the limits to growth. In support of "zero economic growth and zero industrial growth" and in opposition to what it called the "consume-exploit-pollute society," VOW explained that

> the Voice of Women has found that we cannot merely espouse an end to war, we must espouse a way of life free from the gearing toward war. Voice of Women cannot advocate a rise in living standards for the rich nations when this rise means a consequent depletion of the resources necessary for the survival of the poor nations.[25]

Both nationally and in Halifax, VOW had close links to the Quakers. From their beginnings as a group of religious dissidents in seventeenth-century England, the Quakers (or Friends, as they call themselves) have maintained a strong commitment to pacifism and to actively opposing violence, warfare, and injustice by moral pressure and "bearing witness." Dorothy Norvell, a recently arrived immigrant from the United States, a Quaker, and a third-generation peace activist, introduced the Halifax Voices to the Quakers' published critique of modern industrial society, *Speak Truth to Power*. Muriel Duckworth, Peggy Hope-Simpson, and Helen Cunningham were also Quakers. Historian Frances Early credits the influence of these Quaker/Voices leaders with the Halifax VOW's "consensual decision-making process."[26]

When Stoddard Island and nuclear power hit the province's front pages in 1972, the Halifax Friends Meeting, lacking any consensus, felt the need for a more complete understanding of nuclear power issues and their relationship to nuclear weapons, war, and social justice. It asked another newly arrived American member named Susan Holtz to do some research for them. As a researcher for the local Friends meeting, Holtz quickly arrived at conclusions in line with the VOW statement at Man and Resources. "Power for what?" she wrote to New Brunswick anti-nuclear activist Doris Calder. "For a way of life for the affluent in North America which is entirely oriented toward disastrously wasteful consumption? For a way of life which cannot be continued if everyone in our global village is to share together our world's resources?"[27] In a matter of months, Holtz became an activist as much as a researcher and deliberately chose to devote herself to the more technical issue of nuclear risk, rather than ecological limits or environmental justice. Those, she told Calder, could be taken care of by other Friends in her group.[28] In reality, the group tends to follow the leader, and Holtz, who brought nearly endless energy to her role, soon became the de facto leader. Fellow activist Alan Ruffman remembers her as a particularly "intellectual" sort (rather than political), and the same might be said of the group she gathered around herself in 1974 to encourage public opposition to nuclear power and discourage government's nuclear ambitions.[29] The group of Quakers, Unitarians, and VOW members, including Norvell and Duckworth, soon began to refer to themselves as the Conserver Society Group (CSG).[30]

The anti-nuclear CSG spent most of 1974 making connections with like-minded activists and organizations across Canada, gathering information and encouraging the formation of a national coalition to take the fight to AECL and Ottawa. Duckworth, Norvell, and Holtz wrote to activists in Vancouver, Calgary, Toronto, and elsewhere, and tried to persuade organizations like the Canadian Wildlife Federation to form a common front. They also cultivated contacts with sympathetic journalists like Ralph Surette and the editors of the *4th Estate,* much as VOW had done in the 1960s.[31] Their approach was decidedly non-local, however, consistent with their peace movement background, and what they did not do was approach the SSEPA, at least not until SSEPA secretary Anne Wickens wrote to Holtz with an invitation to join the group. It was their correspondence that brought the CSG into contact with a growing Maritime coalition.[32]

As the CSG's activities suggest, shared concern over nuclear power tended to draw activists together despite membership in different groups. It also tended to do so at the same level of geographic integration as the program they opposed. The federal jurisdiction of the AECB/AECL provoked some limited national coalition, but provincial jurisdiction and the actions of the three Maritime governments drew more attention to the regional level. Only three months after its apparent success in October 1973, the SSEPA was confronted with Nova Scotia's possible investment in the proposed Point Lepreau nuclear plant in New Brunswick, geographically closer than Halifax to the association's home in Shelburne and Yarmouth Counties. Once again the provincial government stubbornly refused to share information about the negotiations, and New Brunswick's premier certainly could not be influenced in the same manner that Gerald Regan had been. In response, the SSEPA reached out to New Brunswickers who were organizing against the Hatfield government's nuclear plans.[33] It played a major part in drawing together the first New Brunswick antinuclear coalition, along with representatives of the Moncton branch of Pollution Probe, the Eel River Bar Mi'kmaq Band Council, and two other local groups.[34] In its first incarnation, as the Chaleur Environmental Protection Association (CEPA), the coalition set out in the spring of 1974 with "no immediate plans to seek meetings with public officials" about Lepreau or about another nuclear plant proposed for New Brunswick's northeast coast. Instead, it said, "we're going to bring experts in to inform the public about the dangers of nuclear plants" and provoke popular opposition in the affected areas, much as local opposition in southwestern Nova Scotia had fed into a provincial and regional movement.[35] By the end of the year, nuclear development plans had provoked a wide enough reaction that a broader coalition became necessary, and CEPA gave way to the Maritime Coalition of Environmental Protection Associations, later rechristened the Maritime Energy Coalition (MEC) for publicity purposes. (It was a shorter name, a clearer statement of the group's interests, and it needled the provincial governments by borrowing the acronym of the proposed regional utility, the Maritime Energy Corporation.) Official statements of support for the MEC came in from Women's Institutes, fishermen's associations, nurses' associations, the NSRC, VOW, and the EAC, along with an application for full membership from the Halifax Meeting of the Religious Society of Friends.[36]

Anti-nuclear organization by small rural activist groups under the MEC banner contributed the greatest vitality to the regional movement during the mid-1970s, and kept questions of limits and local economic autonomy at the forefront. In later years, the alleged self-centredness of local single-issue groups would lead to their being labelled "NIMBYs" and dismissed as unsophisticated reactionaries happy to foist the projects they rejected onto some less fortunate community. Such positions were rarely in evidence. Activists initially motivated by personal risk, living near potential nuclear construction sites, consistently joined forces to oppose nuclear development anywhere in the region. Continuing their focus on public outreach rather than bureaucratic consultation, MEC groups planned alternative energy festivals on New Brunswick's Kingston Peninsula and in Middleton, Annapolis County, in 1976, in an effort to convince the public to work towards local energy independence and the dissolution of central energy agencies like the New Brunswick Electric Power Corporation (NBEPC) and NSPC.[37] In Halifax, meanwhile, the EAC was scarcely active in 1974 and early 1975, uncertain of its position on nuclear power and suffering through the end of federal funding and the steep learning curve of charitable fundraising. By the fall of 1975, however, the CSG had merged into the EAC as its new energy committee, bringing the volunteers and financial support of the Halifax Friends Meeting into the EAC's established structure (and into its free office space at Dalhousie University), and uniting most of Halifax's anti-nuclear activists under the EAC name.[38] If unity was truly the prerequisite for effective action, the stage was set in 1975.

CITIZEN-SCIENCE AND POLITICAL POWER

In the mid-1970s, activists from city to farm shared the opinion of Donald Hamilton of the Northumberland Regional Development Association that "unity is the only way that we can effectively combat the nuclear power menace."[39] Moreover, no single group had achieved a dominant position from which to force upon others a position that might alienate them. Local groups each continued to carry on parallel campaigns without cooperation or sometimes even knowledge of the others, despite nominally being in coalition. This would change, but not before the Halifax activists developed a more scientific environmental rhetoric and a willingness to collaborate with the environmental agencies of the state. In the process of doing so, and especially in the process of organizing publicity for the anti-nuclear coalition, a divergence began to show between the more modernist activists and those who wished to persist in the bottom-up promotion of decentralized, low-technology living.

From the inception of the CSG, the Quaker anti-nuclear activists of Halifax were eager to appear respectable and to appeal to federal and provincial bureaucrats (and corporations) in intellectual terms. Even when asserting limits ideas, as she did in correspondence with the deputy minister of the federal Department of Energy, Mines and Resources (EMR) and with AECL managers, Susan Holtz hedged on implementation, suggesting "an immediate and serious energy conservation policy" instead of a policy of zero economic growth.[40] Nor did the CSG ever share the SSEPA's commitment to argument based on local environmental justice, preferring to argue from the general principle to the specific case rather than vice versa. Holtz remained the public face of the group for years, and was a prolific letter-writer who never forgot her mission to highlight the technical risks of nuclear technology. One of the events that reinforced that determination was the Critical Mass conference in Washington, DC, in November 1974, where US consumer advocate and anti-nuclear leader Ralph Nader brought together citizens' groups from all over North America to share information, and where Holtz learned that "from a political point of view, it is just as effective to put real doubt in people's minds as it is to bring them, 100% committed, to your side – and it's far easier."[41] As she told the SSEPA's Anne Wickens shortly after returning from Washington, the lesson for Nova Scotian activists, unsure about how much weight the premier's anti-nuclear promise would carry, was a pragmatic and practical one: to win over decision makers, "one needn't push one's absolute convictions quite so hard, but one does need lots of facts and credible experts."[42] Facts and experts might be just as convincing to the wider public in order to build a mass political movement, but Holtz, who saw her job as being a bridge between the public and the powerful, immediately began planning a venue where decision makers could be convinced by the intellectual merit of anti-nuclear views.

The Energy and People conference took place at Saint Mary's University in Halifax on September 19–21, 1975. Outside of environmental activist circles, its general context was the global "energy crisis," still in full swing since the OPEC cartel moved to reduce the supply of crude oil to world markets in October 1973.[43] Because of its greater dependence on imported crude for electricity generation, Atlantic Canada had felt the sting of rising prices more severely than any other region of the country. Meanwhile, uncertainty surrounding the plans of the three Maritime governments to replace some of their oil-fired generators with nuclear generating stations fuelled continued speculation and anxiety. Despite the promise extracted from him at the Barrington Passage meeting, Nova Scotia's premier had spent the following year issuing statements alternately promising a major nuclear project and denying that any such project was being entertained. New Brunswickers remained unsure whether or when or where a companion project to the Point Lepreau reactor would be announced, and the question of purchasing electricity from Lepreau still lay unresolved in Prince Edward Island. Given the context, Energy and People could hardly have avoided becoming a forum for nuclear debate, but its organizers hoped for, and achieved, a much wider discussion of related energy and economic issues.[44]

The idea for the conference (and the largest monetary contribution) came in the fall of 1974 from several Quaker members of the Conserver Society Group, who hoped that a well-publicized conference catering to a non-expert lay audience might help advance the notion from which their group drew its name. The term "conserver society" was coined by the Science Council of Canada (SCC) in its 1973 report on *Natural Resource Policy Issues in Canada,* in reference to a society, unlike our present consumer society, in which resource decisions would recognize total costs (account for externalities, in other words), respect the limits of the biosphere, and also bear in mind costs deferred to the future.[45] As a general principle with uncertain implications for economic growth, the phrase "conserver society," like "sustainable development" after it, brought together people with varying interpretations of the meaning of "wastefulness" and the possibility of continued economic growth. Once together, however, activists discovered sharp divergences between their respective interpretations and political intentions. When planning for the Energy and People conference began, in accordance with the consensus principle borrowed from VOW and with committees drawn from several co-sponsoring organizations, those differences fuelled conflict: some wanted an event with strictly public appeal and a strong anti-nuclear and anti-growth message, whereas others wished to use the conference to make connections and build support within federal and provincial bureaucracies, where talk of limits to growth could close rather than open doors. After three months deciding and six preparing, the organizers did manage to achieve the mixed audience and "balanced presentation of controversial issues" they sought, but tensions between alternative visions of the conference only grew sharper as the event got underway.[46]

Limits to growth were a prominent theme at the conference, beginning with the keynote address by Gordon Edwards of the fledgling Canadian

Coalition for Nuclear Responsibility (CCNR). The CCNR represented the fruition of the campaign of Holtz and others for a federal-level lobbying organization made up of ENGOs from across Canada, and in 1975 it was in the process of developing a more or less technical rhetoric of radiation hazards and the hidden costs of nuclear energy, rather than an explicit attack on economic growth or modernist society.[47] Though he stopped short of offering specific answers or policy prescriptions at the conference, Edwards spoke at length on the illusion of scientific analysis of mathematically incalculable values such as wilderness (he cited the current debate over the damming of British Columbia's Skagit River) or of unknown quantities such as accident probabilities at nuclear reactors. For him, the path to a conserver society lay not in the recognition of some narrow technical risks and substitution of lesser risks, but in giving up the obsessive "idea of a machine" and admitting the ecological context of society, complete with limits and unmanageable unintended consequences.[48]

Along with Edwards's warnings about the impossibility of continued exponential growth, others presented radical policy proposals and openly questioned the role of government as an honest regulator and interpreter of policy ideas, particularly where the balance of evidence and argument pointed to conclusions that contradicted economic orthodoxy. Dalhousie University environmental lawyer and EAC board member Ian McDougall argued against continued electricity exports to the United States due to the inevitable exhaustion of Canadian energy sources, a theme echoed by Bill Peden of Ontario's Energy Probe. Challenged by government representatives who claimed that a transition to renewable technologies through a period of rising energy use was the only way to avoid massive increases in unemployment in Canada, MOVE member Don Grady replied for the limits theorists that changing the basic nature of society required "unacceptable" actions, and that in order to avoid such actions, governments would always attend conferences like Energy and People "to lie."[49]

Such outbursts of hostility towards the bureaucracy probably went some way towards inspiring the conference chairperson's retrospective assessment that citizens must do more to "encourage governments to trust groups," but in truth there was at least as much opportunity at the conference for government and corporate attendees to present their views, beginning with their presence on the discussion panels. Compromise and consensus in event planning worked against those who wanted an ideologically consistent presentation. Atomic Energy of Canada Limited, Gulf Oil, Nova Scotia Power Corporation, and the federal Department of Energy, Mines and Resources had displays of promotional material throughout; Robert Stanfield, then leader of the federal opposition Progressive Conservatives, gave an anodyne opening speech; and EMR's direct contribution, an energy primer pamphlet called *See Energy Run*, was distributed to attendees despite organizer Bill Zimmerman's complaints that it was "slanted" and not at all what was promised. Organizers even attempted to prevent the drafting of resolutions for the conference, not wanting to alienate the bureaucratic contributors. This last attempt at achieving the appearance of balance came to naught, however, as attendees assembled on their own to vote and approve a resolution that "this conference rejects nuclear power in its present form as the energy source of the future and calls for a moratorium on the licensing, construction, and sale of nuclear power plants until full national, public, and parliamentary debates are held." While the anti-nuclear resolution certainly highlights the perceived urgency of the nuclear issue in Nova Scotia and New Brunswick (which between them supplied much more than two-thirds of the attendees at the conference), the fate of the limits thesis may better demonstrate the will of the organizers. A proposed resolution to encourage priority in both funding and planning decisions for "small-scale, decentralized" projects was voted down.[50]

The Energy and People conference marked a turning point for the anti-nuclear activist community in Halifax. At the time the conference was planned, the CSG was deliberately embarking on a path of technical argument as a means of attracting the ear of government and bolstering anti-nuclear elements within the bureaucracy. The compromises inherent in consensus decision making put their reasonable and unthreatening modernist approach, which did not question the possibility or desirability of economic growth or the value of centralization and the power of expert decision makers, directly next to the attempt of more radical activists to attract media attention and convince the public of the relevance of self-sufficiency, local autonomy, and ecological limits to energy planning. Given the choice, the media unsurprisingly tended to report more favourably on the former; consequently, the more radical conference planners seem to have abandoned the cooperative effort as a vehicle for political pressure.[51] The explicit insistence on limits and distrust of government were absent from the continuing committee's follow-up report in October 1975, replaced by an emphasis on public education and a national lobbying effort, and a commitment to pure "facts and figures," such as were being compiled at the energy library that Holtz built in the EAC's offices with funding from the Halifax Friends Meeting and the Canadian Friends Service Committee. The continuing committee itself, top-heavy with engineers and professional planners, reflected the near-disappearance of radicals from the Halifax coalition as it settled into its new identity as the EAC's energy committee.[52]

The sort of energy policy advocated by the EAC's committee following Energy and People – a technologically novel but economically orthodox mix of wind power and solar, with some conservation measures added – required financial incentives and investment more than social change, and therefore required more convincing of politicians and bureaucrats than of the public. It also encouraged a national perspective, because activists across the country could direct their combined efforts towards the largest relevant energy technology research body, the federal Department of Energy, Mines and Resources. Cultivating those kinds of connections outside of the region could take two forms: bringing the rest of the country and continent to Nova Scotia, or sending Nova Scotians out to meet them. As one might expect, the most persuasive anti-nuclear spokesmen came from those jurisdictions where the industry had been longest established, particularly in Ontario and the United States, and in 1976 the EAC's energy committee led the effort to bring those speakers to Nova Scotia. Following Gordon Edwards, the first prominent visitor was American energy expert Amory Lovins, whose concept of a "soft energy path" was just beginning to achieve global recognition. The two key characteristics of a soft path are renewability (using solar, wind, or geothermal sources, for example) and appropriate scale and quality (warming houses with on-site heat, for example, rather than with distant, central electric generators). The congruence with conserver society ideas was obvious, and the Science Council of Canada eagerly sponsored a speaking tour. The EAC just as eagerly encouraged Premier Regan to attend. He declined.[53] In fact, despite the energy committee's best efforts to attract them, provincial politicians continued to disappoint.[54] Appeals to corporate self-interest were about as fruitful; when activists sent a five-person delegation to the Atlantic Provinces Economic Council seminar on energy in January 1976, one reported back that the regular delegates would be tempted away from their support for nuclear power only if they could be shown "how to make their money back on the initial cost of alternative energy development and begin to show profit."[55] It was a position to which the committee spent more and more time appealing, but it was hardly a recipe for a radical economic revision of consumer society, and it encouraged a disproportionate focus on the technology of the soft path rather than the issues of scale and ownership.

Outside the province, the leaders of the Halifax anti-nuclear network continued to be heavily involved in the CCNR and found, in Susan Holtz's words, "some openness" to public input in Ottawa, especially from EMR. It was a welcome change from the secrecy and stonewalling back home in the country's "most secretive jurisdiction."[56] Yet the CCNR's strategy itself was essentially conservative. In order to "be taken seriously on technical and policy issues," its arguments inevitably circled the familiar ground of radiation risks and reactor safety, and the constant demand to which all of its public efforts were directed – the nuclear responsibility weeks, rallies, and national petitions in which the EAC participated – was for nothing more than a national inquiry into nuclear power.[57] Even so, it was all to no avail, at least in Ottawa. EMR listened, but preferred the advice of AECL vice president A.M. Aikin, who warned against any forum that allowed demagogues to abuse "honest, capable scientists," and who went on in 1977 to co-author EMR's wildly optimistic Hare Report on the management of nuclear waste.[58] The overrepresentation of nuclear science in EMR's research and development budget revealed their preference just as clearly. What the department wanted, and offered, was an energy conservation and renewable generation program that Canadian ENGOs might support, and that might be kept at a safe distance from the work of forming a more fundamental energy policy based on greater use of nuclear energy and fossil fuels. In one telling example, EMR's Office of Renewable Energy, along with the Ministry of State for Science and Technology, sponsored a series of conferences in 1977 on the conserver society concept, the Halifax edition of which focused on renewable energy sources. Local activists did much of the organizational work, but when the EAC's Susan Mayo discussed the preparations with the ministry's Ray Bouchard, her frustration was plain and her assessment blunt: "The fuckers didn't ask us about nuclear power!"[59] Nor was she alone in noticing that, for federal bureaucrats at EMR and Environment Canada, "alternative" energy seemed more often to mean "additional" energy and a reason to avoid discussing the nuclear issue.[60]

Despite its frustrations, the task of working within a coalition of Canadian ENGOs to access the levers of power in Ottawa preoccupied the EAC's energy committee at the end of 1977. Holtz argued to the Canadian Environmental Advisory Council (CEAC), a federally funded panel of experts and activists among whose number she would soon find a seat, that the federal government's power to seize jurisdiction, as it had done over the nuclear industry, meant that ENGOs had to "get beyond local issues" and concentrate on winning over members of the federal bureaucracy.[61] And the perennial dream of recapturing the policy initiative and influencing the most basic assumptions of Canada's energy economy did not fade. When the CEAC invited ENGOs to formal consultations in 1977, so that it might "better advise the minister," activists aware of their creeping marginalization used the opportunity to form a new national coalition, aiming, in the words of its first president, David Brooks, "to raise the issue from particular[s ...] to the question of a conserver society."[62] Their efforts were somewhat confused, however, and the organization that resulted, Friends of the Earth (Canada) (FOE), immediately became a gathering of the more professional ENGOs, who were reluctant to be seen as radicals. The new organization was also supposed to be independent of government funding, reflecting some awareness of the distortions wrought in the conserver society concept by bureaucratic agenda setting, but the need to avoid competing with its own member organizations for donations left FOE no other option but to depend immediately on government research contracts for its operating budget. That FOE still met with a hesitant reception from the EAC's board of directors says something about how cautious the centre had become; some wondered whether the EAC could fully support the more ambitious version of the conserver society notion, or whether it would prove "too political" a goal for the centre's tax-exempt charitable status.[63] Nonetheless, Holtz continued to represent the centre at FOE and to the CEAC's National Steering Committee (which later evolved into the Canadian Environmental Network), and she became part of the effort when the former group acted to put Amory Lovins's soft energy path on the national agenda.

With the financial backing of EMR, the Science Council of Canada, and Petro-Canada, the first Friends of the Earth soft energy path (SEP) study began in late 1978, only four months after the formal creation of the coalition. Though ambitious, it was not without precedent, even in Canada. While leading EMR's Office of Energy Conservation in 1977, David Brooks had drafted a national SEP study with the help of the University of Waterloo's John Robinson, which was itself intended to be a more detailed and complete version of Amory Lovins's SEP paper on Canada, commissioned the previous year by the SCC. Dissatisfied with his work at EMR, Brooks proposed a study that accounted for the full diversity across Canada's provinces. The FOE study, then, was to be yet another refinement of the basic argument Lovins made in 1976: that a future in which Canadians relied primarily on "renewable, decentralized, and ecologically sustainable" energy sources was both feasible and not even particularly difficult to achieve.[64] The influence of Susan Holtz was all over the decision to take the SEP concept to the next (national) level of collaboration. Having sponsored a panel (including Brooks) on Nova Scotia's

SEP in November 1977 for a largely bureaucratic audience, and having pursued provincial funding for a study on the same from early 1978, Holtz's energy committee was clearly eager to advance the concept among the bureaucratic elite.[65]

In comically Canadian fashion, the first set of provincial SEP studies completed and published in the FOE journal *Alternatives* in 1979 and 1980 was written without common metrics and could not be compiled into a single combined set of data. A revised set was undertaken in 1980, this time funded by Environment Canada and EMR, and the results were published in 1983 as *2025: Soft Energy Futures for Canada*. It was by the lead authors' own admission a remarkably conservative document, explicitly disavowing calculation of the social and environmental costs of various technological options in favour of a strictly economic calculus based on projections of future energy demand drawn from Statistics Canada and EMR economic models. Political considerations were absent as well. Amory and Hunter Lovins wrote in the introduction that "this Canadian study's technical assumptions are so conservative that only a concerted drive for *in*efficient energy use and deliberate *suppression* of cost-effective renewable sources could achieve a Canadian energy system needing more fossil or nuclear fuel than is calculated here."[66] Neither they nor the authors suggested what to do if such a policy did in fact prevail.

One of the intriguing practices of the FOE study was called "backcasting," another term borrowed from Lovins's work. Recognizing that typical economic forecasts subsume the categories of what can happen and what should happen into the seemingly objective category of what will probably happen, backcasters pick a desired economic condition at some point in the future and attempt to determine how and whether it can be achieved. The subjective nature of desirability and probability are acknowledged, and feasibility comes to the fore. So do the authors' assumptions about what is politically palatable. In the FOE study, a hypothetical Canadian economy in the year 2025 provided a "desirable" end point from which the "hard" technologies (central, large-scale, non-renewable, and environmentally destructive) were absent. In practice, this meant that the authors ruled out only nuclear energy, Arctic oil, and coal liquefaction as unacceptable.[67] For the sake of a convincing future scenario, it also meant that the appropriate scale of acceptable technologies disappeared in the analysis, along with questions of ownership, whole-system analysis (including non-energy resources), and any doubts about continued economic growth. Considered politically impractical, those ideas fell outside the category of the "pragmatic."[68] The Nova Scotian segment of the study, for example,

Susan Holtz's own work, shared the general premise of "strong economic growth and substantial increases in material standards of living" and assumed an increased industrial output for the province of 1.3 to 1.9 percent per annum, as well as a 50 percent increase in population.[69]

The *2025* feasibility study, addressed in large part to an audience within government, was intended to lay a foundation for policy. Its omissions provide a sense of just what Canada's first national-level, general-interest, nominally independent environmental coalition felt it needed to sacrifice in order to be heard at the end of the 1970s. The EAC and its Canadian allies wished as much as ever for an equitable and clean energy system in the country, but an apolitical feasibility study in which none of the scenarios approaches the goal of a conserver society – not even one so conservatively defined as in the description Holtz and Susan Mayo of the EAC gave in 1979: a "higher efficiency" society with less material throughput[70] – and that carefully avoids any hint of lifestyle changes was a far cry from the kind of populist, limits-aware environmentalism that initially responded to the threat of a nuclear facility on Stoddard Island in 1973. By demonstrating the supposed ease of the transition to a soft energy path, the study's authors hoped to force bureaucrats to acknowledge its viability and justify any different choice of energy policy; in reality, they removed the need for anyone to seriously address the SEP. Presenting the soft path as not only possible but also profitable encouraged, if anything, a feeling that the usual mechanisms of a market economy should produce the desired society with little or no public encouragement.

1979: "It Can Happen Here"

While the Energy and People conference gave the Halifax-based anti-nuclear activist network a chance to set the agenda in discussions of energy policy, the luxury of doing so proved short-lived. The years 1976 and 1977 saw the resurgence of participation in the Maritime Energy Corporation as a viable policy option for Nova Scotia and the beginning of talks to that end between the Nova Scotia Power Corporation, New Brunswick Electric Power Corporation, and federal Department of Energy, Mines and Resources.[71] Word that Ottawa would exempt AECL projects from the new federal environmental assessment program – and news that NSPC might have already been searching for a nuclear plant site in the central or northeastern areas of the province since 1974 – compounded the renewed sense of urgency.[72] Richard Hatfield's government had committed New

Brunswick to a policy of electricity exports to the US Northeast, and EMR's newest "energy strategy," according to Susan Holtz's assessment, "blatantly exclud[ed] political, social, and environmental considerations," as well as other forms of energy, in favour of continually expanding the supply of electric power produced in Canada.[73] With most of the decision-making power between them, it seemed that the NBEPC and EMR might turn the proposed regional utility into little more than an eastern subsidiary of AECL, and potentially remove the ability of the provincial government in Halifax to reject nuclear energy proposals. Facing the possibility of losing what small influence they had already gained over the province's energy policy, the Halifax network increasingly turned to their federal connections in hope of ending Ottawa's love affair with one of its most protected and promoted agencies. In the rest of the province, however, a new popular activism began to take root, and it provided the basis of the burst of political pressure that scuttled the regional utility proposal for good after 1979.

Part of the explanation for the new intensity of local activism lies in the same federal connection sought in Halifax. Offers of funding from Ottawa to small local groups willing to focus on renewable energy and conservation tended to distract activists from anti-nuclear activism while reinforcing their local character. New Brunswickers opposed to the Point Lepreau project suggested that the federal government was using targeted funding to "defuse strong polarized resistance to nuclear power in particular and large scale energy projects in general."[74] If so, it was a successful strategy: during most of the late 1970s, new energy activist groups in Nova Scotia struggled to put public pressure on elected officials, to imitate the success of forestry activists in Cape Breton, and to lift their political profile beyond basic energy conservation advocacy. This was true even when some of their founding members were keen to make a more direct attack on the political scene.[75] Both the Annapolis Valley Energy Centre and the Amherst Energy Conservation Information Centre, new to activism in 1978, looked to the well-established EAC for guidance, learning from the its staff how to access federal funds and how to undermine the nuclear sales pitch with talk of alternative technologies and energy conservation. Even veteran SSEPA activists began to pursue the funded information centre model during those years.[76]

Unexpected circumstances turned this low-profile wave of local energy conservation activism into just what EMR seemed eager to avoid: a renaissance of anti-nuclear political pressure. The Stoddard Island proposal was long dead at the beginning of 1979, but another nuclear island was about to make world headlines: the accident at Three Mile Island generating station in Pennsylvania on March 28, 1979, reinvigorated popular opposition to nuclear energy everywhere and a political style of energy activism in Nova Scotia. In the aftermath of Three Mile Island and with construction on New Brunswick's first Point Lepreau reactor at a peak of activity (along with speculation on the expected second reactor), new groups took on a more explicitly political and anti-nuclear character. One of the first and most active of these groups began in the Annapolis Valley, much of which lies geographically closer to Point Lepreau than to Halifax and, as the new group liked to point out, downwind of Lepreau as well. The Fundy Area Concern for Tomorrow (FACT) group began at a meeting on nuclear energy organized by the provincial New Democratic Party, held, by odd coincidence, on the very day of the meltdown in Pennsylvania. Within a few weeks, a non-political follow-up meeting was held to formally launch FACT, which proceeded to bombard provincial and municipal politicians (and the general public) with the message that nuclear power was unnecessary, unsafe, and most of all unethical, especially from the perspective of the farming communities of the Annapolis Valley that would bear the brunt of contamination from any Three Mile Island–type accident at Point Lepreau, without ever having had a chance to comment on the project in New Brunswick.[77]

The remainder of the year passed in similar fashion, with mass movement anti-nuclear activism at every turn. Concerned Citizens of Caledonia, Opponents of Nuclear Energy, Citizens Against a Radioactive Environment (CARE), and more stand-alone groups arrived, as well as anti-nuclear committees from the Black United Front Yarmouth, Yarmouth Women's Institute, Cape Breton District Labour Council, North Shore Organic Growers Association, and more.[78] The local character of activism remained unchanged, but the drive to cooperate and to take the fight to Halifax and Ottawa surged. The basic critique of the modern consumer economy – once relegated to the nearly invisible local energy centres – returned to visible public presence, though now in the shadow of a more centralist, technocratic national alternative energy movement. The Cape Breton Alternate Energy Society declared its philosophy to be "one of relative deprivation and changing ways of living," and set about to convince the island population to adopt it,[79] while EAC member Ron Loucks wrote to the premier with a lengthy exposition of consumer society's degrading effect on human happiness and enclosed a copy of Dennis Meadows's *Alternatives to Growth*.[80] Loucks did not represent the public view of the energy committee, but in other respects the EAC followed along with the new popular movement. The dominant narrative that all shared was a return to public political pressure based on fear of nuclear disaster and a defence of one's immediate community, one's place. The title of one widely distributed leaflet told readers that "It Can Happen Here," while the SSEPA put words into action by releasing balloons at Point Lepreau, several of which were soon picked up in the Annapolis Valley.[81]

The climactic event in a year of anti-nuclear protest occurred at the Maritime premiers' conference in Brudenell, Prince Edward Island, on June 4, 1979. Having assembled to discuss privately the details of a regional utility, the three premiers were reluctant to accommodate requests for a meeting with ENGO leaders. As a result, nine days before the event, the collected anti-nuclear groups of the three provinces, acting under the name of the Maritime Energy Coalition, called for a rally outside the resort in Brudenell. Six hundred to eight hundred people responded.[82] Unable to ignore the crowd, Hatfield, John Buchanan, and Angus MacLean made a very brief appearance on the steps of the hall and spent ten minutes accepting a four-point statement from a quartet of rally leaders, including Susan Holtz and Elizabeth May, two EAC board members representing Nova Scotia and the Island of Cape Breton, respectively.[83] With the rally coming barely two months after the accident at Three Mile Island, the number of participants is not surprising. Nor is the fact that the three premiers wished to be seen to appreciate their concerns (even if New Brunswick's Hatfield was "clearly upset," according to the EAC's post-rally report).[84] What the event demonstrates best is the extent to which conservative, bureaucratically agreeable, and scientifically optimistic statements had become the default rhetoric of the anti-nuclear coalition's leadership, to the exclusion of the limits to growth. As one of Susan Holtz's collaborators in Nova Scotia put it in a letter to her about a month before the rally, ideas about changing the capitalist consumer society "in their raw state ... are probably unsalable" and "better introduced by the back door" of safety arguments and alternative energy research as a paying investment.[85] Such ideas, already in accord with the kind of action the EAC, FOE, and CEAC were seeking from Ottawa, prevailed in the correspondence of the EAC energy committee in early 1979, correspondence in which Holtz dismissed as unreal "the allegedly widely different assumptions held by proponents/opponents about lifestyle and economic growth," and in which Elizabeth May advertised the Brudenell rally in support of "conservation and the development of renewable alternative sources."[86] The four points delivered to the premiers at Brudenell, and the petition of thousands collected to support them, followed the same script, stressing the safety concerns and asking for a series of public inquiries into nuclear energy projects. "Realistic" alternative energy policies, the brief noted, are "ones which take into account general social goals such as economic growth, jobs, and environmental protection."[87]

Following the Brudenell rally, the resurgence of MEC anti-nuclear activism in the summer of 1979 included renewed protests against the Point Lepreau generating station, as well as against the nuclear fuel plant in Moncton, and a new front of resistance to heavy-water shipments to Argentina. The rhetoric of place defence intensified, reviving the environmental justice arguments of the SSEPA's Stoddard Island campaign and the association's worldly view of shared responsibility for others' places powerfully enough to obscure the differences between the economically radical and the orthodox positions. And in little more than a year, the anti-nuclear backlash bore fruit: the lack of interest from Prince Edward Island and Nova Scotia finally laid to rest any plans for a unified Maritime Energy Corporation (at least until the twenty-first century). A meeting between the premiers and the federal energy minister in October 1980 offered New Brunswick's Hatfield one last chance to convince the others to share the burden of Point Lepreau, but that was the end.[88]

CONCLUSION

Though confirmation was longer in coming, in the estimation of the EAC's energy committee a week after the Brudenell rally success was already at hand. "It seems," the committee wrote, "that the Maritime Energy Corporation as a facilitator of nuclear energy is dead."[89] In fact, the success of the Maritime Energy Coalition in its last real appearance as a genuine regional coalition was even more complete than that. Strong public reaction following Three Mile Island was a crucial factor in the abandonment of plans for a second reactor at Point Lepreau.[90] In the glow of success, however, it is hard to believe that some of the long-standing activists did not feel a profound disappointment at what had been left behind in the race to Ottawa and Brudenell.

The limits thesis never disappeared from the province's environmental scene in the 1970s, but despite occasional warnings that "the ethical and moral problems are overlooked in favour of technological problems," its proponents slowly and steadily receded into the shadow of a dominant, economically orthodox citizen-scientist mode of operations.[91] In the early days of anti-nuclear activism, the South Shore Environmental Protection

Association's fight for environmental justice for local fishermen and Hattie Perry's adept use of public pressure against the premier sat next to the Nuclear Power Study Group's highly technical exposé of nuclear technology and the profound ethical convictions of the Halifax VOW that a high-energy consumer society could never be an equitable society. The closer a group was to the scene of environmental risk, the more radical its activism tended to be, but all participated alike in pressure politics. By 1979 the sense of common purpose had dulled. A temporary resurgence of anti-nuclear political pressure based on feelings of personal vulnerability succeeded in finally killing the Maritime Energy Corporation in 1980 (and with it the common front of Maritime activists), but the environmental movement as a whole was far different from what it had been when the same sort of action crushed the Stoddard Island proposal in Barrington Passage in 1973. Still primarily a common front of small local volunteer organizations, it now faced a division (still unrecognized as such) between a nascent mainstream that eschewed the radicalism of the counterculture or the uncomfortable predictions of the limits theory, and those who clung to both. "The dramatic language [of political radicalism and limits] which raised ecology-consciousness 10 years ago is missing," wrote Amy Zierler, who claimed to see a brief resurgence of it in the nuclear debate. "The laws and procedures we drew up to institutionalize our concern swallowed up much of its spirit, without eliminating its causes."[92]

Led by the Halifax Friends Meeting and the Voice of Women, and especially by the small group of research-inclined activists behind Susan Holtz who eventually formed the core of the EAC's energy committee, the network of anti-nuclear environmentalists based in the city embraced the laws and procedures of the bureaucratic system and turned towards rigorous analysis of nuclear safety and promotion of research into alternative energy technologies. They began to downplay, then conceal, and finally denigrate as "extreme" and "unacceptable" any arguments that focused on the unsustainability of an expanding capitalist economy and consumer society, and especially any that cast government in the role of villain.[93] Apart from the generous continuing support of the Halifax Friends Meeting and their national co-religionists, more and more of the group's funding came from research contracts with the provincial and federal governments. Very much reminiscent of the Quaker notion that everyone has the potential to access divine truth no matter how committed to a wrong course of action they may be at the moment, this science-inclined network sought relentlessly to access and influence the ranks of the provincial and federal bureaucracies and corporate and political decision makers. By mid-decade the constant refrain of "respectability" began to appear in the documents of the EAC, a group derided as "ecology freaks" by the premier himself only a few years earlier. Susan Holtz described the change herself in 1977:

> I've come to feel that one of my most important roles is acting as a human link between people and ideas usually opposed or not in contact, notably environmentalists and decision-makers in the civil service, the Power Corporation, or politicians. I feel that to change, at an emotional level, a situation from one in which people feel they're opponents to one in which they feel they're working on the same problem but with differing views is to change radically the possible outcome not only of that situation but of all future situations.[94]

In September 1978, Holtz travelled to Arlington, Virginia, to attend a Solar Energy Research Institute symposium, one of very few Canadian attendees. There she heard Lee Schipper of California warn the assembly to "honestly follow through the consequences of some of today's attitudes and policies (right or wrong) that our friends are advocating, lest we find that our friends have led us to our enemies."[95] Back home, eight months later, she attended an EMR workshop on Energy Conservation and Community Economic Development in Truro and heard Dan McInnis turn the story of the Antigonish Cooperative Movement into an even more explicit cautionary tale for advocates of a conserver society. The Antigonish movement, he said, was "ultimately crushed by government in its response to profit-oriented business."[96] Both views of activism were utterly different from her own; as far as Holtz was concerned, and as far as the EAC and the Halifax network of energy activists were concerned, environmentalists had no enemies. Within a few years, however, even she would find some.

3

Power from the People
The Anti-Chemical Campaigns

THE SPRUCE BUDWORM MIGHT have seemed an unlikely trigger for Nova Scotia's greatest environmental controversy in the mid-1970s. The endemic insect had eaten itself into obscurity on Cape Breton Island in the 1950s, exhausting its food supply of aged spruce and fir trees and returning to the status of a minor forest species, repeating its population cycle yet again. Although many, perhaps most, residents recognized the budworm as a New Brunswick problem, there was not an immediate recognition of the incipient irruption in the summer of 1975, when fir trees on the highlands began to turn rust red.[1] Foresters working for Nova Scotia Forest Industries (NSFI), the Canadian corporate identity of Swedish pulp and paper giant Stora Forest Industries, certainly recognized the signs, however, and before the season ended, asked the provincial Department of Lands and Forests (DLF) for permission to begin aerial spraying over 100,000 acres with the same chemical insecticide, fenitrothion, in use in New Brunswick.

Initial resistance to NSFI's plans centred on Halifax and a swiftly formed coalition of new environmentalists and older wildlife and resource conservation groups. During the winter of 1976, members of the Ecology Action Centre (EAC) joined representatives from five conservation groups to organize a debate-style symposium on the budworm issue, where speakers in favour of a chemical spray program essayed their arguments against the anti-spray position. It was as even-handed a format as one could imagine.[2] The chief organizer from the EAC, Jim Reid, may have absorbed the lessons of the previous year's Energy and People conference; no resolutions

66

from the floor would mar the objectivity of this symposium. Certainly a wide range of opinions was apparent among the six groups, who admitted in their joint statement that "the problem exists [and] some of us became convinced that aerial spraying of insecticides may at present be the only recourse in some circumstances where there are extreme social and economic imperatives."[3] Whatever the reason for its equivocal presentation, the symposium made desperately poor political theatre. Not long afterward, the Department of Lands and Forests registered its own opposition to NSFI's plan, using much the same data and language it had advanced in the 1950s, and much less equivocally than the activists. The budworm, the department argued, was a natural component of the forest ecosystem, controllable through strategic cutting but not really controllable through chemical means. No one credited the activists with any influence over the department's position, nor did it make much difference; within a few weeks, the provincial Cabinet met and overruled the department's foresters: NSFI would be permitted to spray fenitrothion on the Cape Breton highlands.[4]

Scott Cunningham, the man who drafted the joint statement on behalf of the six Halifax groups, plainly did not think the chemical option was necessary or even viable, and appreciated a more antagonistic approach towards government. He also had access to information about the health risks of aerial pesticide sprays that he decided was best used to generate some bad publicity for the spray effort and Cabinet's decision to grant NSFI's request. As a doctoral student in biochemistry at Dalhousie University and a member of the EAC, Cunningham was aware of the research of Dalhousie's Dr. John Crocker into the incidence of Reye's syndrome among children exposed to pesticide sprays in New Brunswick. Rare, difficult to diagnose, and often swiftly fatal, the syndrome had appeared in several children living near spray areas, prompting Crocker to investigate the cluster of cases. Later research would reveal more about the exact mechanism of the disease, but by the winter of 1976, he had already determined that exposure to the petrochemical emulsifiers used to dilute the insecticide and make it stick to trees could enhance the virulence of otherwise common and mostly innocuous viruses. The research was incomplete – Crocker himself was not comfortable discussing it publicly at first – but it was advanced enough to be powerfully persuasive in the public arena, and Cunningham began searching for someone in the press to break the story.[5] He found Parker Donham at the *Cape Breton Post*.

In Parker Donham and Scott Cunningham, the Cape Breton and Halifax movements to oppose a spray program met, though they had otherwise little contact through the first year of the controversy. From the beginning, the Cape Bretoners had a more directly political approach to activism than the Halifax groups. Resistance in Cape Breton had not gotten underway until February, when the provincial government approved the spray. Then, working quickly, a loosely organized group of residents from communities around the highlands began circulating a petition asking minister of environment John Hawkins to approve hearings by the Environmental Control Council before allowing NSFI to go ahead, a deliberately moderate demand that would have meant the cancellation of the spray program anyway, due to delay. At the same time, they began collecting information on the spruce budworm, chemical insecticides, and industrial forestry for use in direct appeals to the people of Cape Breton. News of Donham's impending story about Reye's syndrome in the *Cape Breton Post* soon reached the group, which decided to coordinate its use of public pressure with his headline. On March 31, 1976, the front-page headline demonstrated Donham's own understanding of the power of public outrage. It read: "Fatal To Children."[6]

The pressure tactics of the newly christened activist group, Cape Bretoners Against the Spray, bore fruit immediately. Overwhelmed by a barrage of telephone protests, Premier Regan and his minister of public health, Cape Breton lawyer Allan Sullivan, emerged from an emergency Cabinet debate the day after the *Post*'s bombshell to announce the cancellation of the spray program. From the initial relief of the DLF's declared opposition, through Cabinet's approval and subsequent reversal, the whole fight – the first of the "budworm battles" – had taken only two months.

The two centres of opposition did not have time to collaborate that winter, but apart from their different tactics, the Halifax and Cape Breton activists were not so different. Both were essentially local movements with few outside connections, composed of both long-time Nova Scotians and a conspicuous number of more recent arrivals, which prompted both groups to attempt to forestall the "outsider" label they knew would be applied to them. In Halifax, the attempt contributed to the retreat into scientific respectability, itself a form of localism in the province's administrative centre. In Cape Breton, it led to the avoidance of publicity by the most recent immigrants. Elizabeth May, for example, who would eventually become the face of the anti-spray movement, admitted a few years later that she initially stayed in the background, aware of her problematic image as a young American woman only two years in Canada.[7] In both areas as well, activists drew on links with local wildlife conservation organizations and with ongoing campaigns against the use of biocides on farms, roadsides, and city streets and parks. As 1976 dragged on and more of the province had time to notice and discuss the flurry of activity during the previous winter, more associations cropped up, and more half-forgotten chemical controversies gained new vigour, especially the Warren farm episode.

The Warren family's frightening story had only become more so in the intervening years, as illnesses persisted or worsened. (Robyn Warren's brother would die of a rare soft-tissue sarcoma in 1978.) Along with their tale came a reminder of the failure of activists in the early 1970s to adequately defend the "ecological logic" of epidemiology. Ian McLaren of the Nova Scotia Resources Council (NSRC) began explaining in April, in terms similar to those John Crocker would soon use to explain his own work, that "nothing short of taking several dozen children and exposing them to the same procedure would ever resolve the question of 'proof.'"[8] The government's role in scattering the first anti-spray movement and stymieing Robyn Warren's efforts to learn even the names of the chemicals contaminating his farm was also remembered, especially among the network of organic farmers who participated in the initial petition campaign in Cape Breton. Over the years to come, how far to trust apparent allies in government would become one of the greatest fault lines of the anti–industrial forestry campaign.

"THE GENERAL PUBLIC'S OVER-REACTION"[9]

Within the Nova Scotia Department of Environment (DOE) and the Department of Lands and Forests during the 1970s, battles were fought analogous to the battle between NSFI and the local activists in Cape Breton and Halifax, though they usually went unnoticed outside of government. In 1976, Lloyd Hawboldt, assistant to the deputy minister of lands and forests, led a faction of foresters and entomologists opposed to chemical sprays against the efforts of his department's director of forest planning, R.M. Bulmer, and a pro-spray group.[10] Both groups attempted to win over the minister and deputy minister. The anti-spray faction relied on Hawboldt's decades-old argument against the "vain attempt to offset a natural trend," and pointedly reminded their colleagues that the company could have prevented a budworm irruption by following the advice of DLF foresters rather than clearcutting in easily accessible lowland woodlots and neglecting the aging highland forest.[11] The pro-spray side, conversely, pressed the advantage of its alliance with industry and with natural resource departments in Maine, New Brunswick, and Quebec, where chemical spraying was already taking place.[12] Though the anti-spray position enjoyed greater success, it was a heavily qualified opposition. All of the department's foresters retained their professional commitment to the ideals of environmental management and control and to the preservation of their status as experts; no one was willing to advocate that the spray option be removed from the table for good. Hawboldt himself worked to restrain his allies' more strident statements in order not to "sabotage the department if it chooses to spray in 1977" or to allow activists in New Brunswick to "use us for their own particular purposes."[13] Despite being so completely submerged in the politics of forestry, and strongly opposed to a spray program, the department's foresters remained thoroughly committed to modernist thinking and could not countenance what they saw as the "politicization" of the expert's natural right to decide.

Despite the minister's decision to oppose NSFI's request, he never curtailed the activities of the pro-spray faction within the DLF. Their cooperation with industry began to bear fruit in the fall of 1976, as NSFI took the initiative against the activists ahead of the winter decision-making season. Its first approach took advantage of yet another jurisdictional rivalry and regulatory power struggle, this time between the province's forest agency and its pro-spray federal counterpart. In late September, the Canadian Forestry Service released its predictions for the following year, forecasting a large increase in the budworm population. The director of the Maritime Forest Research Centre promptly recommended a preventative chemical spray.[14] A public meeting in Truro organized by the DLF's Bulmer spread the news to the largest possible audience, presenting it as a disastrous consequence of the government's refusal to act sooner, rather than the expected progress of an insect population bloom.[15] A month later, another Forest Planning Division man, Ed Cloney, attended a regional meeting in Fredericton on "Forest Protection Against Spruce Budworm," where forest experts concluded – somewhat contradictorily but again as publicly as possible – that the harmful environmental effects of chemical insecticides "are insignificant, short-lived, and sensationalized by the general public's over-reaction – but that environmental monitoring is essential in detecting any long range effects which may arise."[16]

The real offensive push came at the beginning of December. A report issued on the first of the month by the Budworm Committee of the Voluntary Planning Board recommended spraying, after an investigation led by John Dickey, a Halifax lawyer and president of NSFI's Nova Scotian holding company, and including as well the ever-present Mr. Bulmer as DLF representative. Finally, the day after the release of the Voluntary

Planning Board report, the president of Stora Kopparberg, Erik Sunbladt, arrived in Nova Scotia from Sweden with a bombshell announcement: without a campaign of chemical control against the budworm menace, he would surely be forced to shut down the paper mill in Port Hawkesbury within the next five years. To back up Sunbladt's claim, his employees at the mill had produced a sixty-five-page report of their own detailing the future of pulpwood supply on Cape Breton and concluding with a demand for insecticide sprays over not 100,000 acres this time but two million acres – the entire island of Cape Breton.[17]

Environmental activists had not been idle since their unexpected victory in April, though most of the action during the summer was on the Halifax side of the still-disconnected Halifax–Cape Breton axis. What activity there was through the quieter months suggested that the urban activists had finally accepted that the provincial Cabinet's decision on spraying would "be an almost purely political one."[18] The EAC, Halifax Field Naturalists (HFN), and other groups that had worked together during the previous winter turned their attention to the press, and thus to the public, or worked to recruit other interested groups into a strong public lobby. As a result, when NSFI and its allies reignited the controversy in the fall, a host of newly interested parties reacted to the expanded spray proposal, and the Halifax and Cape Breton campaigns finally coalesced into a truly province-wide collaborative effort, with statements of support issued across the map, from the Municipal Council of Shelburne to the Women's Institute of Marion Bridge.[19]

If Halifax provided the organizational push, the most effective *action* in response to Sunbladt's ultimatum again originated from Cape Breton, where Cape Bretoners Against the Spray met to plot strategy two days after his visit. At the suggestion of Ron Caplan, editor of *Cape Breton's Magazine,* the group was renamed Cape Breton Landowners Against the Spray (CBLAS), to emphasize its status as a group of locals facing off against a foreign multinational. Its official response to NSFI's pro-spray blitz included a careful deconstruction of the mill's wood supply predictions by former insurance accountant John May, and a report on "Alternatives to Spraying" written with the aid of Frank Reid, a leader of the anti-spray forces from the Victoria County Woodlot Owners and Operators Association. Reid, who had grown up in industrial Cape Breton, understood well the economic reality of the forest industry, where NSFI's large Crown leases enabled the company to push down the price paid to small woodlot owners. Spraying in the highlands, he insisted, was mainly an attempt to preserve the unused "standing inventory" that allowed the company to control the pulpwood market.[20] The CBLAS analysis met a favourable reception on Cape Breton and earned endorsements from primary producers' associations across the island, but achieving recognition in the Halifax media proved more difficult.[21]

The anti-spray movement's break in Halifax came on January 6, 1977, with a major press conference downtown. NSFI's move in late December to request a permit for the insecticide Sevin (carbaryl) in 1977, rather than fenitrothion, left environmentalists struggling to learn about the new chemical and share the information over the Christmas holidays. In Cape Breton, they posted handbills in restaurants and post offices, but it was at the Halifax press conference that they put into practice what they had learned from watching the pulp company's attack on multiple fronts in the fall.[22] A new petition effort and announcement of support from the provincial Medical Society on the conference day helped draw and keep the media's attention long enough for activists to state their case. And cognizant that they could not rely on fear of Reye's syndrome alone twice in a row, especially with the New Brunswick government working hard to discredit Dr. Crocker's findings, environmentalists struck all of NSFI's rhetorical weak points at once. Two woodlot association presidents, Frank Reid for Victoria County and Dan Alfred MacDonald for Inverness, presented their associations' positions on a softwood market dominated by three large paper mills interested in spraying only to maintain their dominance, while John May spoke as a tourist operator. Biologist Ian McLaren joined Lloyd Hawboldt to offer a scientific perspective on forestry, and Dr. Earle Reid, Chief of Medicine at the Halifax Infirmary, discussed Reye's syndrome and the other dangers posed by human exposure to pesticide chemicals. Together they argued that NSFI's proposal was unnecessary, iniquitous, uncertain of success, potentially counterproductive, and still possibly dangerous. Any pretense of objectivity was abandoned, and the event was a great public relations success.[23]

The province's much-delayed decision on a 1977 spray program came almost four weeks after the anti-spray coalition's appeal to the Halifax media, and not before Premier Regan walked into an unexpected face-to-face meeting with activists, reminiscent of his visit to Barrington Passage in 1973. The Port Hawkesbury Chamber of Commerce might have been a refuge for NSFI's side of the fight – certainly the mill turned out a large number of its employees for the chamber's public meeting – but CBLAS turned out more of its own supporters. Nor were the millworkers necessarily the bulwark of support that the pulp company hoped for. Many followed the lead of Ken Calder, NSFI chemical engineer and CBLAS's best source of information from within the corporation.[24] If Reid's contribution to the CBLAS position can be taken as indicative, forest industry workers on Cape Breton also understood that economic desire, not ecological necessity, drove the company's push for a spray program. The combination of strong attendance by anti-sprayers and lukewarm opposition from millworkers turned the event into an environmentalist set piece, with the premier himself as guest of honour. Not missing a chance to press the advantage, CBLAS released its phone poll results for the island of Cape Breton a day later, showing 75 percent of residents opposed to the spray. Results were swift, only this time it was not the health minister, or even the new environment/lands and forests minister, Vince MacLean, but the premier himself who stepped up to announce the decision to refuse NSFI's request for a second time.[25]

The years 1977 and 1978 saw the refinement of environmentalists' use of the power of popular pressure. Appeals to the public along all possible lines of argument obviated any need for consistency among arguments: the economic case for full industrial exploitation of the forest but without chemicals might sway one segment of the population, while the ecological case against all pulpwood-focused forestry practices could sway another group. So long as the objective was to convince the public rather than the premier or any of his ministers, contradiction was irrelevant. As a tactic for generating pressure on political leaders, it was hugely effective.[26] As NSFI became progressively more antagonistic towards the Regan government, and MacLean in particular, anti-spray activists began to reach beyond provincial borders (imitating their industrial opponents) to recruit expert supporters, and Elizabeth May drifted towards the original Halifax-based coalition's conciliatory methods, out of a desire to support MacLean's position.

The end of 1977 and the beginning of 1978 were Elizabeth May's coming-out season as the public face of the anti-spray movement. Having come to the attention of the media during another anti-spray coalition press conference, May then participated in a pair of televised debates that put her squarely in the public eye, a position she quickly grew to enjoy.[27] Further publicity came from a series of running debates for local audiences across the province, pitting May against Kingsley Brown, the maker of a NSFI-sponsored pro-spray documentary called *Mr. Regan's Choice*. Brown too had a measure of public recognition, at least among those employed in forestry. In the early 1970s, he had been an advocate for small woodlot owners, and despite coming off worse in his broadcast exchange with May, still enjoyed a positive reputation in the province. By the spring of 1978, as the public awaited a third decision on a chemical spray program, May had already become a seasoned activist, an eager participant in government-sponsored consultations, and a convert to the economically and politically unthreatening style of activism advocated by the EAC. At times, she also defended the Regan government. Only a few years later, she would remark on her position during this third protest season: "I believed then, and to this day, that they [Regan and MacLean] acted out of personal conscience and informed, rational judgement when they opposed spraying."[28]

On March 17, May's faith appeared to be vindicated when MacLean once again refused to permit aerial insecticide spraying on Cape Breton Island. Even better, the following fall produced sound evidence (much to the distaste of the Canadian Forestry Service [CFS]) that the budworm irruption in Nova Scotia was finally collapsing on its own. Three years of effort had met apparently unlikely success; environmentalists had prevented Nova Scotia from following New Brunswick's lead into a permanent spray program despite the industry's best efforts. They had won. Celebrating what they took to be a new policy of ecological forestry, few activists noted the fine print on the province's five-year, $62 million investment in "silviculture." Far from accommodating the will of natural systems, the new policy encouraged replanting with "commercially desirable" species, especially white spruce and tamarack, in single-aged, single-species stands suitable for mechanical cutting, and suitable as well for future insect blooms. There was also too little recognition that an additional $35 million available to dry-store budworm-killed wood over the following decade would effectively insulate NSFI from the negotiating power that the budworm had granted to small woodlot owners, and preserve the corporation's growing political influence.[29] Finally, almost no one seemed to appreciate that the fine balance between pro- and anti-spray factions within the Department of Lands and Forests (as well as around the Cabinet table), which had lent such decisive power to activists' own orchestration of public pressure, could shift abruptly, or that the logic of industrial forestry guaranteed a return to the battlefield.

AN UNCERTAIN RELATIONSHIP WITH POWER

The position of government, either provincial or federal, had never been to side unequivocally with environmentalists. Rather, it wished to shape the movement. As early as 1976, the federal Department of Environment recognized the value of environmental activist groups as a constituency, a tool with which to turn public opinion in favour of the department's legislative agenda. Like any other legislative constituency, environmentalists required careful management, perhaps more careful than most given the difficulty in separating and discouraging any members who held on to unlegislatable ideas about the unsustainability of industrial society as an enterprise.[30] The federal department's cultivation of the movement began with informal meetings between Environment Canada's Atlantic Regional Board and a select few activists, and progressed quickly to invitations for formal participation in national Canadian Environmental Advisory Council (CEAC) meetings.[31] Funding made available directly from the department brought activists from across the country to Montreal in 1978 for two days of meetings to draft "position papers on environment, wildlife, pesticides, and the conserver society."[32] It was only one of many such meetings convened during the last half of the 1970s in which the logic of consensus could work on squeezing out ideas that might seem too extreme. Federal funding placed only one major restriction on participation: groups receiving funds had to maintain "non-political" registered non-profit status.[33] Those selected soon provided their own additional strictures; after resolving in 1978 to create a permanent committee of environmental groups beneath the CEAC (what would become the Canadian Environmental Network), a steering committee went in search of "broadly based" groups capable of responding quickly to queries from the Advisory Council – in other words, professional groups rather than unincorporated "single-issue" groups composed of local activists.[34] By the following year, much of the advice conveyed by those groups to federal bureaucrats consisted of requests for ever closer integration, and for dedicated funding to the groups who would participate.[35]

Those groups in Nova Scotia that saw federal consultations as a route to real influence sought to enjoy the same sort of relationship with the provincial government, and the budworm spray issue evoked from them a concerted effort to achieve it. The EAC and CBLAS, working together closely by the end of 1977, each attempted to convince MacLean to impose an anti-spray member or two from their ranks on the new Task Force on Wood Allocation.[36] EAC leaders also pushed for the Environmental Control Council (ECC) to work more closely with environmentalists and put funds towards research conducted by professional activist groups.[37] This quest for access and funding soon led to even greater emphasis on those areas where some environmentalists could agree with professional foresters' insistence on environmental management and control. EAC and CBLAS propaganda, often jointly produced with conservation groups like the

Canadian Nature Federation, Halifax Field Naturalists, or Nova Scotia Bird Society, lent support to the provincial government's new large industry-oriented silviculture plans, which Minister MacLean insisted would obviate the need for budworm control and also "increase the productivity of our forests by two and one-half to three times its present allowable cut."[38] They also enthusiastically endorsed non-chemical control measures meant to achieve the same effect as chemical insecticides, apparently willing to undermine their and their allies' ecological argument that the budworm belongs in the forest and must be allowed to run its course.[39] Elizabeth May was particularly keen to encourage aerial applications of the biological control agent *Bacillus thuringiensis kurstaki* (*Btk*) as an alternative to insecticides.[40]

Even if some environmentalists were willing to shift their positions towards the Regan government's ideal of industrial promotion, or take on an "advisory arm" made up of businessmen to boost their orthodox economic credentials (as the EAC did in 1978), government proved less flexible. Meeting in the middle works only if both sides move, and the province was never willing to match the federal Department of Environment's efforts to court activist participation. Bureaucrats in Halifax favoured secrecy over manipulation as a tactic for the management of public dissent, and federal/provincial rivalries did not spur the search for legislative constituencies in Nova Scotia as powerfully as interdepartmental rivalries did in Ottawa. MacLean's response to requests for environmentalist representation on the new task force was a casual "no," and his rationale for refusing to order an ECC public hearing was transparently inadequate: he claimed that the council had never requested authorization.[41]

Doubts about the wisdom of professionalization and of accepting the economic growth assumptions of the province's industrial development policy were never far away. With decision-making power within the organization growing ever more remote from the membership, the EAC's leaders defended their role as a "counterweight" to the power of business and government within the existing system, prompting one member, Eve Smith, to reply that the fundraising required by that approach "has become a way of life, and leads at times to modification of approach or policy, or is unequally distributed. It sometimes gives more power to a few who control policy ... this is a money oriented society and we may be corrupted by it, almost without recognizing our own corruption."[42] A few years later, the centre's closest ally on the ECC, the ecologist Dr. Gordon Ogden, insisted that the ECC would not fund action groups, for their own good.[43]

Until the very end of the peak period of forestry conflict, from 1976 until 1983, misgivings about environmentalists seeking professional status or a direct role in government remained at the level of Ogden's advice or Smith's warning, and did not flare up into open recrimination. That could have been due in part to the short time since the EAC's transformation into a professional group, and the even shorter time since Elizabeth May and CBLAS formed their organization amid a direct challenge to government. It was likely also due in part to the incompleteness of both groups' drift towards conciliatory activism: the EAC still regularly debated its own structure and methods during those years, and May, ever more the de facto spokesperson for the Cape Breton group after 1977, remained equivocal for years, alternately defending government actions or participating in direct consultations and then insisting that "power is not achieved through government grants, large budgets, or paid full-time coordinators. Power is people."[44] Perhaps because of such statements, environmentalists making firmly ecological and anti-managerial arguments, even the few still making anti–economic growth arguments, could still see a measure of common ground with the ecomodernists leading the publicity drive. More important, so long as the tactics of the anti-spray campaign encouraged environmentalists to reach politicians through the intermediary of public pressure, all lines of argument – health, economic, ecological, social justice, emotional, or epistemological – and all types of activist could coexist. Adopting the opposing side's terminology and assumptions in a battle of ideas does have consequences, however, and the longer the conflict over industrial forestry dragged on, the more those consequences began to reshape the face of the environmental movement, driving a wedge between the ecomodernists and those who remained skeptical of government's willingness to change.

THE OTHER SPRAY

The budworm spray controversy of the late 1970s and the herbicide spray controversy of the early 1980s tend to be remembered as quite separate events. In reality, they were two sides of the same policy coin: both the government/industry axis and the environmentalists carried forward into the new decade much of what they had learned since 1976, including what they had learned from each other. The ensuing controversy revealed that the political context of environmental activism mattered a great deal to its effectiveness, as a change in government brought the full power of the state into action opposing the environmentalists' anti-spray campaign.

Herbicide sprays were even more familiar in Nova Scotia than insecticides in 1979, when environmental activists took note of their increasing use in forestry. The connection with the brief anti-herbicide campaign of the early 1970s was certainly more direct; one of the first actions by the EAC in 1979 was an attempt once again to stop Nova Scotia Power from using chemical herbicides on its power line rights-of-way.[45] Local agitation against roadside spraying of farm weeds by the Department of Agriculture also continued apace, feeding into the province-wide movement, and organic farmers had for years maintained their case against the use of herbicides, even more than insecticides.[46] In each case, the chemicals in question were old and well-studied agents, most often 2,4-dichlorophenoxyacetic acid (2,4-D) and 2,4,5-trichlorophenoxyacetic acid (2,4,5-T) – albeit often used under the trade names "Tordon" or "Brushkiller."[47] But if environmentalists could arm themselves with more and better information about such long-used chemicals, they also faced even more entrenched opposition.

Arguably dangerous chemicals on their own, 2,4-D and 2,4,5-T saw their first military application in Vietnam in 1962, where a 1:1 mixture of 2,4-D and 2,4,5-T went by the code-name Agent Orange.[48] Unfortunately for the Vietnamese, and for the American and Canadian soldiers and civilians made unwitting test subjects for the wartime defoliation program, the mixtures used during the war were heavily contaminated with 2,3,7,8-tetrachlorodibenzodioxin (TCDD), a particularly toxic form of dioxin. The consequences – death, disease, and deformity – among those exposed in Vietnam or in North America were horrific, but it took years for the US and Canadian governments to grudgingly admit that the chemicals were dangerous. By 1979, neither the US nor Canadian governments had yet repudiated the chemical manufacturers' claim that preventable TCDD contamination was responsible, and not the 2,4-D/2,4,5-T mixture itself, despite the accumulation of studies suggesting just the opposite. Critics of both governments' actions met a stonewall of regulatory indifference and bureaucratic secrecy.[49]

Around the world, chemical disasters seemed to pile upon disasters in the late 1970s, profoundly shaking public confidence that the balance of benefits in fact outweighed the costs of the postwar chemical revolution.[50] Infamous names like Love Canal and Times Beach entered the public narrative in the United States, alongside Agent Orange, and in 1979 the largest-ever class action suit in American legal history pitted veterans exposed to toxic herbicides against their own government.[51] In Canada, however, the first major challenge to the continued use of the same chemicals came not from veterans but from environmental forestry activists in Nova Scotia.

In the forest industry, a single application of chemicals like 2,4-D could kill birch, oak, ash, and the like and leave behind a pure softwood stand for easy mechanical harvest, or wipe out the raspberries and low shrubs and forbs that spring up in a recent clearcut, leaving replanted softwood seedlings with full access to sun, soil, and water. The latter operation, called "conifer release," accelerates the growth of seedlings but leaves the soil impoverished; without the first stage of succession to restore nutrients, or the deep roots of hardwoods to stabilize the regrowing trees, exhaustion and erosion threaten (usually answered with the promise of chemical fertilization, and of insecticides to protect the weakened trees).[52]

Herbicide treatments were well-practised techniques by 1979, yet it took some time for environmental activists in Nova Scotia to take note of the province's nascent forestry herbicide program. Concerned with insecticides, they were slow to shift attention to herbicides, while industry pursued both as part of the same policy of ecological control. In 1978, the NSRC alerted the ECC to a series of experimental applications conducted by the DLF. The ECC attempted to investigate further, but the new minister of environment, Roger Bacon, showed little interest in approving new hearings, in reviving the council's public relevance, or in any action that might draw attention to the issue.[53]

The political context of the fight over industrial forestry had changed sharply with the election of John Buchanan's Progressive Conservative government in September 1978. While some environmentalists continued to praise what they saw as a turn away from industrial conifer monocultures, the pro-spray faction within Lands and Forests continued to promote the industrial model from a new position of strength. The new deputy minister, former forest industry association head Don Eldridge, had supported NSFI's position during the spruce budworm debates, and with the retirement from public service of anti-spray stalwarts like Lloyd Hawboldt and A.M. Wiksten, there was little to impede Eldridge's promotion of industrial forestry.[54] Certainly the new minister of lands and forests would be no obstacle; George Henley, the incumbent from 1978 to 1983, proved an equally staunch supporter of the forest industry's chemical ambitions. In 1979, his department undertook further spray tests with 2,4-D, glyphosate (Roundup®), and fosamine ammonium (Krenite®), including a large plantation site near Trafalgar, Guysborough County, adjacent to the headwaters of both the Saint Mary's River and the East River of Pictou. Challenged by some Pictou County residents, Henley explained that the failure of the prior government to control the spruce budworm meant that reforestation was urgently required, and that once planted, softwood trees required chemical "protection" to speed their growth and forestall a disastrous wood shortage.[55] In general, the Buchanan government pursued a much closer relationship with the pulp and paper industry than had the Regan government, ensured that herbicide spraying on forest land got started with minimal public attention, and encouraged the industry to proselytize its view of forests as crops rather than living systems.[56]

One of the most effective means by which industry and government could promote the strictly economic agro-forestry perspective was to do exactly as environmentalists had demanded since 1976: not use chemical insecticides against the spruce budworm. The DLF eagerly seized upon every chance to employ the relatively new bacterial agent *Btk*, endorsed by CBLAS and the EAC as an organic alternative to synthetic chemicals, even after the collapse of the budworm population in 1978. The DLF sprayed 20,600 acres of forest with *Btk* in 1979 and 70,260 acres the following year, and continued the program indefinitely thereafter.[57] Dubious necessity paled to irrelevance beside the opportunity to advance the idea and practice of industrial forestry – to insist on the need for "control," by one means or another – with a method already declared safe and acceptable by the leading voices against chemical sprays. Thus environmental activists began their anti-herbicide campaign at a severe disadvantage, fighting a practice that had already begun, and one that could be presented by government as a mere extension of the long-established use of the same chemicals on farms and roadsides, all while having undermined their own ability to use ecological arguments against the managerial logic of control.

The move towards annual use of *Btk* did arouse some activist resistance in Nova Scotia, despite the refusal of leading anti-spray activists like Elizabeth May to cease defending it. Biological though it may have been, *Btk* tests by Environment Canada included additional anti-evaporants and adhesives (plus a chitinase enzyme), and most often measured the effect on budworm populations and defoliation rates to the exclusion of wider ecosystem monitoring.[58] That sort of tunnel vision alarmed those who saw in it echoes of chemical insecticide testing. Opposition in Cape Breton led some members of CBLAS to form their own organization in response to the "unacceptable compromise" made by its leaders. The Crowdis Coalition, named after the primary test site at Crowdis Mountain near Baddeck, accused May of "selling out" the ecological argument in favour of a purely scientific approach to chemical safety and a managerial idea of forestry. At a time when the anti-herbicide campaign was warning the public how "in the fast world of chemical discovery and analysis 'safe' is a risky word," the new critics wondered why a broadcast biological agent should be held to a lower standard.[59]

The EAC attracted some criticism on similar lines after sponsoring an equivocal public lecture on agricultural chemicals in February 1980, but both critiques failed to blunt the attempt to achieve respectability and expert status.[60] Convinced more than ever that their victories in the "budworm battles" had rested on sound scientific argument first and public pressure second, Susan Holtz, Susan Mayo, and others at the EAC, along with May (who joined them on the centre's board of directors in 1980 while continuing to represent a loosely organized group of Cape Bretoners[61]), poured ever more of their attention and energy into winning the battle of facts. Wholly in the citizen-scientist mode, they carefully avoided being seen to "blindly oppose any action which may affect the environment."[62] Too much faith in scientific fact, though, can just as easily blind a person to the power of politics, a desperate liability when called upon to formulate new tactics against an unsympathetic government.

Unlike the proposed massive insecticide sprays of the previous decade, herbicide applications in the early 1980s were individual and relatively small operations carried out by various forestry companies, subject to DOE and DLF approval. Accordingly, the campaign against herbicide sprays gained momentum in a piecemeal fashion, jumping from one local battle to another until coming together in a province-wide effort, something industry and government tried very hard to prevent. Henley and Eldridge at the DFL bore responsibility for regulations around public notification, and they took every opportunity to limit the time between notice and spray. Whereas environmentalists had enjoyed months of foreknowledge even for the first 1976 budworm spray proposal, herbicide spray applications became closely guarded secrets, received, reviewed, and approved behind the closed doors of the DLF and announced with only weeks to spare. The DOE signed off on any spray application using chemicals approved by Environment Canada and showed even less concern for public awareness. Secrecy, in short, was policy. An opposition motion in the Legislature in the spring of 1982 would have forced the DLF to publish applications upon receipt; the government voted it down.[63]

But if secrecy made activism difficult, it also sometimes provoked it. In the summer of 1980, NSFI received government permission to use 2,4-D on five hundred acres of leased Crown land at Big Pond, Cape Breton

County. When news of the impending spray reached the community two weeks before the event, residents were incensed. Public notification rules did not specify who should be directly notified, and the pulp company made minimal effort. As one farmer later told *Atlantic Insight* magazine, "it's the goddamn way they were going to do it. We have a priest, fire chief, school principal, and Community Council in this town and NSFI said they didn't know who to contact." DOE and DLF officials reacted to the controversy with a redoubled commitment to secrecy, but Big Pond residents took their case to the Nova Scotia Supreme Court and won an injunction against the spray.[64]

Within months of the Big Pond settlement, another of NSFI's plans faced local opposition in the village of Lochaber, in Antigonish County. The area approved for herbicide treatment was only about 150 acres this time, but the chemical would be a mixture of 2,4-D and 2,4,5-T – the infamous Agent Orange. Once again a community reacted en masse, and this time, with the assistance of Antigonish MLA Bill Gillis, pressured the DOE into a "reinspection" of the site – and NSFI into abandoning the plan – without resort to the courts.[65] In Lochaber, as in Big Pond, it was local activists who began the agitation against herbicide spraying. Most of them had never before been involved in the province's environmental movement, demonstrating once again the centrality of place-defence in generating environmental activism. All of the newcomers reached out to the established groups, the EAC and CBLAS, for advice and help in acquiring the factual ammunition with which to fight, but decided which course to take on their own, with two results. First, this new generation of activists discovered a provincial network in need of new energy. Rather than settle their own problems and retire from the field, they pushed for a united front. Vicki Palmer of Lochaber was at the forefront of the effort. "Although the issue is resolved for the moment in Lochaber," she wrote, "it is plain that the time has come for the government to take a good hard look at their policy on herbicides. Local skirmishes are just symptoms of a greater problem."[66] In the New Glasgow *Evening News,* she was quoted calling for the creation of a provincial organization to carry the fight beyond one small controversy at a time.[67] The second result of the new activists' work, however, was a stark choice of tactics that made close cooperation difficult. Big Pond had enjoyed enviable success in convincing one judge of the potential risks of chemical sprays, while Lochaber did equally well in cowing the DOE. Obviously, an extended campaign would have to be mainly a political effort, but it is a rare environmental campaign that takes its impetus from anything but an imminent threat, and the question of whether to respond to the immediate threat in the legal or political arena would have to be answered. Complicating the question, the pro-spray forces had drawn their own lessons from the season of failure in 1981 and would not so easily succumb to either tactic again.

The new united front of forestry activists took the form of a committee of the EAC during the winter of 1982, a choice of venue that immediately put the group's focus on information dissemination and attempts to directly influence government. On the first account, the Forestry Committee can only be counted a success. Vicki Palmer from the Antigonish Environmental Coalition and Dan MacGillvray from the Big Pond Environmental Association brought the previous year's experience to a group comprising scientists, foresters, and activists.[68] As Don Eldridge feared, the dual controversies of 1981 had given "the advocates of no spray a platform,"[69] and they refused to relinquish it, sending their most persuasive speakers around the province to high schools and community halls to explain once again the dangers of chemical sprays and argue for alternatives.[70]

Unfortunately for the activists, their second principle of action – to directly influence government – turned much of their proselytizing into wasted effort. The Buchanan government readily obliged their desire for formal consultation, but lacking the established infrastructure of Environment Canada's public participation process, reached instead for a time-tested tool and declared a Royal Commission on Forestry. Public inquiries have long functioned to legitimate "the idea of the state" when an organized citizenry attacks government policy.[71] They are also effective distractions from the usual political process. Alexa McDonough, leader of the provincial NDP, wrote the EAC in April to caution against placing too much faith in a process "really only intended to be a further delaying tactic and a ruse for the industry interests."[72] Three weeks later, just as the Forestry Committee noticed a "drying up of information sources regarding the granting of spraying permits," the government announced its official policy that permits and applications would be kept secret from the public.[73] Previously faint hope that the province might prohibit all spraying during the Royal Commission's deliberations faded entirely, only to be replaced by anger when the continued advance notice of approved sprays promised by the environment minister turned out at times to be a week or less.[74] Nevertheless, most activists persisted in asking the public to turn their attention to the three Royal Commissioners, in the hope of convincing them to recommend against continued spraying. No hope was ever so vain. Though the records of the Royal Commission show a tremendous intellectual variety among anti-spraying advocates, including a strong

showing by witnesses arguing in favour of emotion and experiential knowledge as a counterweight to scientific reductionism, the three commissioners were hostile to any but the managerial and economic perspectives on
forestry, and eventually became open public advocates of industrial forestry.[75] In the meantime, the process provided a screen behind which the
premier and his ministers might hide in a time of crisis.

On June 21, the DOE granted permits to all three large pulp companies
in the province to use a 2,4-D/2,4,5-T mixture ("Esteron 3-3E" to the
department and companies; still "Agent Orange" to activists) on fifteen
thousand acres throughout the province.[76] The DOE proved surprisingly
forthcoming with news of the permits, making them known almost immediately, and activists faced a dilemma: try to pull together an effective
pressure campaign against an intransigent Cabinet (after having invited
the public to direct their letters to the Royal Commission), or attempt to
halt all three spray programs in court.

The first reaction was political and could hardly have been otherwise.
As locals learned about the spray plan, committees formed in communities
near spray sites without any outside encouragement. Public meetings,
petitions, and delegations to Halifax followed, the same tactics that had
proven effective in Lochaber. Under the tutelage of the EAC-based coalition, however, nothing disturbed the respectable, scientific appearance of
the movement, at least not until the first week of July. With time running
out and no hint of compromise from government, the Whycocomagh
Mi'kmaq Band had earlier decided to issue its own deadline: an NSFI spray
site on Skye Mountain, near the community's water supply, outraged Chief
Ryan Googoo, and he vowed to uproot one thousand of the company's
seedlings if the permit was not withdrawn. It was not, and on July 7 the
band turned out en masse to fulfill the promise. As other activists at other
times have learned, nothing spurs a government to action like a challenge
to its legitimacy, and that is what Whycocomagh's tree-pulling day represented. Inverness South MLA Billy Joe MacLean arrived immediately with
a promise of personal intervention, and (with Chief Googoo's threat of a
repeat performance weighing heavily) Cabinet moved the following day
to suspend all aerial spraying permits granted for 1982 and until the report
of the Royal Commission on Forestry.[77]

Victory was short-lived. By the end of July, spraying of 2,4-D/2,4,5-T
from trucks had begun on some mainland sites. It took a few days longer
to learn why, but in the early days of August, the DOE revealed that the
aerial spray permits suspended by Cabinet had been automatically converted to ground spray permits. Activists were stunned and faced once

again the choice of tactics: pressure (demonstrably ineffective, short of vandalism, which Elizabeth May and the EAC called "a defeat for the democratic process") or litigation.[78] And this time they deliberated without the luxury of delay. NSFI published its newspaper notices on August 4, promising to begin spraying on the 11th. Driven to their "last resort," in the words of Vicki Palmer, the activists chose to go to court.[79]

PLAYING BY THE RULES: THE HERBICIDE TRIAL

The rules of the courtroom are never simple but the principles are usually straightforward. The court, according to Justice Merlin Nunn of the Nova Scotia Supreme Court, is the "final and proper forum" for determining the veracity of facts and their adequacy to a certain standard of proof.[80] That far, and no further. To win their temporary injunction, the plaintiffs seeking to stop herbicide spraying in Nova Scotia needed only to prove the possibility, not the probability, of harm to themselves or their property, and to do so to the satisfaction of Justice C. Denne Burchell, who had heard and been swayed by many of the same arguments from the residents of Big Pond a year earlier. In addition, they needed to promise to pay the costs incurred by the defendants if the case ultimately went against them. It had been a relatively quick task in 1981, but the pulp companies were better prepared to argue in 1982. And argue they did, for six days – the longest chambers proceeding in Nova Scotian legal history – bringing experts from across North America to testify. Eventually, Scott Paper and Bowater Mersey were dropped from the injunction application when Burchell ruled that no plaintiff lived close enough to the western spray zones, and NSFI alone faced seventeen plaintiffs from Cape Breton and the eastern mainland who found that they had successfully argued themselves into a neat trap. The pulp companies' procedural intransigence had driven legal costs high enough already that for the plaintiffs to withdraw would invite financial ruin (and allow the spray to go ahead), while a loss at trial could be much worse. Having won their injunction, they had little choice but to go ahead with a protracted courtroom battle against an expanding cast of opponents. NSFI's name may have appeared on the suit, but Scott and Bowater kept their lawyers on the case, and were soon joined by the US multinational Dow Chemical, manufacturer of 2,4-D and 2,4,5-T.[81]

Dow's interest was only one part of the internationalization of Nova Scotia's forest controversies. The anti-herbicide movement in Nova Scotia had indeed "unwittingly stumbled into a battle with the international pesticide industry," as environmentalists themselves quickly realized, and if anyone doubted the costs of defeat, they were swiftly educated by Scott Paper. Scott had no official role in the proceedings after the first four days of hearings in Justice Burchell's chambers, but for those four days the company demanded $23,000 in costs from the plaintiffs. Appeals reduced the amount by about a third, but having effectively already lost their case against Scott (and despite the ongoing case against NSFI), the plaintiffs were held liable and given a week to pay.[82] It was an ominous beginning, but driving home the reality of the threat also helped draw attention and supporters to the plaintiffs' side.

The herbicide trial, as it came to be known, was one of the milestone events in the formation of a provincial environmental movement that was more than a mere congeries of independently operating parts. Groups that had existed before the herbicide issue turned much of their attention and energy to it, and new associations found their raison d'être in support of the plaintiffs. Rudy Haase's Friends of Nature (FON), oldest of the new groups formed since 1960, pledged to raise $10,000 towards the legal costs.[83] At the same time, a new organization in Annapolis County, People for Environmental Protection (PEP), which had been speaking out against chemical biocides only since mid-year, legally incorporated in the fall of 1982 and set about fundraising for the case.[84] The plaintiffs even found a lawyer through the provincial network – Richard Murtha, a member of the Sackville Environmental Protection Association and a Vietnam veteran who attributed his own chloracne affliction to exposure to Agent Orange.[85] To avoid duplication of effort and share news quickly, the leading activists formed a phone tree, and by the time the trial began in May 1983, the list of individuals and group representatives they had compiled constituted the first so-named Nova Scotia Environmental Network.[86]

The mobilization of public upset and activist energy around the trial looked very different from the budworm battles of a half-decade earlier, when multiple lines of argument had converged on the Cabinet table in Halifax. Quite apart from the possibility of having to pay NSFI's court costs, simply fighting the case was a massive financial undertaking for seventeen plaintiffs. Though some expert witnesses could be recruited from supporters within the province, such as the veteran anti–budworm spray activist and surgeon Dr. William Thurlow, others could only come from abroad. Ultimately, nine of the plaintiffs' fourteen witnesses lived outside the province, and each one had to be brought to Cape Breton, housed for the duration of their testimony, and returned home. Sympathetic lawyers could serve at reduced rates, especially with the assistance of Elizabeth May and some of her fellow Dalhousie law students, but reduced is not free. Necessarily, then, most of the work done in support of the plaintiffs was fundraising. A band of Cape Breton supporters quickly organized an association – the Herbicide Fund Society (HFS) – dedicated to collecting money for the trial, and other groups began to direct donors to them.[87]

The environmental movement as a whole had only so much effort to expend, and however necessary the fundraising effort was, it could not help but draw attention away from the work of generating political pressure. PEP, for example, after participating in one of Environment Canada's public consultation meetings, writing a brief for presentation to the Royal Commission on Forestry, and soliciting donations to the HFS, might have laboured for half a year without even once coming to the attention of the provincial Cabinet if not for its work in organizing a phone-in day to Premier Buchanan's office.[88] Even there, however, political efforts suffered the additional handicap of having to penetrate the bubble of shifted responsibility that the trial and Royal Commission had placed around Province House. Whatever could not be dismissed with "it is before the court" could be handily redirected with "tell it to the Royal Commission." For some activists, the chance to prove their case "objectively" was a welcome alternative and much more respectable behaviour than forceful lobbying. For others it was a handicap, tolerated out of the necessity to support the plaintiffs, who had put so much on the line on everyone else's behalf.

One new development that under better circumstances might have proven a potent political weapon was the extent of collaboration with environmental groups outside Nova Scotia. Certainly there had been exchanges of information and nominal association with other Canadian and American groups since the early 1970s, when the infant EAC reached out to Ontario's only slightly older Pollution Probe. And the "budworm battles" had seen more of the same, as well as some genuine influence on the course of a similar campaign in New Brunswick, in which the Reye's syndrome episode in Nova Scotia provoked the first mass popular resistance to insecticide spraying across the border.[89] But the end of 1982 saw the first active collaboration between Nova Scotian environmentalists and their foreign peers, aiming at achieving victory not only in a Sydney courtroom but also in a much larger campaign. Cape Breton's trial became news around the world. As the newsletter of the worldwide Pesticide Action Network (PAN) put it in 1983, "the potential implications of the court case are more far reaching than the plaintiffs imagined in that first day in court. Proving to the court's satisfaction that the use of admittedly dangerous substances in dilute quantities according to government approved procedures constitutes nuisance, actionable at law, would broaden the potential for environmental litigation against other hazardous materials."[90]

By early 1983, the EAC's Forestry Committee was also talking about a ban on 2,4-D/2,4,5-T "across Nova Scotia and Canada."[91] Like the writers at PAN, most out-of-province environmentalists tended to see the widest implications to their cooperation – a chance to use the Sydney proceedings as political ammunition – while the Nova Scotians with whom they connected, mainly in the EAC and CBLAS, remained caught up in the fundraising effort. The EAC quote on national ambitions, for example, came quite typically in the course of a fundraising appeal letter. Speaking tours by herbicide trial plaintiffs to Ottawa, Vancouver, Washington, and points between were also, for the speakers transfixed by their financial peril, mainly fundraising tours.[92] The connections built between Nova Scotian environmental activists and Swedish environmentalists in particular brought profound pressure to bear on Stora Kopparberg's headquarters – which probably forced the company to seek a settlement with the plaintiffs at the end of 1983[93] – but never achieved any noticeable pressure on the government of Nova Scotia. In that sense, it, and most of the out-of-province collaboration built around the herbicide trial, were mostly wasted potential.

The reason Nova Scotians had to reach beyond the provincial border to recruit witnesses was the extreme complexity of the set of ideas they had to argue in court. At trial they would be expected to prove the potential for harm within a narrow definition: human health could only be taken as isolated from environmental health, affected by the latter but never part of it, and a legal/scientific standard of proof would apply, meaning that all other possible causes of a given effect would have to be ruled out before the court would accept any herbicides as being responsible for it. The kind of medical research that might produce such results is expensive and rare, and even bringing the researchers themselves from Sweden or the United States could not prevent NSFI's lawyers from arguing the absence of direct, verifiable links. It was the same argument used by the New Brunswick government to defend its insecticide program during the Reye's syndrome controversy. At that time, it led Dr. John Crocker to complain that, short of experimentation on humans, no researcher could ever produce the kind of proof they were demanding of him.[94] The plaintiffs could only hope to educate the court on the nature of epidemiological evidence as the trial progressed. Even so, they would still have to overcome an insurmountable problem of scientific uncertainty, arguing for the effective prohibition of 2,4-D and 2,4,5-T when even the best research sometimes failed to make clear whether the possible danger stemmed from the named phenoxy compounds themselves, from the products of their breakdown over months in storage or in nature, or from dioxin contaminants that occurred in vastly different concentrations from one chemical or one manufacturer to the next. And all the while they would face the attempts of NSFI's lawyers to prolong the court's confusion, arguing the need to sort out every nice distinction before pinning any blame on the chemicals in question, and insisting on the clearest "smoking gun" evidence of their harmfulness. In effect, the plaintiffs had shouldered the nearly impossible burden of transforming a precautionary case into a deductive one – a "probably" into a "definitely." Justice Burchell had warned them in the summer of 1982 that the issue of chemical safety belonged properly to politicians, not judges, but once he granted his injunction, there was little chance to back away.[95]

Given the clearly poor odds of success, the question "why go to court?" was on many minds in late 1982 and through much of 1983, though the urgency of the process precluded its becoming a matter for much open debate until after the settlement with NSFI.[96] The leading activists' having had so little time to decide on their course of action, and the profound fear of what Agent Orange exposure might do, were certainly major factors. For some activists, injunctions were seen as primarily a delaying tactic anyway. Yet haste alone cannot explain it; the first successful challenge to the budworm spray in the winter of 1976 had hinged upon a Cabinet decision in a matter of weeks using political tactics. One reason for the difference was surely Elizabeth May's entry into law school at Dalhousie University. May enjoyed a well-earned respect among anti-spray forces, especially on Cape Breton, and she had led every legal effort since Big Pond in 1980. Most of all, however, the reason for May and her allies in the EAC and other established Halifax groups to pursue the legal route was their maturing faith in scientific argument and the ability to sway politicians (or judges) with statements of pure fact. Since 1975, the EAC had pursued an image of respectability, based on the understanding that a place at the policy-making table and a chance to state its case would be enough to convince anyone; Susan Holtz's insistence that the environmental movement had no real enemies epitomized that attitude. Its allies in forestry activism, the old-style conservationists, were the heirs of a long tradition of even more strict scientific optimism, not always as keen on public education and democracy as the new environmentalists, but very much committed to the idea that technocratic foresters, free of the corrupting influence of politics and commercial interest, could be counted on to follow the dictates of sound science. May and CBLAS might have begun in 1976 with some antipathy towards government, but the experience with Vince MacLean and with Environment Canada's public consultation had turned some heads, especially hers, and close cooperation with the EAC encouraged the change.

With confidence in their facts and experts, then – shaken only slightly by Justice Merlin Nunn's decision to hear the case alone, without a jury[97] – the plaintiffs put together a set of arguments around four essential points: (1) the physical evidence of spray chemicals' mobility beyond the spray site; (2) the ecological evidence of their damage to the forest system; (3) the economic evidence of the lack of necessity for herbicides in pulp-wood forestry; and (4) the medical evidence of their harmfulness to human health. Their witnesses' combined testimony would present a damning description of NSFI's practices and of the government's oversight. Optimistically, supporters hoped that politicians, bureaucrats, and Royal Commissioners might "hear the crucial evidence that will help them make sane decisions."[98] In reality, none of them were listening, and if they had been they would have heard Justice Nunn dismiss each of the first three approaches summarily as irrelevant to the question of human health and safety. If the chemicals could not be proven harmful, he reasoned, NSFI might waste money, kill forests, or spray water supplies at will, even when instructed not to, and the court should still be satisfied that no criminal trespass existed.[99] Arguments that had won over the public against insecticide spraying fell flat in front of Nunn's insistence on the strict legal standard of proof of harm.

According to Nunn's preference, the majority of testimony from the first day of the trial on May 5 to the last day on June 1 concerned the effects of phenoxy herbicides on human health, and it was here that NSFI came prepared to fight. The plaintiffs' witness John Constable, surgeon at Harvard Medical School and one of the world's foremost epidemiologists regarding the effects of Agent Orange in Vietnam, started the contest by detailing the very recent evidence of birth defects there, and suggested that though newer phenoxies had less dioxin, no one could yet know if it was little enough to be harmless. "It is unreasonable," he said, "to use human subjects to determine the minimum toxic dose of a very deadly chemical."[100] It was exactly the argument that the plaintiffs offered again and again, even as the central point of Elizabeth May's end-of-trial summary: to proceed in the face of scientific uncertainty amounts to human testing. NSFI responded by minimizing both the scientific disagreement and the potential harm, producing experts to contradict each of the plaintiffs' experts, and yet more experts to insist on the relatively higher cancer risk from, variously, vitamin A, aspirin, cigarettes, contraceptives, diet soda, peanut butter, milk, and oxygen.[101] As testimony went on, witnesses attacked other witnesses' work. Lawyers for each side attacked the other side's experts for their experimental procedures, grasp of statistics, or closeness to industry. It became, in Richard Murtha's words, "the world series of scientific evidence."[102]

If the trial was a ball game, the plaintiffs struck out often. They seemed to be playing by rules different from those imposed by the umpire. Mikael Eriksson, a Swedish cancer researcher, objected to NSFI's simplistic numeric assessments of risk. "Risk to whom? Benefit to whom?" he asked. With the herbicides themselves as well as their various dioxins and other contaminants understudied, he added, "we just know for sure about sarcomas and lymphomas." Other cancers might well be caused by the same array of toxins.[103] Susan Daum, an epidemiologist from New Jersey, carefully explained to Justice Nunn that rare cancers and birth defects may be "markers" for more common ones whose causes can't be discerned with enough certainty. If thalidomide had caused a common birth defect, she said, its effects would have disappeared into the statistical background and no one might ever have realized what it was doing.[104] In granting the injunction in August, Justice Burchell had mentioned thalidomide and DDT, saying that people do have a right to fear "approved" substances.[105] Nunn would not have it (or simply could not grasp it).[106] The question of risk inequity was beneath mention, but during the trial as well as in his final ruling, Nunn insisted that any chemical as bad as environmentalists made TCDD dioxin out to be should have obvious effects.[107] Barring such effects, no evidence would satisfy him. When plaintiffs' lawyers pressed one of NSFI's witnesses about full or partial bans on 2,4,5-T in Sweden, Italy, Holland, Norway, Japan, and the Soviet Union, Nunn interjected to dismiss "political" matters: "I have received no evidence of any country that has banned them on the basis of scientific evidence." On another occasion, he vented his frustration with inconclusive studies and suggested that the scientists "scrap them all and start over again," as though one good experiment would settle the question forever. Finally, on the last day of the trial, the plaintiffs attempted to call Robyn Warren to the stand, hoping to use his story of herbicide poisoning to "rebut the theory that nothing happens in real life." Nunn refused to hear him.[108]

Justice Nunn's ruling, when it came on September 15, could hardly have been a great surprise. In insisting on the strictest standard of proof, he had earlier said that the "reasonable fear for safety and health" criterion could shut down almost any industry if consistently applied.[109] Those who had attended the trial might have heard echoes of the startling honesty of Dr. Marshall Johnson, witness for the defence, who said that "if you took everything that causes terata [birth defects] off the market, we wouldn't have anything."[110] Only "smoking gun" evidence could have met Nunn's standard, and that (e.g., "John Doe's cancer was definitely caused by 2,4-D") is exactly the kind of evidence epidemiology cannot produce. There was no shortage of criticism of the ruling during the late months of 1983, but in truth Nunn had carried out his assigned task as well as should have been expected. The court is an inherently conservative institution. Arguments in favour of precautionary principles cannot be expected to move a judge when the law he applies has no space for such considerations. May, Murtha, and Wildsmith crafted a case best suited to the court of public opinion and gambled on its success in a court of law.

Criticism of Nunn's ruling on the merits of the case quickly fell away behind rising criticism of his ruling on costs. The plaintiffs had indeed gambled, and stood to lose everything. Not even pausing to hear arguments from either side, the judge awarded full court costs to NSFI. Though the plaintiffs had acted in the public interest, normally a mitigating factor in costs rulings, the final ruling seemed better suited to a frivolous suit. This, along with Nunn's direct criticism of the plaintiffs' witnesses' "lack of objectivity" caused the greatest anger and worry among environmentalists.[111] Regardless of the outcome of the trial, the feeling that a ruling on costs had been used to punish activists and discourage further opposition to chemical forestry incensed their supporters. Sydney City Council (already upset during the trial when one of NSFI's witnesses suggested that the city's tap water was more carcinogenic than 2,4,5-T) passed a unanimous resolution asking the provincial government to pay the costs on behalf of the plaintiffs, and fundraising efforts increased with the help of the Dalhousie University Student Union, the Nova Scotia Liberal Party, and the provincial Federation of Labour, along with environmental groups in several other provinces. Pollution Probe bought an ad in the *Globe and Mail* asking for donations in support of the seventeen Nova Scotians and their families facing financial ruin; Friends of the Earth Canada did the same in the *Ottawa Citizen*.[112] Nevertheless, the precedent set by Nunn's ruling could scarcely be undone by a simple show of support, no matter how strong. The provincial minister of environment made it clear that he had no intention of interfering in the case in any way, and saw "no need to finance the court battles of environmentalist groups,"[113] and the EAC reported that a group of activists in Calgary had abandoned court action against Amoco Petroleum over a sour gas leak in 1982, for fear of a similar ruling on costs.[114]

In the fall of 1983, the herbicide issue was as vital as it had ever been. If government and industry had hoped to squelch opposition in the wake of a harsh court ruling, they were disappointed. Measured by fundraising effort, press attention, and the geographic reach of both, the protest was, if anything, gaining momentum. Yet the whole effort in Nova Scotia – and by extension the connected efforts beyond – was still tethered to court proceedings, and to the shaken confidence and fading energy of seventeen average Nova Scotians. None of them could have expected in the summer of 1982 that sixteen months later they would be contemplating appeal proceedings that might drag on for months or years longer, and the strain of Justice Nunn's costs ruling was wearing them down. The example of Scott Paper's costs award during the injunction hearing was never far from their minds: if NSFI made a similarly sudden demand for payment, the plaintiffs, despite all of the fundraising, could not hope to raise the amount needed. Some of them also questioned the value of an appeal, when the injunction that had grounded NSFI's planes had expired with the end of the trial. They might go through all of the additional expense of an appeal only to be sprayed before ever meeting another judge. Peter Cumming wrote:

> They had become representatives of all Nova Scotians, personally responsible for reforming Canadian law for all environmental and citizen groups who might take a corporation or government to court over anything, figureheads, martyrs, and torch-bearers for people across Canada, the United States, and Sweden ... sooner or later the question must be asked as to how much any group of people should be expected to bear.[115]

For plaintiff Vicki Palmer, the answer was already clear: "People are burnt out."[116] For almost three months the plaintiffs debated whether or not to proceed with an appeal. In early December, they decided to "get out of a bad situation as cheaply and quickly as possible."[117]

The settlement that the plaintiffs signed with NSFI was a divisive one. The final debate over whether to accept the deal was tense and ran late into the night, and when they finally came to a decision, it was based in part on the advice of a corporate lawyer who enjoyed less than perfect trust from all seventeen plaintiffs. The settlement would mean turning over remaining funds raised to NSFI (not a significant amount) and surrendering the right to appeal, but would also finally end the plaintiffs' financial peril. Ryan Googoo, keen to appeal Nunn's brisk dismissal of the Aboriginal rights argument, and Elizabeth May, who wished to keep the debate in a legal forum, initially refused to sign the settlement, though Googoo eventually agreed to abandon an appeal in order to preserve the settlement for the other plaintiffs' sake.[118] The Herbicide Fund Society, not itself a plaintiff, did not need to sign but was asked to give up its funds or risk scuttling the settlement. After some debate, its members decided to capitulate, and also to dissolve their society and begin anew, hoping to raise funds to repay the costs left out of the settlement and to operate at a greater remove from most of the former plaintiffs.[119] Money questions strained the cohesion of the anti-herbicide forces – HFS's Peter Cumming believed NSFI had drafted its offer with that result in mind[120] – but almost everyone was reluctant to criticize too heavily the plaintiffs who had done so much. Financial disagreements alone did not drive the acrimonious debate of late 1983 and 1984; instead fundamental disagreements about how to wage the campaign were breaking through after months of enforced solidarity.

THE STING OF DEFEAT

For a certain subset of the anti-pesticide movement (well represented in the EAC, and including Elizabeth May), court action presented the ideal vehicle for environmentalism: objective, scientific, and respectable. At a time when environmental activists were being accused of harbouring anti-business feelings – dangerously close to anti-capitalist, with all of its sinister Soviet connotations – any method of argument that could borrow the legitimacy of the judicial system was an advantage. Unfortunately, the tactical choice that was supposed to "balance the image" of the movement did nothing to increase its influence on forest policy or alter the growing frequency of attacks against environmentalists in the press, except perhaps by restraining their ability to respond effectively.[121]

Industry spokesmen rarely missed a chance to criticize environmentalists and indeed went out of their way to do so, for example, in newspaper advertisements like those shown in Figure 2, but predictably so and to muted effect. Attacks from high-ranking members of the Buchanan government were far worse. With the pro-chemical faction in ascendancy within Lands and Forests and the DOE, there were few curbs on comments such as deputy environment minister E.L.L. Rowe's, associating activists with "violence and civil disobedience," or Attorney General Harry How's

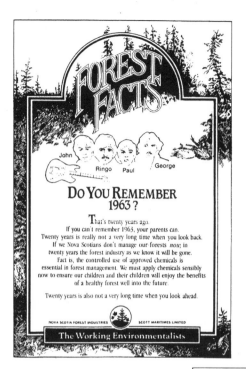

FIGURE 2 The backlash against activists included a mostly fruitless attempt to usurp the word "environmentalist" and a much more successful attempt to present them as a meddling leisure class. *Source: Chronicle-Herald,* December 10, 1983, 7 *(top); Chronicle-Herald,* December 16, 1983, 7 *(bottom).*

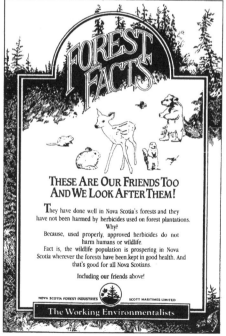

suggestion that half of the movement in Nova Scotia was made up of Americans.[122] The long-serving and prominent minister of lands and forests George Henley gave the most thorough denunciation of environmentalists, as a small group operating in Nova Scotia with the "support of subversive elements from both within and without the nation by both political philosophy and financial assistance and under the guise of environment." The solution to this pernicious influence, according to Henley (and despite the efforts of the most scientifically inclined environmentalists to appropriate managerial language), was to "base our educational program on facts, on scientific facts so that we may go forward with our forest management despite the preoccupation of those I have mentioned who through distortion, through vandalism, through supposition, through emotion, based without truth would destroy the very principle of forest management."[123]

Activists understood what the critics intended. One remarked that "Mr. Henley ... is well aware that about 50 per cent of all those who heard or read his statement already have implemented in their minds the connection between anti-spray and communism."[124] Yet their response was remarkably confused. Since the end of the budworm fight, the largest environmental coalition in the province had grown lax in its public outreach even as it pursued legal solutions and bureaucratic access. As one measure, the EAC's formal membership declined to about three hundred in 1982, from over six hundred just two years earlier.[125] Members who self-identified as part of the movement were replaced by supporters, who stood outside of it. And while some in the movement fretted over the potential loss of social influence as a consequence of the drift towards elite or expert status, it is not clear that anyone anticipated how much easier the change made it for people like Henley or How to portray them as a clique of subversives and outsiders. Nor does anyone seem to have realized how badly losing in court had undermined their own claims to scientific expertise and credibility, or the power of the propaganda weapon that Justice Nunn's decision would place in the hands of the movement's critics. By impugning the scientific objectivity of the plaintiffs' witnesses in his ruling, Nunn effectively gave the endorsement of the court to the statements of the defence, which Lands and Forests' Eldridge immediately began circulating to forestry agencies across the country. (The PAN cited a particularly egregious example by a witness supplied by Dow Chemical, who described Agent Orange as "a mythical substance which caused tremendous damage in Vietnam in the newspapers, but nowhere else."[126]) Even when environmentalists attempted to buttress their mass-movement credentials, they faced criticism designed to undermine their reputation as honest information brokers. A public opinion poll that showed 61 percent of Nova Scotians opposed to the use of 2,4-D and 2,4,5-T on forests prompted a DOE spokesperson to suggest that the numbers had been "cooked."[127]

Henley's talk of an "educational program" was much more than a rhetorical stick with which to beat environmentalists. It was policy. In an ironic reversal of the trend in the nascent environmental mainstream, the Department of Lands and Forests avidly pursued public outreach starting in 1983 and continuing under Henley's successor, Ken Streatch. Active support of industrial forestry had been growing in the department and in the DOE since shortly after the Progressive Conservative government took power in 1978 and brought Don Eldridge from the Nova Scotia Forest Products Association into the deputy minister's office, but it took the herbicide trial to finally shock the chemical proponents out of the narrow reaches of interdepartmental committees and the Eastern Spruce Budworm Council and into acting on Eldridge's exhortations to publicly "answer [the] anti-spray people."[128] The year 1983 brought active cooperation between pulp and paper companies and government on public woodlot tours to sprayed and unsprayed stands, and on attempts to counter negative publicity by seeking out media attention. As momentum grew for mass public appeals by industry during the winter of 1984, plans for the first Nova Scotia Forestry Exhibition were drawn up and funding was secured from Lands and Forests.[129]

Critics of the industry operating within the reach of government agencies found their positions increasingly untenable in this new era. Some, like the ECC, simply swam with the tide, calling it "encouraging" to see industry "beginning to combat this [environmentalist misinformation] with information and education programs."[130] Others resisted. Minister Streatch personally took over as the chairman of the Forest Practices Improvement Board, which had given a voice during the controversy to small woodlot owners opposed to chemical forestry. The former chairman, Hugh Fairn, complained that Cabinet was stacking the board with "people dedicated to the destruction of the [Forest Practices Improvement] Act," while board member and fierce critic of industrial forestry Murray Prest accused the minister of attempting to "cripple" the board and with it one of the few means for small landowners to resist the pulp companies' market control.[131] But industrial forestry advocates refused to cede either media dominance or control of the board to their critics. Just as environmental activists had learned from their opponents during the budworm controversy, their opponents now borrowed environmentalists' tactics and appealed to aesthetic arguments (contrasting the "terrible looking grey mess of trees" killed by the budworm with the "lovely little green trees" in herbicide- and insecticide-treated plots).[132] They also continued to consolidate their claim on scientific expertise, and began crafting forestry education curricula for elementary students. Thanks to "public education" subsidies included in federal/provincial forestry agreements, Canadians' own money brought the inaugural "People of the Forest" lesson to Pictou County at the end of 1983, from which students learned the value and necessity of chemical treatments.[133]

Environmentalists recognized what was happening. Some could even appreciate the irony of their unintended achievement. In one of the first newsletters from the HFS's successor organization, Citizens Against Pesticides (CAP), Peter Cumming noted on a list of activist accomplishments that, while they had earned support from literally all around the world, "we have also mobilized the forest industry, Lands and Forests, Canadian Forestry Service, Truth in Forestry, etc. etc. into trying to sell the chemical forest to Canadians."[134] It is questionable, though, how many realized that public education was necessary only as a weapon against environmental activists. After all, unlike environmentalists, industry had no need of public pressure to turn policy decisions in its favour. The provincial government had made perfectly clear its intention to continue herbicide spraying even as the legal drama unfolded. While waiting for a decision, the environment minister publicly vowed to treat the upcoming ruling as applying only to the few thousand acres covered by the injunction, and Lands and Forests finally removed the last official requirement for prior public notification before spraying. Aerial application of 2,4-D/2,4,5-T was still off the table thanks to the pressure tactics of the Whycocomagh Band the previous summer, but there was nothing to prevent spraying from the ground. In 1983 as in 1982, Lands and Forests approved ground permits for scattered sites across the province and even conducted its own program on five hundred acres.[135] (See Figure 3.) The secrecy was imperfect – the Scott Paper Company was more open than government, and the information could be extracted from the DOE with enough persistence – but it hardly mattered. Letters of protest from the EAC and the provincial New Democratic Party were no more effective than last-minute protest marches by the residents of Orangedale, Inverness County. Government had simply stopped listening.[136]

In the aftermath of Nunn's ruling and the subsequent settlement, as bureaucrats and elected officials joined industry spokesmen in denouncing "ignorance and irrational fear,"[137] the rain of secretly approved herbicides resumed. New rationales were found for insecticide applications as well, as the gypsy moth moved into southwestern Nova Scotia.[138] Environmentalists, largely cut off from information sources in government and fighting on multiple fronts (now against a revived roadside spray program with 2,4-D in various counties), drew meagre comfort from the fact that 2,4,5-T, suspended from use by the US Environmental Protection Agency in 1979 and finally discontinued by Dow Chemical, was no longer available. The herbicide program in 1984 would see instead the first widespread use of glyphosate on Nova Scotia's forests.[139] But the change was due entirely to outside factors, and the last stockpile of 2,4,5-T still made its way into the forest, albeit by the more laborious method of ground spraying. The herbicide trial, epitome of a provincial movement based on science and the law, had in the end achieved only the peculiar and unintended effect of driving the provincial government to abandon any pretence of impartiality. There were now, at least, very clearly opposed camps on the issue of industrial forestry, though not everyone in the movement was willing to acknowledge it.

CONCLUSION

The campaign to prevent insecticide and herbicide spraying on Cape Breton Island garnered unprecedented public support across Nova Scotia, but the court challenge that had effectively locked non-modern arguments out of the contest for over a year had proven disastrous, and mistrust of government among those who would make such arguments was stronger than ever. It was joined by a growing mistrust of those who had led the movement into court. The failure of the legal effort and the shock of Justice Nunn's costs ruling preoccupied the province's environmental activists, and the eventual settlement even more so, but it also freed them from the enforced solidarity of the courtroom proceedings. Peter Cumming, who had pushed his alternative views fruitlessly before the Royal Commission during the trial preparations, wrote several essays in the aftermath. In "The Stink of Defeat," he called it "amazing ... that our shaky structure has held together as long as it has,"[140] but admitted that the effort had left the entire movement "demoralized, burned out, and fighting among themselves."[141] In "Out of the Courts and Back to the Issue," he suggested that "the legal child [had] gobbled up the larger parent, the herbicide issue itself."[142] In

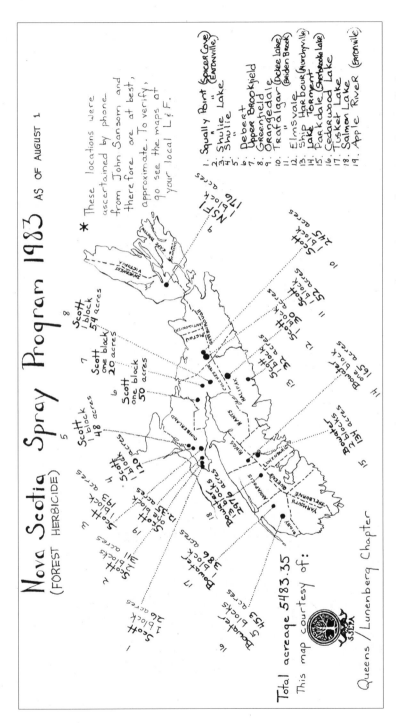

FIGURE 3 Map of spray sites for 1983. *Source: Queens/Lunenburg SSEPA News 2, no. 2 (1983), Nova Scotia Archives, Betty Peterson fonds, MGI, vol. 3470, no. 6.*

both essays, the advice was the same: return in earnest to the political pressure tactics of the budworm era and leave the divisive post-mortem analysis for another time (perhaps never). Too many activists, though, were unwilling to let it go at that. Freed to express their frustration, groups like the Cape Breton Wildlife Association lashed out at a "red herring" legal effort that focused on human health and left no room for defence of wildlife or landscapes,[143] while others – likely influenced by the activist schism around uranium mining (see Chapter 4) – saw behind the question of tactics a deeper division between those who would work within the boundaries set by government and those who would challenge them.[144]

The power of governments to shape social movements has to do with more than simply tempting offers of consultation or research funding. It also involves their withdrawal of the same, as well as of basic information, in order to protect their prerogative of final decision making, and the powerful instruments – such as Royal Commissions' terms of reference, parliamentary procedure, court rules, and bureaucratic compromise – with which they influence the sorts of arguments and ideas deemed legitimate in official proceedings, in the press, and in the public mind. The Queens-Lunenburg South Shore Environmental Protection Association (SSEPA) complained in the summer of 1983 that

> we have been telling the government how we feel about its forestry and public notice policies, especially regarding herbicide spraying. We have followed all the proper channels – letters, phone calls, telegrams, petitions, and even litigation. We have made submissions to the Royal Forestry Commission. Still we are ignored. Still government will not meet with us. Still government issues permits while the Royal Commission on forestry is deliberating; while the Nova Scotia Supreme Court weighs the evidence. Still the government reduces further the feeblest of public notice regulations.[145]

The SSEPA members were feeling the effects of this whole suite of conditions as well as describing the sort of activities that it is designed to evoke. Confronted with such an apparently insuperable challenge, activists were forced to decide between acquiescence and rebellion, but the process of following "all the proper channels" had already set a large proportion of the movement on the path to acquiescence by narrowing the parameters of acceptable argument to suit the institutions of power.

The contest over industrial forestry demonstrates the power of the modern state to shape social movements, but the state never acts alone. These conditions, this exercise of government power, require as well the tacit consent of the governed. It requires the latter's own agency, and in the summer of 1983 a number of environmentalists in Nova Scotia had already demonstrated their determination to remain within the boundaries of respectable discourse, regardless of the cost.

4

Two Environmentalisms
Uranium and Radicalism

I N THE LATE 1970S, Nova Scotians witnessed a boom in uranium prospecting. As prospectors homed in on deposits, moving from aerial
surveys to drilling and trenching, their activities became more noticeable
on the ground, and more and more alarming to Nova Scotian landowners,
some of them already certain that uranium should not be mined, others
still only curious and concerned to find out the risks.[1] The province's anti-
nuclear movement was well prepared to provide information. Uranium
and its dangers had long been recognized as a fruitful avenue of anti-nuclear
argument: granted a hypothetical accident-free nuclear energy system,
uranium mines and tailings piles would present the largest single source
of additional radioisotope releases by the nuclear industry, and the federal and provincial governments had been steadfast in their support of
the industry. The established groups therefore had information ready on
the anti-uranium experience in Saskatchewan, British Columbia, and the
United States.[2]

Organized activism that went beyond merely sharing information
gathered steam slowly during 1979 and the early months of 1980. Prodded
by a growing stream of letters and phone calls from worried landowners,
and enjoying a partial respite from campaigning against the *use* of nuclear
fuel in the region after the Brudenell rally, established groups turned their
attention to cooperation on the issue of its production in the winter of
1980.[3] In January, the Community Planning Association's inveterate coalition builder in Halifax, Joanne Lamey, began assembling interested parties
from around the province into a common front, before quickly deferring

to the Energy Committee of the Ecology Action Centre (EAC).[4] There
was a gathering on February 20, but the EAC was initially cautious and
conservative. Susan Holtz was determined to cultivate a bridge-building
mode of operations, in line with which the EAC made direct calls upon
the minister of mines and energy, Ron Barkhouse, to "follow BC's lead,"
but offered him little reason to comply.[5] The EAC's information-sharing
role certainly helped draw more attention to the issue, but it (as well as
the Fundy Area Concern for Tomorrow [FACT] group in the Annapolis
Valley) generally integrated anti-uranium campaigning into their well-
established routine of anti-nuclear activism; there appears to have been
little effort to collaborate on a strategy with the growing number of citizens
alarmed about uranium mining quite on its own.

The first significant new citizen action against uranium exploration in
Nova Scotia came from an unexpected source: the Women's Institutes.
Nova Scotia's Women's Institutes were established early in the twentieth
century as service clubs for rural women, promoting education, civic
engagement, and cultural activities. By the 1970s, however, they were often
dismissed as conservative assemblies of older women.[6] Yet they were far
from moribund or unresponsive to changing times, and had much in
common with the feminist peace groups that were drawn to the earliest
anti-nuclear activism in Halifax. The pesticide debates of the late 1970s
attracted a great deal of attention in agricultural communities and among
institute members, who considered the health of farm families a traditional
women's issue. Some institutes were also reinvigorated by the arrival of
back-to-the-land families, including women with experience in peace and
social justice activism. Early in 1980, several Women's Institutes received
information and assistance from the Department of Environment to set
up environmental awareness committees; within months, Institutes in
Hants and Kings Counties were already at work gathering information on
uranium mining.[7] By November, the Women's Institutes of Hants County
moved from gathering information into building public support for an
anti-uranium movement.[8]

In early 1981, one of the rare Maritime-wide anti-nuclear gatherings
under the banner of the fast-fading Maritime Energy Coalition (MEC)
united interested parties in demanding a moratorium on and inquiry
into uranium mining, but a common set of demands alone made for
neither a full-scale movement nor a strategy for organizing one.[9] What
was lacking was a triggering event, something personal, something analogous to the Genelle blockade in British Columbia, which launched
the process of protest, Royal Commission, and eventual moratorium on

uranium prospecting in that province. The winter of 1981 provided one, as news spread that one of the companies with claims in the Vaughan/ New Ross area southwest of Windsor was no longer looking for uranium so much as looking at a mineable deposit of it. If any single factor transformed uranium from the obscure preoccupation of a relatively small number of peace activists, anti-nuclear groups, and Women's Institute members into the third major environmental controversy since the 1960s, it was the prospect of an actual uranium mine operating within a few years at a known site. With the encouragement of Women's Institute members who had spent most of the previous year studying the issue, statements of support for a British Columbia–style moratorium on uranium mining and prospecting came from the Hants and Digby Counties Federations of Agriculture, and from the provincial New Democratic Party leader, Alexa McDonough. Most worrying of all, from the industry's perspective, the vote of the West Hants Municipal Council to request a provincial moratorium was the direct result of the work of the Women's Institutes.[10] And the local leaders of the anti-uranium forces from Hants County promised more to come, continuing their drive for support during the winter and spring of 1981, urging more action from other members of the Voice of Women (several "Voices" were already among them) and from other groups in the province.[11]

As opponents were lining up against uranium mining, Aquitaine, the French mining company that had made the discovery near Vaughan, and its allies in the provincial government began a counter-effort. At a public meeting at the Windsor exhibition grounds in April, Aquitaine's senior vice president of explorations and special projects, Mike Hriskevich, joined environmental consultant Leo Lowe and the company's regional office head, Don Pollock, on a mission to defuse local opposition. In the co-ordinator's chair sat Jack Garnet, Nova Scotia's director of mineral resources and a champion of uranium mining. One of the province's up-and-coming anti-uranium leaders, writer and English professor Donna Smyth, later described the meeting as decidedly hostile towards the presenters. Certainly the men from Aquitaine gained few allies by underestimating the store of knowledge built up by local activists over the previous year; claims that yellowcake uranium was "not radioactive," or that Ontario's Elliot Lake mines (with their long, dead river) represented safe and successful industrial practices, were instantly rebutted and were featured in anti-uranium propaganda for the next two years.[12] A similar performance soon followed at the West Hants Municipal Council, where Pollock gave a rebuttal to the Women's Institute presentation a month earlier and insisted that there was no additional radiation measurable in the town of Elliot Lake (an arguably true claim, but quite beside the point of radioisotope contamination of food and water). The council declined to withdraw its moratorium request.[13] Pollock was one of two leaders of the mining industry's propaganda effort, but his extreme statements and accidentally revealing gaffes consistently provided his opponents with ammunition.[14] The provincial government, on the other hand, apart from Jack Garnet, tried at first to evade rather than confront public fears by appointing an inactive Select Committee of the Legislature to investigate.[15]

As the campaign turned into a contest, the growing activist group in Hants County decided to organize formally as Citizen Action to Protect the Environment (CAPE). Its open letter to Premier Buchanan at the end of June displayed all the hallmarks of the group's activism: requests put to the premier served more to inform other readers of alarming facts, such as that the ministers of health and environment had not been chosen to sit on the Select Committee on uranium mining, or that the Department of Mines and Energy was both regulator and promoter of mining, or that exploration continued while the Select Committee supposedly sat to determine its dangers.[16] The members of CAPE had already decided that the Select Committee was a dead-end process, but writing as though it was not enabled them to point out the de facto support the government gave to mining and the lack of effective regulation in the province. Publicly needling politicians in order to attract the support of people who did not already identify as "environmentalists" was an effective strategy for CAPE in 1981, though it did not always please its allies at the EAC, who persisted in a conciliatory approach.[17] CAPE's direct appeals to the public were less controversial but still populist, such as the much-publicized map that showed areas of the province under claim by uranium prospectors. As geographer Brian Harley remarked, "maps are never value-free images";[18] CAPE's choice to map claims rather than simply focus on the one existing site of potential development encouraged people in broad areas of the province to think of themselves as being personally under threat. (See Figure 4.)

The success of CAPE's more aggressive tactics, along with the steady contribution of the established groups' publicity and public education, drew fresh countermeasures. Aquitaine's Don Pollock travelled to the annual meeting of the Mining Society of Nova Scotia in June with a stark warning and a request: "If these groups [of environmentalists] are successful in creating a seven-year moratorium in Nova Scotia as they have done in

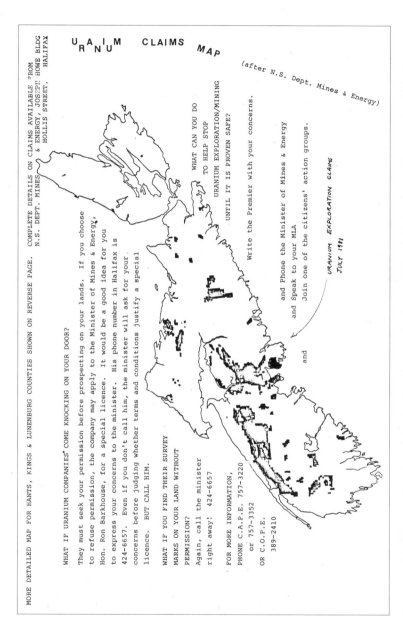

FIGURE 4 CAPE's map of uranium claims in Nova Scotia, 1981. *Source*: Dalhousie University Archives and Special Collections, EAC fonds, MS-11-13, box 30.10.

BC, exploration in the North West Territories could also fall and Canada could wind up with no uranium whatsoever" – a fate preventable only if mining interests could organize political pressure of their own.[19] Whether or not Pollock truly believed that Saskatchewan's entrenched uranium industry was under threat, his advice was sincere. Like the spokesmen for pulp and paper interests in the province, he wanted industry to strike back publicly against environmentalists. By the end of the year, his prodding would result in a new agency, the Chamber of Mineral Resources, to advocate for industry, but Aquitaine's commitment to confrontation was more urgent: on August 28 Nova Scotia's Legislature dissolved for nearly six weeks of election campaigning, during which Alexa McDonough's NDP promised to give the anti-uranium forces a voice that government members could no longer ignore.[20] Under its corporate successor name in Nova Scotia, Kidd Creek Mines, the company brought in its head of environmental affairs, Roy John, to lead a counterattack.

To the members of CAPE and its peers, an election campaign in 1981 was a precious opportunity. Armed with the results of a year and a half of research and self-education, organized, and drawing on the support of agricultural and medical advocacy groups, the activists were better prepared for the campaign trail than some MLAs. In print, in person, and on the airwaves they repeated the facts on radioisotope contamination of water and agricultural produce, reminded their audience of the limits of humanity's technological prowess, and challenged politicians to state a clear position. And they urged more people to join the fight. "The government of Nova Scotia seems in a mad rush to encourage this industry," wrote Muriel Siemers of Centre Burlington in the *Chronicle-Herald*. "Uranium is a relatively common ore. It is mined in places where public opposition is weak, or where the public is not aware of the hazards."[21]

Making the public aware meant appealing to people's personal identification with their home place. The combined claims map did that. So did the constant refrain about the incompatibility of uranium mining and agriculture, an echo of the economic justice arguments made by south shore fishermen during the Stoddard Island nuclear debate. But the greatest coup in the effort to personalize the issue for Nova Scotians was the discovery of a uranium claim overlapping the Pockwock Lake watershed, which supplied drinking water for the entire city of Halifax. When the EAC exposed the claim (by the German company Saarberg) two weeks before polling day, and revealed that the provincial Department of Environment was apparently not even aware of Saarberg's activities in the watershed, it threatened to turn the mainly rural issue into a major urban issue as well, and hugely increase its press coverage.[22] Politicians on all sides jumped on the new information. Alexa McDonough accused Premier Buchanan of attempting to "absorb and silence the protest" with "un-enforceable" voluntary guidelines for prospectors and the unproductive Select Committee.[23] The government, having vested control of exploration licences in Cabinet in August in a bid to reassure the public ahead of the election, found itself directly responsible for the Pockwock claim, and had little choice but to respond. Within three days of the EAC's press release, mines minister Ronald Barkhouse announced a freeze on new exploration permits until the Select Committee submitted its report on exploration. Existing permits would not be renewed, and the last active permit would expire in May 1982.[24] Representatives of Saarberg also came forward im-mediately to announce that nothing more than aerial surveys had been done near Pockwock Lake, and no more exploration would be conducted there.[25] After nearly two years of silence and misdirection, draft explora-tion guidelines and second-draft guidelines, never with the force of true regulations – a "talk and dig" policy anticipating British Columbia's infamous "talk and log" – the provincial government had taken its first substantive action on the uranium issue by committing to an investigation that included exploration, just what the activists had aimed at since early in the year. Success might never have come without the support of the NDP during the election, or without the early alliance with established anti-nuclear campaigners, but public pressure is what finally compelled the Buchanan government to act, pressure that could never have been brought to bear without local upstart activists' aggressive publicity.

If Buchanan's government (returned to office after polling day) or Kidd Creek Mines hoped that their desperate concession during the elec-tion would quiet opposition or finally channel activists' energy in a less public direction, their hopes were soon crushed. Few in the anti-uranium camp were prepared to trust the government to produce a report truly addressing their concerns. In the four months following the election, into early 1982, activists redoubled their efforts to reach the public and persuade Nova Scotians of the danger and foolishness of uranium mining. The Annapolis Valley Branch of the Nova Scotia Medical Society resolved in November to join the call for a full moratorium, followed two weeks later by the General Council of the provincial medical society.[26] Agricultural groups continued to lend their names to the effort: the Cream Producers Association, the Kings County Federation of Agriculture, and more.[27] And new local anti-uranium groups sprang up like spring grass. Rather than expand the CAPE group geographically, its members helped local

activists start their own in Kings County (Kings Association to Save the
Environment [KASE]), Vaughan (Residents Enlisted to Save Communities from Uranium Exploration [RESCUE]), New Ross (Communities
Organized to Protect the Environment [COPE]), and Chester (Citizens
Against Uranium Mining [CAUM]). In Cumberland County and in
Colchester County, established anti-nuclear activists launched into anti-
uranium campaigns as well, all of them like the southern groups in borrowing heavily from the EAC's collection of videos and documents on
radiation health risks.[28]

Local groups borrowed more than just books and pamphlets from their
Halifax peers. Elizabeth May became the environmentalist equivalent of
Kidd Creek's Roy John, travelling from one local event to the next, where
she and he would replay some version of their initial meeting.[29] John, who
quite readily admitted having been hired by Aquitaine to combat "the
anti-nuclear activist groups," kept up a constant stream of critiques of
activist statements and aimed always to bring the debate back from the
unscientific realm of nuclear weaponry and technological uncertainties
to the firm ground of fact and comparative risk, a battleground where
he expected to hold the advantage but where May presented a uniquely
capable opponent.[30] While his allies in government employed emotional
language of their own (at times verging on red-baiting, such as the insistence of the Department of Health's radiation expert, Ted Dalgleish, that
activists "are only trying to gain some personal notoriety or wish to expand
upon some personal anti-social dogma"[31]), John insisted on "a rational
judgement based on logic and truth rather than emotion and lack of information."[32] And environmentalists replied in kind, with peace activists
pointing out the contribution of Canadian uranium to the global nuclear
arms race while others, like May, hammered back at John with an equal
command of nuclear jargon, exposing the unspoken assumptions beneath
his statements (for example, that tailings can be contained for millennia
with yet-undiscovered technology, or that radiation exposure can always
be expressed as a whole-body average).[33]

Neither side stopped at the provincial border in recruiting new authorities to join the fight. As would soon happen in the lead-up to the herbicide
trial, Nova Scotia's environmental controversy became the focus of attention from far beyond. The quartet of Jack Garnett (Mines and Energy),
John, Pollock, and Dalgleish (Health) regularly joined forces with men
from Atomic Energy Canada Limited (AECL) and Environment Canada
who often found themselves addressing points put by Gordon Edwards

of the Canadian Coalition for Nuclear Responsibility (CCNR) or Dr. Rosalie Bertell, whose presentations on the "bureaucratic exclusion" of the public from decision making and government's deliberate misrepresentation of health risks at Wolfville and Halifax provoked Dalgleish enough to comment on activists' supposed sinister self-promotion.[34] Dr. Robert Woollard, one of the authors of the British Columbia Medical Association's anti-uranium report, proved a champion of the cause in Nova Scotia as well. Indeed, the battle over uranium mining in Nova Scotia became one of the three great nationally significant challenges to the industry in the years around 1980, alongside Saskatchewan and British Columbia.

The level of cooperation and coordination among anti-uranium groups in 1981 was greater than it had been at any time to that point. By the start of 1982, the new acronyms on the scene – CAPE, KASE, COPE, and so on – could field capable public speakers well versed in the technical jargon of nuclear risk. The EAC and its library had played an important role in education. So did the networks of existing anti-nuclear and social justice groups, drawing on the resources of national and international activist allies.[35] But the vigour in organizing the public into an effective force for political pressure came always from the local level, from residents wanting at first to protect the integrity of their relationship to the natural environment – their farms, gardens, and wells – and discovering by accident that the one issue came hitched to a whole system of political ecology, a system that required them to become true political activists and to fight for the recognition of an ecological perspective and for a forum in which there existed a possibility for meaningful public input into policy decisions, before those decisions were made. Unsurprisingly, there were also differences of opinion among local activists as to how profoundly they should oppose the system; different networks reinforced different views, and acted at times less like neutral repositories of resources and contacts and more like ideological police.

The Cracks Appear

Differences in activists' approach to government surfaced early in the campaign against uranium in Nova Scotia, well before the election campaign produced such encouraging results. As time passed, those differences seemed more strongly linked to the geography of dissent, with rural activists presenting the most consistent political pressure and stridently non-modern arguments against uranium mining as a threat to local communities and economies, and urban activists trying to convince regulators of the factual merits of the anti-uranium position.

When the FACT group joined the Bear River Board of Trade to organize a public information meeting at Bear River, Digby County, in May 1981, Jack Garnett attended to defend his department's handling of mineral exploration and tout the strength of his draft exploration guidelines. The guidelines, he said, the "most stringent in Canada," had been redrafted after "constructive comments from numerous exploration companies and environmental groups."[36] It was a well-practised line. Garnett, at that point the leading pro-uranium figure in the province, offered much the same defence each time his voluntary, accommodating, and still-unfinished (after five years of exploration) guidelines came under attack.[37] In response, Robbie Bays and David Orton, aghast at how debate had been cut off in Bear River without an effective anti-uranium speaker, issued a press release deriding the guidelines and "strongly repudiat[ing] any claims that environmental groups contributed to or approve of these guidelines, which do not protect the health of Nova Scotians."[38] Garnett was not lying, though, even if he did put the most favourable spin on the truth. He had sought input from at least one source within the environmental movement – Susan Holtz at the EAC – and had received it.[39] For her part, Holtz remained entirely opposed to uranium mining and exploration, and she did not believe that offering comment on Garnett's first-draft guidelines compromised her position. Rather, she saw it as a second front, pushing for the best possible rules and a place at the negotiating table if in fact exploration did go ahead. Unfortunately, the mere fact of her commenting did provide political cover for Garnett, and her refusal to admit as much proved to be an ongoing bone of contention between the EAC and environmentalists who, like Bays and Orton, saw little difference between government and corporate actors.

Differences of opinion on strategy or theory brought tension, but internal confusion at the Ecology Action Center as to its own power structure and role in the anti-uranium fight caused the most significant fracture among allies in 1981. Since the winter of 1980, the EAC's Energy Committee had been the nominal gathering place for anti-uranium activists, but for much of the following year the committee did not meet. Instead, uranium was folded into the activities of a person-to-person network of anti-nuclear activists. After the events of April 1981, a uranium subcommittee began to meet, bringing together CAPE and EAC members with a few other peace activists and environmentalists, mainly from

Halifax.[40] From the start, confusion reigned over the question of their autonomy from the EAC's board of directors.[41] By the end of May, a confrontation over the board's power to veto the group's more overtly anti-government statements provoked the resignation of David Orton and the eventual departure of most of the members from rural areas.[42]

David Orton exemplified the growing ideological diversity of the environmental movement in Nova Scotia since the late 1970s. Moving to the east coast from British Columbia in 1979, he had brought with him long experience as an organizer for various leftist groups in Ontario and Quebec, and a familiarity with direct-action protest.[43] The networks of peace activists and scientific conservationists who had so powerfully shaped the province's environmental scene through the Stoddard Island episode and the "budworm battles" were often politically conservative, and their members within the Ecology Action Center and the peace organizations that initially took up the uranium issue were uncomfortable with overtly political critiques of the government/industry relationship. The new network of politically leftist environmentalists in the province, however, shared a structural view of social and economic power in which government was never neutral and could be moved to act against the interests of its corporate partners only if sufficient numbers of citizens demanded it. This was the thinking behind Orton's proposed coalition statement for the EAC subcommittee, which dismissed the government's Select Committee as a political sedative and insisted that "our [i.e., environmentalists'] main task should be one of convincing and mobilizing the public."[44] Despite agreeing with much of his position, other members of the subcommittee dismissed his draft as "seditious," "one-sided," and "too revealing."[45]

The conflict that began at the Bear River meeting with Jack Garnett's "environmentalist-approved" guidelines festered for months, and was not resolved by Orton's departure from the EAC's subcommittee scarcely a month later. Discontent over the EAC's close relationship with government was openly discussed, and finally erupted into public animosity around the issue of the speakers selected for a public lecture series at the Halifax library, for which EAC planners had scheduled one entirely pro-uranium panel.[46] Three critics offered much the same opinion in September and October, ahead of the November 5 event, but only one, Sherri Cline from the north shore group CARE, offered it without appending further and more profound criticism.[47] On behalf of his new Socialist Environmental Protection and Occupational Health Group (SEPOHG), Orton gave a pointed and public reminder in a letter to the *Dalhousie Gazette* of Susan Holtz's inadvertent hand-up to Garnett (one of the speakers lined up for the library), and even quoted her assessment of his guidelines as "a fairly good first draft."[48] It was the third critic, though, who struck closest to the heart of their various objections. A long-time anti-nuclear ally, the South Shore Environmental Protection Association went so far as to issue a press release instead of direct criticism, decrying the slate of speakers on the simple grounds that "claims by government and mining companies are not reality," and taking the analysis of the guidelines incident one step further: "We [SSEPA] neither solicit nor accept money from corporations or the government to fund our organization, [and] although our association is one of the most prominent environmental groups in the province, we were *not asked to comment* on the guidelines for uranium exploration."[49] In the end, the EAC did accept the judgment of its peers, and on November 5 Elizabeth May was on hand at the library seminar to offer a formal rebuttal.[50] By then, however, Susan Holtz had already moved to defend her methods against what she termed "gratuitous attacks," and to vent lingering ill-will for the "spiteful and unscrupulous" David Orton, whom she accused of trying to "take over the [uranium sub]committee as a political vehicle for his Marxist-Leninist philosophy."[51] As for her commentary on Garnett's exploration guidelines, she insisted on the value of "a precedent for consultation" in case the prospectors could not be stopped, and reassured her critics that, after all, "our two major points were not incorporated into the final version," though how she imagined that this would help her case is unclear.[52]

The two months of strained and bitter correspondence that followed, between Holtz and Anne Wickens at SSEPA or Holtz and Sherri Cline at CARE, was about as public as private correspondence can be, and each page laid bare the mistrust many activists felt towards the EAC, especially those at the greatest remove from the city of Halifax. In the sharpest blow, Wickens explained that the SSEPA had decided on a press release in order to achieve "an element of surprise against the pro-nuclear people," something of which the EAC was obviously not considered capable. She repeated the earlier accusation that, due to its reliance on government funding, the EAC could not be expected to be as aggressive against the uranium industry as "we ... who are being poisoned first and worst."[53] On the same theme, Cline asked two pointed questions: "Do you feel it is better to be conciliatory and let the mining companies/government get away with their misleading and/or false statements? If so, is this because EAC would not jeopardize getting the next corporate contribution or government grant?"[54] Holtz's personal criticism of David Orton prompted a similar rebuttal. Orton's SEPOHG had worked effectively with several other anti-uranium groups in the province after his departure from the EAC's subcommittee, and "as for his Marxist-Leninist views," wrote Anne Wickens, "they may well exist ... [but] SSEPA does not, and never has refused membership to, or assistance from, any person or group because of race, colour, or creed."[55] According to the critics, it was much more likely that his politics had proven incompatible with the EAC's "respectable" image.[56]

Demanding as they did proof of direct opposition to government, in the form of public criticism, as evidence of the EAC's environmentalist credentials, the EAC's critics held a very different view than its staff and directors about what it meant to be an environmentalist. Despite the warning from one of their own in 1979, when former board member Linda Christansen-Ruffman described the organization's development through the 1970s as a turn away from the public and towards experts and policy makers (a "professionalism and legitimacy ... which will undermine EAC's long-standing advocacy of public participation"), the "two Susans"–era EAC remained committed to conciliatory methods and believed that no insurmountable differences divided them from less-established groups.[57] As Holtz insisted on the EAC's behalf in January 1981, "I see little evidence that 'professionalism' has weakened grassroots support."[58] Christansen-Ruffman had the better eye, though. As the winter of 1982 wore on, the war of words between the EAC and its critics petered out. The president of the EAC's board of directors took over the correspondence and closed the file with a bland insistence on its independent voice, regardless of funding.[59] No one, though, would call it a resolution; the major collaborative effort of the winter, a six-group mission to lobby Gerald Regan, included none of the EAC's critics.[60] And though it continued to debate the propriety of government and corporate funding internally from time to time, the EAC remained committed to its respectable path: "We have achieved, over these ten years, high credibility across the province and indeed all over Canada, and have no intention of compromising that."[61]

THE ROYAL COMMISSION ON URANIUM MINING

The Buchanan government returned to office in 1981 in a difficult position regarding uranium. Rather than continue attempting to reassure activists with political attention, the government returned to a policy of distancing itself from the issue and channelling activist energies into a less damaging forum. Reaching once again for the quasi-judicial form that granted government so much power to define the terms of debate, on January 22 the

Buchanan government announced a Royal Commission of Inquiry into Uranium Mining, set to officially begin on February 9 under Judge Robert McCleave.

Anti-uranium activists in Saskatchewan and British Columbia had learned to recognize the potential for inquiries to marginalize opposition or compel participation in a specific discourse (usually scientific or legalistic, but not emotional or ethical), and the lesson was not lost on their Nova Scotian peers. If the Buchanan government's intention was cooptation, however, it could not have chosen a less appropriate commissioner. If ever a man could test a dissident's commitment to cooperation with government, it was Robert McCleave, A sixty-year-old judge of the Provincial Court, former Progressive Conservative MP for Halifax, and current chairman of the Nova Scotia Labour Relations Board, in which position he had helped quash the unionization of the Michelin Tire plant at Granton, McCleave was well known but not well liked among labour activists in the province. His intense attachment to judicial propriety extended to his other public roles, where he felt compelled to defend his own authority from any perceived slight. As an unnamed Halifax lawyer put it to a *Toronto Star* reporter in 1983, McCleave's politics and his judicial role couldn't be separated: "He's firm in his conviction he always knows what is right."[62] In short, he was a democratic authoritarian, suited to the courtroom perhaps, but immediately ill at ease in the commissioner's chair.

In keeping with their year-old strategy, environmentalists were initially pleased at McCleave's appointment. The effective use of public inquiry proceedings in British Columbia had enabled activists there to intensify the pressure on politicians rather than be pushed aside. The first step towards repeating the process in Nova Scotia would be to achieve the widest possible terms of reference for the inquiry. The terms set out by the Order in Council establishing the inquiry eschewed "moral" issues such as the connection between uranium mining and nuclear weapons manufacture, but terms of reference are open to interpretation.[63] An appeal to McCleave himself was clearly in order.

The results of a multi-group meeting of activists in Truro on February 14 offered the first major clue that McCleave might not present the picture of reasonable accommodation that normally draws participants to an inquiry. The nine groups meeting in Truro included SEPOHG and CARE. The EAC's Uranium Committee had a representative there as well, though the centre itself later disavowed involvement. Despite their well-established differences, the activists in Truro agreed to act as if they accepted the inquiry as a genuine venue for public participation in policy making, at least until and unless it became clear that McCleave would not allow them to use the proceedings to generate publicity and political pressure.[64] A CARE press release following the meeting expressed support for the inquiry and asked that McCleave (who had not yet set out any rules of procedure) hold preliminary hearings on the conduct of the inquiry, and that the government consider appointing two additional commissioners and establishing more specific and comprehensive terms of reference.[65] McCleave reacted angrily. Already feeling "insulted"[66] and "pressured"[67] by the advice offered by the EAC and extra advertisements for the inquiry published by CAUM, he lashed out in interviews against "some Colchester groups ... anonymously spreading false information" and "making unprincipled attacks on the inquiry," and he threatened to suspend three unnamed people from the inquiry.[68] Nor did it end with CARE. As the judge's plans for the inquiry slowly became clearer, more reactions from environmentalists appeared – more "attacks," in McCleave's eyes – and he moved beyond threats of suspension.[69] Threats of subpoena and of contempt charges followed, and after McCleave took it upon himself to investigate the fairness of some newspaper reporting, prompted by an editorial in one paper that mildly rebuked him for his overreaction, the *Truro Daily News* briefly refused publication of any inquiry-related material for fear of the same threats.[70]

Reactions to McCleave's unusual behaviour and apparent intention to treat a public process as if it were taking place in his courtroom ranged from total non-cooperation to apology and favour seeking. Activists already skeptical that the judge would allow a truly free debate took his intemperate reaction and his interference with the press as a sign that he would work actively against any attempt to use the inquiry as a vehicle for publicity. The logical next step, then, was to turn the inquiry itself into a public issue. Some continued to participate, like Robert Whiting, the veteran pollution fighter from East River, Lunenburg County, who recognized no distinction between government Royal Commissioner, and who informed McCleave of his intention to pursue charges under the Federal Fisheries Act if the Nova Scotian government allowed uranium mining.[71] His strategy was simply to make a publicity-worthy presentation within the inquiry when his chance came. Others mocked McCleave's overdeveloped sense of propriety, like Judy Davis of CARE, another veteran activist who had attended the Truro meeting and wrote to the judge explaining that she saw his job as deciding "questions of how mining will be done," not if it should be done, and accusing him of scaring the public away from his own inquiry.[72] Others needled McCleave, aiming to draw him further into a debate that could only cast doubt on his political neutrality. Winston Settle made a public response to McCleave's public critiques. In a letter copied to multiple politicians and the press, he refuted the judge's accusations against CARE (that they had corresponded with him anonymously) and called his conduct "paternal, if not threatening." The public "consider themselves as respectable," he wrote, "and do not intend to be talked down to as if they were little children. If this is the type of inquiry we are to have, I for one will have no part of it, and I do reserve the right to write and talk to anyone as is the right of a free citizen of this country."[73] Settle's political tactics and those of several groups from the Truro meeting who wrote to the attorney general to demand McCleave's removal were rewarded by the entry into the debate of provincial Liberal leader Sandy Cameron, who asked for McCleave's removal due to his "contempt for free speech."[74] It was not enough to move Buchanan, but pressure from Cameron and NDP leader Alexa McDonough did inspire McCleave to retreat from his legal threats for a while.

Some on the anti-uranium side persisted in trying to guide the province's mercurial uranium commissioner into a more populist/democratic position. One sent McCleave a copy of the proceedings of the 1979 National Workshop on Public Participation in Environmental Decision-Making, perhaps hoping that he might appreciate its warning against an approach that is "highly discretionary, favouring the rich, the well-informed, and those who have access to the corridors of power, [and which] ... has helped to frustrate many groups, and has tended to make them believe that confrontation, rather than cooperation, is the best way to deal with government."[75] McCleave, however, remained adamant that he would offer no funding to presenters and would treat volunteer organizations no differently from the nuclear industry.[76]

Given McCleave's well-known conservatism and his open resistance to any action that might turn his inquiry into "some form of popularity pressure contest," those attempting to nudge him in the opposite direction faced a daunting task.[77] One of the most common tactics during the initial controversy was to put distance between those who had already drawn the judge's ire, whom he called "the lunatic fringe," and the rest of the movement.[78] Here the activists from Halifax and the Annapolis Valley area had an existing hostility upon which to draw, and in David Orton an ideal figure from the political left upon whom to place the blame. CAPE member Ralph Loomer wrote to McCleave in February to express his support for the judge's criticism of CARE, and to explain why the Truro meeting behaved in so "unprincipled" a fashion:

> The valley group with which I am associated did not send a representative to this meeting because we are aware of an attempt by a declared Marxist-Leninist person to dominate groups in the Colchester area. His tactics and attitude are repugnant to those of us who are members of Ecology Action Centre and our valley groups who oppose the idea of uranium mining here. We rejected this person's attempts to compromise us in his pursuit of class struggle. After he declared his politics and was excluded from further discussions of our committee he became involved with the Colchester and Amherst groups.[79]

Apart from the few early boycotters like Winston Settle and David Orton, the vast majority of the anti-uranium movement decided to participate in McCleave's inquiry. Despite the tight deadline imposed by the judge for people to request time to present to the inquiry, letters poured in from activists as well as those who had never before considered themselves activists. Some still hoped to use the proceedings for publicity, counting on attention from news media that never did muster great interest in the minutiae of inquiry hearings. Many truly believed in the inquiry as a vehicle for public input into policy, while others seemed unsure to what extent they ought to attempt to win over McCleave or to keep their attention on building the movement. One thing immediately apparent was the wisdom of the decision to ask for a public inquiry, at least inasmuch as new groups of activists continued to gather across the province, inevitably forming around a small set of local leaders and extending over a single town or set of villages.[80] The official vehicle of an inquiry also attracted vastly more attention to the issue from church groups of every denomination, whose insistence on addressing the moral issues may have convinced McCleave to give up any attempt to rule the nuclear weapons connection out of bounds.[81] Despite these gains, however, active opponents of uranium mining remained a small minority of the overall population, easy enough to ignore if they ceased to accumulate support. As the winter of 1982 melted away and Nova Scotians prepared for the first hearings of the Royal Commission on Uranium Mining, members of the Buchanan government could have been forgiven for thinking they had finally shunted the uranium issue off to a politically safe venue. Whatever new local opposition arose could be directed towards McCleave, away from the daily conduct of politics in Halifax and out of view of the general public.

HOMELAND DEFENCE

The testimony given at Judge McCleave's forty-four hearings represented a true cross-section of Nova Scotian views on uranium mining in 1982, and revealed a movement divided between those who sought expert status – the citizen-scientists – and the disciples of political ecology, who relied upon various non-modern normative arguments to make their case. Among the latter, a small number of activists (like native Haligonian and filmmaker Ian Ball) were still willing to base their presentations on the limits to growth thesis or appropriate technology movement, a larger number were intent on denouncing the environmental injustice of the distribution of risks and benefits between rural and urban areas, and numerous witnesses presented anti-uranium activism as a defence of home place.[82] The most common presentations by far, however, were those assailing the modern politics of expertise.

From the very first hearing, in New Ross, Lunenburg County, where Michael Keddy warned the audience that "it is only after exploration has taken place that the Landowner sees the folly of putting his trust in some-one whose interests lay not in the land but in the provincial deficit,"[83] presenters returned again and again to a claim of authority based on a close relationship with the land. The home place theme was neither paro-chial nor always confined to the countryside (though it did predominate there): the small activist group RESCUE explained the plural "commun-ities" in its name as an acknowledgment of the duty to stand up for others in the same situation, and Dr. C.J. Byrne in Halifax complained about "some bloody economist or systems analyst talking about costs as if he or she were talking about buying jellybeans down at the corner store or Woolies [when] they never talk about the other and more serious cost, the heartache and sorrow brought about because people have to leave an area they have learned to live with and love."[84] By implicit, and occasionally explicit, contrast, a mining company could make all sorts of legal and economic commitments to a community, yet, as Ron Leitold of New Ger-many said, "the one it can't make is a personal commitment – concern, devotion, loyalty, love (call it what you will) for a particular area and its way of life – only the people who live there permanently can."[85] Though it is sometimes common to attempt a distinction between environmental defence of a home place and economic defence of the same, it is clear from the testimony of those who made such claims that the idea of pristine nature and the division between human and environment held little sway over their minds. The most articulate statement of their indivisibility came when Muriel Maybe and the Lunenburg County Women's Group drew upon Aldo Leopold's land ethic to describe how "we are obligated to respect and cooperate with the land if we hope to ensure our continued existence ... we are, in fact, members of a community of interdependent parts. We need the soil, the water, the plants, the animals."[86]

Presenters who made place-defence arguments were aware of their vulnerability to attack, particularly regarding two distinctions that clearly did prey on the minds of many witnesses, between native Nova Scotian and recent arrival from outside the province, and between reason and emotion. Frequent accusations that environmentalists were "foreign troublemakers" were well remembered. In a significant way, the claims of authority based on close relationships with a given place served to circumvent the discount on come-from-away opinion, or even turn it back against the critics. As Erin Gore said at the Chester hearing on April 30, "we are not outside agitators; we have lived here eleven years and are permanent residents. Our would-be corporate neighbours, the mining companies, are only temporary residents; what responsibility are they willing to accept?"[87] More than a few presenters also took time out of their presentations to defend the role of emotion in normal decision-making processes, decrying in some form or other the fallacy of rational choice (the idea that any decision can be made without reference to first principles based on emotion) and reminding the audience of the positive role of emotion in the history of the anti-slavery movement, struggles for economic justice, or democratic political reform.[88]

The more explicitly political presentations to the inquiry frequently included environmental justice arguments. In this, the presenters drew upon a durable tradition in Nova Scotian environmentalism going back to the SSEPA's defence of south shore fishermen's interests against the nuclear industry in 1973, but they also reflected a national trend. In fact, the discontents of metropolitanism formed a shared language of environmental activism across Canada. In British Columbia and especially in Saskatchewan, anti-uranium activists had vigorously challenged the imposition of environmental risks on western Canadian hinterland areas in order to produce benefits that would accrue mainly to urban centres and to the national capital.[89] Much the same arguments also appeared in the chemical forestry controversy, still in full swing in Cape Breton and the northern mainland even as the uranium inquiry progressed. The economic politics of the province since the 1920s have consisted largely of a series of rebellions against an exploit-and-export economy imposed by a Central Canadian–dominated system, and it had not escaped notice that since Aquitaine's withdrawal from Nova Scotia, the Millet Brook project had been pursued by the federal Canada Development Corporation, with the support and encouragement of AECL.[90] "They are here in Nova Scotia," argued CAUM's Brian McVeigh, "because this province acts as a hinterland for exploiting cheap resources to feed the manufacturing mecca of the central region of Canada, where one in three light bulbs are powered by nuclear power."[91] Worse yet for several of the rural presenters was the compounded imperial pressure from the provincial capital; as an angry Robert Finck complained to McCleave in Bridgewater, "it's just another example of second-class citizens getting the dirt while the Halifax gentry get the gravy."[92]

Nearly two hundred witnesses can cover a broad and diverse rhetorical territory. More than even the defence of home places and environmental justice, however, what united the makers of normative arguments at the inquiry was a rejection of the politics of expertise. When McCleave held his first hearing at New Ross on April 2, one of the first complaints was from a sawmiller at the Ross Farm Museum, Kenneth Seaboyer, one of scores of non-expert laymen self-educated in the nuclear industry's track record. "The experts on the safety of uranium seem to me to be experts only when everything functions properly," he said, inaugurating a seven-month-long litany of criticism of the technological optimism – the hubris – of scientists who presumed themselves able to contain mine wastes that would remain a radioactive hazard for half a million years or more.[93] "We must face the simple reality of Murphy's Law," insisted Muriel Maybe shortly after Seaboyer. "What can go wrong, sooner or later will. The Titanic did sink, Three Mile Island did leak, the Ocean Ranger did go down. Uranium tailings cannot be 100 percent contained."[94] With unintentional irony, the Atomic Energy Control Board's Kenneth Bragg appeared at the inquiry in June to claim that "it is reasonable to assume that future generations are going to be at least as smart as we are," and to detail the new methods in state-of-the-art tailings disposal at Key Lake, Saskatchewan, and Quirke Lake, Ontario (really doing himself no favours by describing Quirke Lake's deep-lake disposal scheme as being "completely out of the environment"). He was answered two weeks later by Valerie Wilson of People for Environmental Protection (PEP) in Annapolis Royal, quoting Hannes Alfven: "If a problem is too difficult to solve, one cannot claim that it is solved by pointing out all the efforts made to solve it."[95]

The practice of science, in addition to its capabilities, came in for occasional critique by the most politically savvy activists. FACT's Robert Bays made reference to the "gambling game" of scientifically derived but constantly revised safe exposure standards (once more conveniently supported by a remarkably candid AECB brief describing the "as low as reasonably achievable" (ALARA) principle of occupational radiation exposure as having its basis in "social and economic factors."[96] But Dr. Linda Christansen-Ruffman and Dr. Karen Flikeid for the Nova Scotian branch of the Canadian Research Institute for the Advancement of Women offered the most comprehensive deconstruction of the sociology of science: the unequal distribution of resources, the assumption of safety until proven otherwise, and the use of politically convenient assumptions in the design of studies.[97] Science and politics could scarcely be distinguished in Nova Scotia's uranium debate, the commissioner heard, when the Department of Health dispatched its Radiological Health Officer to discredit Dr. Rosalie Bertell in the press.[98]

Unusual as it may seem for environmentalists with a non-modern perspective to have come in such numbers to present their views to Judge McCleave, who had in one of his rare clear statements of intention promised to base his report on scientific fact and consult heavily with experts of many sorts during the second phase of his inquiry, those were the presenters with strategic considerations foremost in mind, less intent on convincing the judge and more on reaching and politicizing other Nova Scotians. Judy Davis expressed the attitude in *Rural Delivery* during the early days of the inquiry: "CARE does question whether or not our group – or any other environmental group – can receive a fair hearing from the Inquiry," but it would participate nonetheless.[99] A veteran of the Anil Hardboard campaign (see Chapter 1), Robert Whiting, demonstrated much the same sentiment at the inquiry, virtually ignoring McCleave to lecture the audience on industrial pollution as "political murder" and warn, "don't trust the government!"[100] Similarly skeptical presenters took the opportunity presented by McCleave's invitation to "be creative" and performed music impugning the honesty of supposedly neutral leaders in Halifax and Ottawa,[101] and Susan Hower took the creative pursuit of publicity several steps further than anyone else, at the Liverpool hearing on April 27, when she delivered a short speech on the need for a "responsible, informed electorate" who would care enough to notice events like McCleave's inquiry, then pulled a black hood over her head and performed a mock suicide with a loaded starter's pistol.[102]

Hower's shocking performance was only the most spectacular of many attempts to make people take note of what was going on at the inquiry hearings. As most activists were painfully aware, apart from Donna Smyth's regular reports in *Rural Delivery,* there was precious little press coverage of the inquiry's progress in the press or on the air. It was rare that a reporter would even show up to witness a hearing. Partly this was because Royal Commissions are known for their dry and technical hearings; partly it was due to the press's conditioning to view them as fact-finding exercises, newsworthy only when making their final recommendations to government; but it was also a failure on the part of environmentalists to make full use of their allies in the press. In Nova Scotia, the major news media are concentrated in the city of Halifax and emerge only reluctantly to cover events in the rest of the province when those appear most newsworthy. Few of McCleave's hearings were held in the city, and the environmental groups based there, with the best contacts in the press, sought the legitimacy of expertise and dedicated themselves more to influencing the commissioner than the public, failing to create the kind of spectacle that might have drawn greater attention.

The command of nuclear and geological science brought to bear on the McCleave Inquiry by Nova Scotian environmentalists was impressive. Following the lead of activists in British Columbia during the Bates Inquiry (Royal Commission of Inquiry, Health and Environmental Protection, Uranium Mining), they recruited from the medical field as much as possible,[103] and a battery of professional and citizen-scientists from the EAC, CAPE, KASE, and CAUM seldom let up on their barrage of facts related to the failures of tailings management and the viability of alternative energy systems. Ralph Torrie, Friends of the Earth Canada's expert on uranium, travelled from Ottawa to present for CAUM in Chester and gave an impeccably thorough description of all the many failures of the industry-standard "modified dumping" process. (He refused to use the terms "management" or "disposal" because, he said, "they aren't.") Again, the influence of a continent-wide anti-uranium movement came to the fore, as Torrie described the enormity of the Church Rock tailings spill in the United States, which only three years earlier had spread thousands of tons and tens of millions of gallons of radioactive mine waste across parts of New Mexico and Arizona. He drew special attention to acid leaching at tailings dams in Ontario. His presentation concluded with a list of potential avenues of technical development, including vitrification and the removal of radium and thorium from tailings – none of which were being pursued by the mining industry, nor were likely to be as long as the industry was permitted to dump radioactive elements in tailings heaps.[104] The EAC's own presentation included a similarly technical dissertation on the soft energy path, the failure of tailings containment, and the dangers of exposure to low-level radiation. The EAC also detailed an acceptable regulatory regime, in case the province decided to ignore the rest of its advice.

The presentations of the EAC, CAUM, KASE, and, to some extent, CAPE suggested nothing so much as a spirit of technological optimism equal to the best the AECB could offer. For them, it seemed as though there was nothing mankind could not do, only that which for reasons of ignorance and greed it chose not to do; and the remedy, far from being a renewed commitment to the local place or a re-evaluation of economic or ecological justice, was the recognition of scientific truth. Their moral arguments – for they were far from amoral technologists – revolved around the contribution of uranium to the nuclear arms race and carefully skirted the political ethics of dissent and public participation that so enraged McCleave. As for publicity, they seemed not to connect the inquiry hearings with the wider campaign for political pressure.[105] While the technically inclined presenters prided themselves on their ability to "make the uranium companies squirm," in Donna Smyth's words, their willingness to burnish the legitimacy of McCleave and his inquiry caused at least as much discomfort among the province's environmentalists, many of whom saw uranium companies as nearly irrelevant distractions from the real work of making government squirm.[106]

A Parting of the Ways

Their attitudes towards McCleave and his inquiry remained the single most salient dividing line among anti-uranium activists in Nova Scotia, reflecting all of the unresolved tensions from the previous two years about the politicization of environmental issues, the propriety of government funding, and the participation of environmental groups in non-public processes of consultation like the one concerning Jack Garnett's exploration guidelines. Unlike the courtroom setting of the herbicide trial, McCleave's inquiry presented no barriers to alternative modes of argument, and despite his continued and ever more desperate attempts to impose courtroom conventions on the inquiry and discourage debate in the press, McCleave could do nothing to prevent activists from using the question of the inquiry's legitimacy as a political weapon, as Paula Scott in Chester did in a letter to mines and energy minister Ron Barkhouse. Barkhouse had inaugurated a trend among MLAs by refusing to attend the initial hearing in New Ross, his own hometown and constituency, and Scott chided him for his absence:

I'd like to believe that we – the people – have the last word, but our cynicism tells us that you – the government – have already made up your collective mind under pressure from the mining industry and that the inquiry is merely a formality undertaken to quiet public opinion by going through the motions of asking our opinion. We've been disappointed too often to believe you easily.[107]

Her letter was copied to the three political party leaders, seven newspapers, and Judge McCleave.

Few if any environmentalists were willing to suspend their anti-uranium activities while McCleave made his wandering way around the province. Lectures continued, as did letters to politicians, the collection of petitions, and attempts to win the support of municipal councils.[108] But even among those who did not openly challenge the inquiry's legitimacy there was suspicion that the mining industry hoped to "wear out the energies of the industry's opponents" in the forum of a public inquiry.[109] McCleave's declared intention to have three phases of increasing scientific and legalistic complexity exacerbated such fears, though some persisted in distinguishing between the judge's intentions and those of the industry. For those who did not, the obvious solution was not only to use the inquiry to generate publicity but also to publicize the very fact that the inquiry served to stifle meaningful dissent. Those already on the fringes of political life had no great difficulty challenging McCleave. Sitting in front of the judge in Chester, Robert Whiting barked, "If I sound like a radical, then I damn well am!"[110] But it was the self-identifying leftists who were most successful in irritating him, correctly judging that "every time McCleave opens his mouth, more people are mobilized against him,"[111] and gambling that a collapse of the inquiry, or at least its transformation from easily ignored sideshow to source of political embarrassment, would be of greater benefit to the anti-uranium effort than seeing it through.

Conveniently, McCleave's conservative political history and his continued position as head of the Labour Relations Board gave him a strong contempt for persons of the left, who made excellent use of his prejudice. After a presentation in Amherst by Don Rushton of Concerned Citizens of Cumberland County (CCCC), on government collusion with corporate capitalism, a presentation that included material critical of the judge's conduct during the inquiry, McCleave traced the ownership of a slideshow used there back to another group in Halifax (specifically to Charles Lapp), noting in his records that "the groups did not seem to be related except in political philosophy, which was violently opposed to the Commissioner and the Inquiry, and the beliefs of more than 99% of the people living in Nova Scotia."[112] The Nova Scotia Federation of Labour took subtle aim at McCleave's labour board, and obliquely at his inquiry, when it insisted that government alone could not be trusted to keep uranium miners safe; "over the years any progress that has been made has been more as a result of confrontation than by any rational process of scientific enlightenment."[113] And Tony Seed, freelance journalist and candidate of the Marxist-Leninist Party, who had twice run against Robert Stanfield in Halifax when McCleave stood down for him, managed to get under the skin of both the commissioner and his supporters at the EAC by speaking well over his allotted time at a Halifax hearing in September, forcing the EAC presenters to reschedule for another day.[114] The irritants accumulated, and McCleave wrote to a friend that he felt under attack by "an unholy crowd of Marxist-Leninists, some fellow travellers in the Legislature [the NDP], some pretty irresponsible journalists ... and a few paranoid parties."[115]

If the voices from the left saw reason to question groups that refused to take issue with McCleave's behaviour or with his inquiry's legitimacy – if they wondered, with David Orton, "what kind of openness is it when the inquiry process is seen as one of educating Judge McCleave and not the public"[116] – their frustration was matched on the other side by those who questioned why anyone would hand more ammunition to a pro-uranium effort that habitually painted all environmentalists with the same red brush. What began early in 1982 with the Department of Health's Ted Dalgleish telling a *Digby Mirror* reporter how, in his view, environmental activism led to "mob violence," grew in intensity and frequency later in the year, after the overwhelmingly negative response to uranium mining at the inquiry became clear.[117] Kidd Creek's Roy John tried to be subtle at an Air Pollution Control Association meeting in Saint John, New Brunswick, in September, referring to "a segment of the population who have different social and political aspirations," but he was able to rely on his ally Greg Isenor, president of the Chamber of Mineral Resources, to offer more explicit context by borrowing lands and forests minister George Henley's term "subversive" to describe an "anti-development lobby" opposing uranium mining.[118] Instead of allying with environmentalists, the deputy minister of environment joined their critics early in 1983 with the most elegant innuendo yet against protesters of "particular political persuasions" and their association with "violence and civil disobedience."[119] None of this was unique to Nova Scotia; similarly targeted activists in the United States eventually named the anti-environmentalist campaign of the 1980s a "green scare," referencing the "red scare" persecution of anyone with left-leaning politics.[120] For environmentalists hoping to gain a place at the regulatory table, any taint of "subversion" could only be seen as counterproductive.

The easiest way to counter the charge of disreputable political leanings (aside from directly, as was often done[121]) was to redouble one's visible support for the legitimate consultative process, that is, for McCleave. Statements of support during the hearings were usually sent to McCleave himself. A good example is Ginny Point (formerly of the EAC) and her expression of gratitude for the inquiry's "enabling [of] people to publicly voice their thoughts through a legitimate process."[122] After the first stage came to a close and Kidd Creek Mines announced its withdrawal from the process in November, however (to be replaced at the head of the pro-uranium side by the Chamber of Mineral Resources, and soon by the chamber's new president, Don Pollock), the EAC had to resort to a press release in order to be seen to "reaffirm its commitment" to the process.[123]

Unfortunately for those seeking a reputable route to influence, Judge McCleave was not one to forget his enemies. Despite having been requested to make time for the north shore CARE group to speak about inquiry procedure and organization at the Pictou hearing on June 15, McCleave reacted with hostility to the brief read by CARE's Dean Whalen. Among other critiques, Whalen objected to the fact that inquiry transcripts were available only in Halifax and could be obtained only by being photocopied in the presence of either McCleave or the inquiry coordinator, Stanley Forgeron, or by being borrowed to be copied elsewhere.[124] He also asked McCleave to explain, at last, just what he had found "false, misleading, or unprincipled" about CARE's February press release.[125] Claiming to have been blindsided by this "attack on the inquiry," the judge wrote a letter the following day barring Whalen from any further role in the hearings until he apologized for the "slur" of implying that McCleave and Forgeron had been absent from the office without reason during Whalen's visit.[126]

The personal animosity between CARE and Judge McCleave coloured the remainder of the inquiry. Despite confusion on the part of the public as to how Whalen's story could be construed a slur, or why McCleave refused to consider his request to place hearing transcripts in regional libraries outside of Halifax (leaving, as one writer pointed out, the supposedly villainous CARE as the only ready source of information on the north shore[127]), the judge refused to back down or explain himself. He even went so far as to suppress the CARE brief when he finally relented and sent copies to the libraries.[128] The facilities for photocopying also became more accessible after the Pictou episode, yet CARE members received no credit for inspiring the reforms. Instead they remained personae non gratae at the inquiry (officially, only Whalen, "for his deceit," and Sherri Cline, "for her insolence" during the Pictou hearing, remained barred from participation[129]), and enjoyed scant support from their peers in the more southerly groups. Donna Smyth largely avoided publicizing the drama in *Rural Delivery*, which, publicity being the whole point of challenging the judge, prompted an angry Don Rushton to ask why she would "rather identify herself with McCleave."[130] In addition, the EAC's board of directors voted not to "publicly affiliate itself with the positions of other groups addressing the inquiry," when asked by CARE to speak out.[131]

Rather than attempt to repair the gulf between McCleave and CARE, or join the latter in further foredoomed criticism of the former's conduct, anti-uranium groups in the city and in the nearby mainland instead moved to formalize their own coalition ("publicly affiliate," one might say) ahead of stage two, isolating the north shore groups and the leftists. As the first stage of the inquiry closed, a committee of four activists from the central mainland area circulated (in their areas only) a proposal for the second stage, primarily requesting funding for their own expert witnesses, and suggesting that McCleave take over all questioning of witnesses himself.[132] Reaction from the north was predictably negative. Sherri Cline (CARE), Gail Fresia and Don Rushton (CCCC), and David Orton (SEPOHG) (who was on the verge of moving from Halifax to the North Shore with his family) wrote together to *Rural Delivery* to decry "a group putting itself forward as *the* representatives of the environmental movement – even though there was no open invitation to all interested parties," and a proposal that "reeks of faith in the system and authority."[133] The coalition's reply, that the northerners ought to make their own proposals and "embrace a range of divergent attitudes," left the distinct impression that the move to unify attitudes in and around the city had little to do with diversity and much to do with delegitimizing those who would not accept the premises of the supposedly impartially scientific second stage.[134]

IMPLOSION

Events do sometimes overtake expectations, and though no small number of activists in the province clearly expected a long and bitterly controversial second stage of Nova Scotia's uranium inquiry in 1983, in the end the battle was decided inside a single Halifax courtroom – perhaps even inside one man's mind – over the course of two angry days in March, a catharsis that forced both sides of the environmentalist conflict to finally acknowledge the deep roots of their differences. The departure from the script began with a letter sent by McCleave in February to the participants in the first stage of the inquiry. Apparently feeling pressured by activists eager for word on the planning of the second stage (much as he had felt ahead of the first), the judge asked everyone to "please hold your fire," and enjoined all parties to avoid "speculation" on the inquiry's future.[135] No one really did. Faced with a bitter exchange in the press between deputy environment minister E.L.L. Rowe and Elizabeth May, and wishing to pass judgment on some of the presenters whose "perverse ideology" had so bothered him in recent months,[136] McCleave convened a "special session" of the inquiry at the Halifax Law Courts on March 4, and requested the presence there of May, Rowe, Dean Whalen, Sherri Cline, Don Rushton, and a *Toronto Star* reporter (and yet another former Marxist-Leninist Party member) named Alan Story. Charles Lapp, creator of the slide/tape show presented by Rushton in Amherst, titled *Uranium: The Nova Scotia Experience,* was subpoenaed and arrived with a lawyer.[137] Story was there because he had interviewed McCleave by telephone the day before, acting on a tip from Lapp, and McCleave felt it "most improper that a witness should be talking to the press."[138] That the member of the press in question was a man who had only recently embarrassed the entire Nova Scotian judicial system by exposing the now-infamous wrongful conviction of Donald Marshall Jr. surely added to the impropriety. Over the course of the afternoon, McCleave made a remarkable series of rulings: that Lapp should return to court in two weeks to show and be judged for his slide/tape show (for reasons the judge refused to specify); that Story was forbidden to use two words from his interview with McCleave, "censorship" and "kangaroo," on pain of a contempt charge; that Rushton apologize to the inquiry for alleging slander by McCleave; and that Alan Ruffman, Howard Epstein, Tony Seed, and Gail Fresia were in "default of the inquiry" for not having produced written copies of presentations, and also had two weeks to comply or face the unspecified consequences of an unheard-of ruling.[139] It was by even the most generous assessment a bizarre performance, made only more so when McCleave addressed the Rowe/May controversy by asking the assembled audience to deliberate on "free speech [and] ... the limits that should be made on anything that is being said" in or out of the inquiry, presumably without using the word "censorship."[140]

Reactions to McCleave's extraordinary performance certainly exceeded any environmentalist's grandest hopes for publicity from the inquiry. His treatment of Alan Story in particular inflamed other members of the press, who repeated and reprinted the story of an "arrogant" and "paternalistic" judge making a reporter sit on the prisoner's bench and refusing him access to a lawyer when requested.[141] Inside the Legislature, McCleave came under repeated attack, and both the Liberal and NDP leaders requested his removal from the inquiry.[142] Perhaps worst of all for McCleave's immutable sense of the respect due his position was the ridicule; posters soon appeared around Halifax advertising a public screening of Charles Lapp's slide/tape show, and they were decorated with a picture of a kangaroo.[143] By the time of his second "special session," McCleave had clearly reached the end of his ability to handle the pressure.[144] "Beset by a radical group and beset by certain members of the press," the judge treated the assembly on March 18 to a long diatribe on the responsibilities of the press, while a crowd of protesters from CARE, CCCC, SEPOHG, and some Haligonian allies milled about the entrance to the Law Courts, holding signs reading "BOYCOTT THE INQUIRY" and "STOP ATTACKS ON ENVIRON-MENTALISTS."[145] Those inside had been made to pass through a metal detector and a line of police to reach the courtroom. After Lapp's slide/tape show was played to loud applause, McCleave simply ended the session. "We leave the courtroom wondering what has happened," Donna Smyth wrote. "Nobody has been charged with anything."[146]

No one was ever charged with anything, nor could they have been. Although the attorney general's examination (pointedly not an "investigation") of the situation ended publicly with a reaffirmation of McCleave's power to conduct the inquiry as he wished, privately the deputy attorney general informed the judge that his powers as a commissioner allowed him to compel only testimony and evidence under threat of contempt, and not to dictate anyone's speech or conduct inside or outside of the inquiry. In other words, while acting as a commissioner, he had not the powers of a judge.[147] McCleave, disappointed with "so little protection" offered him, retreated from public view, leaving environmentalists to debate the future of the inquiry among themselves without any hint of whether or when stage two would begin, or who might be called to account in court before then.[148]

Debate they did. Rather than unite against a commissioner whose own suspect political neutrality offered a clear chance to avoid the objectively scientific phase of the inquiry and return the debate fully to the political realm, the anti-uranium forces' internal divisions only deepened in response to McCleave's apparent breakdown. Susan Holtz did write to the attorney general on behalf of the EAC to lodge a formal complaint over the "curtailment of freedom of expression," but refused to join the chorus of calls for McCleave's ouster and replacement, advising instead a six-month recess.[149] Beyond the single complaint, in fact, those who had previously supported McCleave continued to do so. CAPE's Ralph Loomer even wrote again to the judge to "share [his] repugnance and distaste for the sleazy fanatics who would replace the institutions of democracy and jurisprudence of British tradition with a one-party dictatorship. Their strategy is intentionally disruptive and destructive of any worthy cause in which they participate."[150] Only slightly less divisive, but much more public, the EAC's Uranium Committee wrote in an open letter to the premier that "the recent series of criticisms and allegations in the House, the Courtroom, the media, and on the streets would seem to place the future of the Uranium Inquiry in jeopardy. Ecology Action Centre has not participated in these activities, nor does it intend to, because they are damaging to the process."[151] As their choice of language suggests, being seen to support the process meant more to the EAC than merely availing of another chance to reiterate its position on the science of radiation exposure. Its board of directors made it clear that the "Centre has been careful not to be entangled in any of the 'side shows' around the Inquiry and hopes to maintain its image as a responsible, credible organization whose attention remains focussed on the issues which generated the Inquiry."[152]

Those whose participation in any future inquiry stages was dubious at best maintained that a process without potential for organizing the public into a political pressure group could be no more than an "expensive pressure valve for public opinion" and a force for delegitimization of non-scientific positions.[153] They objected to any support given McCleave as a distortion of the truth – that he had attempted for a full year to stifle any dissent against his right to make the final decision – and they resented the refusal of CAPE and the EAC, as the best-known groups in the fight, to speak out against McCleave's attacks on leftist environmentalists. Only a little more than a year earlier, Susan Holtz had been bitterly upset at Sherri Cline and Hattie Perry for promoting "disunity" within the movement, and protested her toleration of political philosophies other than her own. Yet after McCleave's letter and his first special session made it clear to all that his anger was directed at "perverse" leftists, her concern was to protect the inquiry and the judge from criticism. A CAPE spokesperson explained to a *Mail-Star* reporter at the time that McCleave was upset at

FIGURE 5   A drawing of Judge McCleave and the EAC.
Source: Dawna Gallagher, in Don Rushton, "So Long, Stage II:
McCleave Gets Set to Ride Off into the Sunset," *New
Maritimes* 2, no. 6 (March 1984): 11.

"a few people isolated from the environmental movement [who] had it
out for him" from the beginning.[154] The northern groups, for their part,
renewed their criticisms of the EAC as "establishment bound," dependent
on government and corporate funding, and (along with CAPE) simply
politically naive.[155] (See Figure 5.)

Rather than the strength in diversity that some optimists had hoped
for, the stalemate between participants and non-participants in the inquiry
reflected the most basic differences in political assumptions. While Donna
Smyth lamented that personalizing the conflict with McCleave meant that
the "moderate, reasonable people who put such a lot of hard work into
Stage I are being ignored and forgotten,"[156] Don Rushton insisted that "the
discussion can never be completely separated from the forum in which it
takes place." And if the two camps willingly debated in the press, they

could not manage to discuss strategy in person. Rushton's attempt on behalf of the CCCC to convene a provincial meeting to discuss whether or not to pursue a boycott of the inquiry by all groups was not so much rebuffed as ignored by all of the leading groups other than SEPOHG, CARE (whose boycott could just as well be called a ban), and SSEPA.[157] Both sides had come to recognize that their positions were not only incompatible but at cross-purposes. One held that participation in and endorsement of the official system of decision making was the only effective way to convince political and industrial leaders of the truth of environmentalists' claims, the other that only political pressure from large numbers of citizens could overcome the established unity of political and industrial interests that the official system was designed to uphold, and that "playing the game" made it look like the problems were well in hand and therefore hindered the growth of political consciousness. Each side attacked the legitimacy of the other.

CONCLUSION

Nova Scotia's anti-uranium campaign was brief but spectacular, and was crucially significant to the formation of the provincial environmental movement. While it confirmed the lasting trends – the power of political pressure, the influence of global environmentalism on the provincial movement, the defence of home places as a motive, and the relevance of the modern/non-modern distinction in environmental arguments – it also impelled the makers of modernist arguments into closer cooperation with government and industry, and their non-modernist peers into their firmest yet rejection of the state's power to set the parameters of acceptable discussion.

The Royal Commission on Uranium Mining ended not with a bang or even a whimper but with a long shrug of confusion. Judge McCleave's disappearance from the public eye as an inquiry commissioner lasted a full year, and his reappearance in the winter of 1984 consisted of nothing more than the announcement of the premature end of the inquiry. The final report of the McCleave Inquiry was submitted to the Lieutenant Governor on January 30, 1985, nearly three years after it began (and about three and a half years after the moratorium began).[158] It was released to the public on March 19, and the reception among environmentalists revealed just how little had changed since March 1983. Despite McCleave's complete repudiation of most environmentalist claims about the dangers of radiation exposure, the impossibility of safe tailings disposal, and the inseparability of nuclear energy and nuclear weapons, the response was remarkably positive in Halifax and in Hants County.[159] The Buchanan government had accepted McCleave's recommendations to extend the moratorium until 1990 (on uranium only, releasing prospectors from the legal bind that prevented them from seeking other minerals in uranium claims) and erect a regulatory system based on "scientific assessment of risk and level of risk considered acceptable."[160] McCleave had also expressed a "personal preference" that any uranium mined in Nova Scotia be used in the province for electricity generation only, at least unless the tailings disposal could be proven safe, in which case export might be acceptable. Elizabeth May, Susan Holtz, and Donna Smyth insisted that the recommendations meant that uranium mining would never take place in Nova Scotia, despite warnings from others that the report could as easily be interpreted as an instruction to wait five years before declaring the tailings "safe" and carrying on with mining.[161] A regulatory system that made an honest assessment of the science, they believed, would find a safe nuclear energy system "of course impossible."[162]

Optimism aside, the close relationship between politics, the law, and the nuclear industry in Canada had certainly not changed during McCleave's absence from the scene. Even some of the faces remained the same. After a disastrous spill of radioactive water from a tailings pond at Key Lake, Saskatchewan, in the winter of 1984 – the same tailings system presented to McCleave as state-of-the-art – there was considerable work to be done to rehabilitate the image of uranium mining in Canada, work contributed to by the federal government's National Uranium Tailings Program and its newest recruit, Roy John.[163] And Kidd Creek's Nova Scotian lawyer, Ronald Pugsley, had filled his time since the hearings representing Dr. Leo Yaffe in the latter's libel suit against Donna Smyth. Smyth's trial was a nationally infamous bit of litigation in which only the author of the supposedly libellous text faced trial. The fact that the publisher was left out of the suit convinced activists that the accusation was meant only to silence and punish a particularly outspoken anti-uranium leader. Having waited two years for a trial (the same two years spent waiting on Judge McCleave), Dr. Smyth took two days to convince a jury that there was no risk to Dr. Yaffe's reputation in being described as "one of many 'experts' that the nuclear industry will parade in front of us."[164] A good deal of her success can be attributed to her own foresight in electing a jury trial, apparently having decided that, in her own case, faith in a judge's impartiality was probably not the wisest course. Indeed, the presiding judge seemed inclined to convict.[165] In any event, during the two years of waiting, Smyth was partially handicapped as a campaigner, unable to comment publicly on the case.

From the earliest days of the struggle in 1979 and 1980, Nova Scotian environmentalists had been fighting against not only (not even mainly) the mining industry but also the provincial and federal governments and their commitment to nuclear technology. They had been fighting, without always recognizing it, against a modern conception of economic development and risk assessment that devalued the personal experience of place and of home, discounted the inequity of metropolitanism, and preserved the privilege of expertise. In this, Nova Scotia serves as a lens through which to view the trends in Canadian (and worldwide) environmentalism. The Royal Commission on Uranium Mining, like the herbicide trial and the Royal Commission on Forestry, exemplified the use of judicial or quasi-judicial forums to dissipate activist energy and to enforce that same modernist discourse. McCleave may have been an unusually enthusiastic guardian of the traditional prerogatives of experts and duly constituted authority, adding to the value of the provincial story as an exemplar of environmentalist history, but it was not an accident of personality (his, or Orton's, or Holtz's) that the process of the inquiry completed the schism of the environmental movement in the province. None of them (not even McCleave) was a singular force of nature; they represented groups of like-minded activists or officials, who represent in turn the strands of environmental thought common throughout the international movement.

That the McCleave Inquiry ended when and how it did was almost entirely the work of the "radical" environmentalists he so despised, and given McCleave's repudiation of most of the arguments put to him by environmentalists, it would have been reasonable, in 1985 as it is now, to conclude that they were responsible for the moratorium that prevented uranium mining in Nova Scotia for years thereafter. They were responsible for turning the inquiry into a source of political pressure rather than a brake on it. But the mainstream groups in the province did not say so in 1985, because they could not accept the idea that conciliatory environmentalism had failed to do what it promised – namely, to gain a seat at the regulatory table. (So complete was his disdain for the activists' position that the government committee McCleave recommended be created to dictate safe standards had no room for even token public representation.[166]) The cost of victory against the uranium industry was an admission that such differences could no longer be bridged by blithe assurances of unity in the movement. Given the opportunity that McCleave provided, Nova

Scotian environmentalists first drifted then raced in opposite directions entirely under their own power, to the point that formal coalition was no longer possible. There was no longer an environmental movement in Nova Scotia; there were two. The rupture had been exhausting and embittering, and for most of the anti-uranium activists, McCleave's moratorium was victory enough.

5

Watermelons and Market Greens
Legacies of Early Activism

THE NUCLEAR ENERGY AND uranium mining industries profoundly disappointed the hopes of development promoters in the 1980s, as cost overruns and soft international markets achieved what environmental activists alone could not. Industrial development in general did not slow appreciably, however, and Nova Scotia remained an exemplar of the activist trend, with new independent small groups springing up wherever great enough numbers felt sufficiently threatened by new development, and with small rural groups ready to offer more radical solutions to the downsides of modernity.[1] By the middle of the 1980s, the division of Nova Scotian environmentalism into mainstream and fringe was complete, but the two streams were in frequent contact with each other. In Cumberland County in 1981, for example, residents opposed to construction of a central Maritime hazardous waste dump sought aid from the Ecology Action Centre (EAC), but staked out their own, more radical position: if the experts could not be trusted, they said, the only morally consistent response was to "learn to live without the products these companies manufacture."[2] Nearly a decade later, Cape Bretoners belonging to the Save Boulanderie Island Society attempted a court challenge with EAC support, after the federal government cancelled an environmental assessment process for the new Point Aconi coal-fired power station, but they were just as prepared with threats and civil disobedience when the court ruled against them.[3]

Activist cooperation did not exist in a political vacuum or rely solely on the capacity of mainstream and fringe to abide each other. The state also maintained a role in their relationship, for better and for worse. Official processes were often fruitless and divisive avenues of dissent, as those activists learned who tried to force the federal and provincial governments to clean up the residue of Sydney's steel industry, in Sydney Harbour and the tar ponds site. Despite air pollution up to 6,000 percent higher than the national standard, pollution in industrial Cape Breton had attracted little attention in the 1970s. As one resident recalled, "we just didn't want to hear, 'cause we wanted those damn jobs so bad."[4] It was, oddly, the Department of Fisheries that spurred the first major organized activist effort in 1982 when it closed the lobster fishery on the south side of the harbour, citing as justification the 735 pounds of phenol, 10,447 pounds of ammonium, 919 pounds of cyanide, and 2,058 pounds of thiocyanate dumped there every day by the Sydney Steel Corporation.[5] Once initiated, however, public activism accelerated rapidly. Faced with contamination of such magnitude – approximately 250 acres of tar ponds and former coke ovens sites, to a depth of 24 metres, arguably the largest concentration of toxic chemicals on the continent – there was no question that activists would target government directly, and groups of every sort contributed. Even the most determined opponent of government consultation could support direct lobbying for the relocation of residents away from the edges of the site (combined with a public pressure campaign, of course). The lessons of the 1970s were not lost on the environmental agencies of Ottawa and Halifax, however, and in order to contain the threat of radical/ mainstream cooperation, the federal, provincial, and municipal governments created a Joint Action Group (JAG) to decide on clean-up methods. Ostensibly meant to include members of the public in the decision-making process, the JAG served equally well to focus discussion on the very questions – scientific versus experiential knowledge and the legitimacy of political positions – that put environmentalist participants at odds with each other. In the long run, the JAG proved little more than a tool to leach activist strength and a cover behind which politicians might hide.[6]

The tar ponds were the best known of the decade's controversies, but possibly the best illustration of the capacity for collaboration among environmental activists was the fight to prevent the demolition of Kelly's Mountain in Victoria County at the very end of the 1980s. In 1989, site preparation began for a "mega quarry" on the edge of St. Anne's Bay, a project that would have blasted out and crushed six million tons of granite annually to make gravel for sale to the United States. Local reaction was swift and typical: the Save Kelly's Mountain Society (SKMS) immediately began a campaign to have environmental assessment hearings, and sought help from the EAC resource centre.[7] It also reached out to allies among

Mi'kmaq traditionalists on Cape Breton Island, who objected to the presence of a quarry next to a sacred site at Gluscap's Cave. In the fight for Kelly's Mountain, Mi'kmaq activists made use of racial rhetoric in a way that Chief Ryan Googoo and the other Native participants in the herbicide trial had only begun to explore in the early 1980s. Traditionalists stood to gain both in their own communities and in the wider Canadian culture by promoting the image of an "Ecological Indian," whose unique cultural traditions gave him or her a privileged relationship with the natural world.[8] The SKMS, meanwhile, recognized the political power of the Native leaders' argument and did all they could to support it. Differences among environmentalists certainly did not disappear during the controversy, but they were contained by an agreement on rhetorical tactics and a refusal by all parties to be drawn into discussion of amelioration or remediation of environmental damage. As so often before, the provincial government was not very interested in permitting any obstruction to industrial development, but it was very difficult to ignore the combination of scientific arguments about noise, dust, toxicity, and fisheries from the SKMS, vandalism along the road to the quarry site by unknown agents, and promises by the Mi'kmaq Warrior Society to "wage war" in defence of the mountain. Though the "Battle of Kelly's Mountain" nearly became a genuine battle in the process, the activists got their hearings, preserved their common front, and, unlike the tar ponds clean-up advocates or the Point Aconi power plant opponents, emerged victorious.[9]

Successful collaboration on new issues was dependent on the ability of mainstream activists to refrain from attacking their allies in order to buttress their own legitimacy. That in turn relied on a measure of goodwill and a perception of common goals between the two groups. Stopping a certain project, be it power plant or quarry, was an appropriate common goal. Changing a broad policy was not. Activists concerned with industrial forestry in the 1980s had great difficulty agreeing on which policy to endorse and how to go about achieving it in the aftermath of their great failure at the herbicide trial.

While undeniably discouraged by the ignominious denouement of the trial settlement process in 1983, those activists who had led the legal effort remained determined to fight the use of herbicides in forestry (as well as the resurgent use of insecticides) by direct appeal and through the courts. In 1984, the EAC proposed a mandamus lawsuit against the provincial government, essentially an attempt to convince the Supreme Court of Nova Scotia that the Buchanan government, by refusing public hearings, had been negligent in its duty as a regulator. This "plan B," as it was called, carried less personal risk than a nuisance suit against the pulp companies, though everyone admitted that it might at best be considered a "stalling tactic."[10] Meanwhile, the EAC pursued a more cooperative relationship with the federal bureaucracy, applying for funding to produce reports on the risks of various pesticides or run conferences on "the ethical dimensions of risk."[11] Not surprisingly, Ottawa was reluctant to underwrite anything so public, but it was happy to offer support for the Atlantic Environmental Network or for Environment Canada's "stakeholder meetings," where the same issues would be discussed out of the public eye. Environment Canada was even happier to recruit Elizabeth May to work for the minister of environment as a liaison with the environmental movement and a distributor of funds. Minister Thomas McMillan's trust was well placed; May directed the bulk of funding to the Canadian Environmental Network (CEN), and not to any public advocacy efforts. Some activists even complained that she tried to stifle criticism of McMillan's Environmental Protection Act.[12]

A great many activists in Nova Scotia felt differently from May and the EAC about the efficacy of direct appeals to politicians' better natures, and very differently about the usefulness of further legal efforts. Premier John Buchanan and his ministers, who held the true decision-making power, had made it clear that they did not wish to listen to environmental activists and would do whatever possible to discourage them and quash dissent. As journalist Ralph Surette put it, "we may safely assume that if the government of Nova Scotia knew of hazards [from chemical spraying] it would not admit it."[13] The environmentalists' next step could only be to force them to listen by raising the number of voices, and voters, in the game. Even before the decision had been made to abandon an appeal of the herbicide trial verdict and settle with Stora Kopparberg, several groups in the province had soured on the search for legitimacy. A large coalition of groups planned a major publicity campaign in 1983, designed to embarrass the government at the peak of the tourist season with a coordinated, province-wide distribution of information on the "Dioxin Trail," a play on the province's promotional names for its coastal highways, such as the Sunrise Trail and Cabot Trail. Only days before the campaign was to begin, however, the EAC, Herbicide Fund Society, and Women's Health Education Network abandoned the plan and sent the printer's plates for the campaign leaflet, unused, to the Queens/Lunenburg South Shore Environmental Protection Association (Q/L SSEPA). "The only explanation we could get," wrote the latter, "was that those concerned in the pull-out thought the pamphlet was an unwise tactic." Activists on the south shore and north shore felt "anger and betrayal" but could only begin planning for the following year's campaign.[14] (Someone in Cumberland County did go ahead and erect the Dioxin Trail signs, but without the accompanying literature, it must have been a puzzling protest to the few who noticed it.[15])

The strongholds of radical activism were located on the province's north and southwest shores, as well as on Cape Breton Island. There, at some remove from Halifax, activists continued with their more populist style of advocacy without much assistance from the city. The Q/L SSEPA joined its north shore peers in the Scott Boycott Committee in late 1983, and the Concerned Residents of Clare and South West Environmental Protection Association organized public meetings on the continued use of 2,4-D in the province's roadside spray program. One prominent speaker for the two groups was a familiar face in anti-chemical circles: Robyn Warren.[16] On forestry matters, the rhetoric and action of the rural populists in the mid and late 1980s began to move towards overt challenges to government consultation. Charlie Restino and the Cape Breton Coalition Against Pesticides (CAP) declared that "more headway can be made by mobilizing public opinion" than by visiting politicians, and worked with David Orton and the North Shore Environmental Web (NSEW) on public appeals.[17] NSEW was even more forceful, uniting as it did many of the activists targeted by Judge Robert McCleave and many who had been dropped from Justice C. Denne Burchell's anti-herbicide injunction, who were overlooked in favour of the Cape Breton trial while the Scott Paper Company remained free to spray chemicals at will. Its members insisted that "it is usually foolish to look to governments (or the court system) to significantly redress environmental damage."[18] Diana Cole of the Concerned Residents of Clare group took such feelings one rhetorical step further. She had participated in one of Environment Canada's national environmental non-governmental organization (ENGO) conferences in 1983 and returned home describing the experience as an exercise in "totalitarian democracy," "empty rituals for the sake of the prestige and perpetuation of those in power," and an "exhausting and debilitating" distraction from real change. What was more, she suggested, this was exactly the intention of the agency, which "exists to preserve a repressive society and neutralize opposition." Activists from the north shore and Cape Breton applauded her statement.[19] Later in the decade, when the provincial government began drafting a new Pest Control Products Act and seeking responses from environmental groups, the harshest critics of consultation recalled the Department of Environment's testimony at the Royal Commission on Forestry in 1983, when its representatives spoke of the need for new legislation solely to raise "public confidence [and] reduce the level of public opposition to forest management programs involving the use of pest control products."[20] Rather than go along with the province's consultation as the mainstream groups did, unwilling groups followed the NSEW's lead in promoting an "informed consent or informed rejection" policy among municipal councils, which would have given local residents living within one kilometre of a woodlot a veto over chemical applications.[21] Ironically, despite refusing to participate in the formal consultation process, their challenge may have helped block Lands and Forests' attempt to exempt woodlands from regulation under the new act.[22]

Radical/mainstream conflict was never entirely limited to forestry debates. Since the early days of the uranium mining controversy, government funding of environmental groups had been a bone of contention, and the issue had not faded with the end of the Royal Commission on Uranium Mining hearings in 1983. When funding or political philosophy came up for discussion, sparks flew. When activists associated with the Sprayers of Dioxin Association in New Brunswick, a group representing victims of Agent Orange testing at CFB Gagetown, attempted to organize a Maritime Environmental Coalition in 1984 as a lobby group successor to the Maritime Energy Coalition, the response among more radical groups indicated just how far apart the factions had drifted. "We would not be involved in any group that accepts funds from those we're fighting," wrote Sherri Cline and Judy Davis of CARE, NSEW, and the Scott Boycott Committee, and "we prefer to put our energy and any funds into raising public awareness rather than into establishing a coalition oriented toward lobbying politicians or trying to match the opposition financially to fight on their terms through their channels."[23] Their critique targeted the EAC and its taste for legal tactics as much as any possible regional coalition. Unwilling to admit that the herbicide trial had been a disaster (Elizabeth May insisted it had prevented 2,4,5-T spraying), and dependent on government funding for its survival, the EAC drew heavy criticism from the radicals.[24] Diana Cole's reaction to the trial was as sharp as her critique of Environment Canada: it was, she said, a case of "poor leadership ... worse than no leadership at all because it lures the people to defeat in a dead end, making the failure appear as victory."[25] Rather than raise money for use in futile lawsuits, the radical activists preferred action, and in 1988 they blockaded roads to a woodlot in Colchester County for six weeks to prevent herbicide spraying there.[26]

Differences over funding were bound up with more profound disagreements about the relationship with government. The NSEW developed a written policy that "environmentalists should not work with corporations or government" on principle, and the more often instances of disagreement arose, the more clearly the radical activists articulated a philosophy that rejected economic growth, the primacy of scientific expertise, and homocentric ethics. These were the articles of faith for modern society that they believed had led the mainstream down its mistaken path. Nor were they alone in staking out an ideological territory (though the radicals were usually more explicit in their rationale); the mainstream redoubled its own commitment to cooperation with government and industry throughout the 1980s. Nova Scotian environmentalists played as great a role in the promotion of the soft energy path (SEP) in the late 1980s as they had at the end of the 1970s. A 1988 update to the Friends of the Earth SEP study maintained the original document's insistence on the viability of the alternative energy scenario "under conditions of strong economic growth and substantial increases in material standards of living."[27] In 1984, and again in 1986, the province's flag bearer for SEP promotion, Susan Holtz, repeated the study's premise, that lifestyle change was a "primarily research question" and should be secondary (in environmentalist and government minds) to "a clear focus on environmental quality as the overriding value."[28] In doing so, she articulated what had become the basic assumption of the mainstream position: that it was possible to address environmental problems without significant or even noticeable change in the nature of society.

The logical extension of mainstream thinking about the minimal importance of social change was the expectation of government action. If environmental problems were "primarily the unintended effects of human activities and technical capabilities," then all that was required to solve them was to muster the political will needed to overrule those profiting from the status quo and simply "change our institutions to avoid or correct" the problems.[29] Pursuing such a goal meant launching ever more appeals to those in power, and sparing ever less attention for the public – not a new condition for the EAC and its national allies in the 1980s, but pursued with greater self-awareness than ever before. The EAC's board of directors openly described the centre's role in the early 1980s as changing "from one simply of creating environmental awareness to one of identifying the issues and proposing alternatives."[30] In 1988, they further specified the audience for their proposals: "We'll be expected by business, industry, labour, and government to act co-operatively in new forms for multistakeholder consultation on environmental and economic development."[31]

Governments, especially the federal government, did what they could to encourage mainstream environmentalists to cooperate, offering more opportunities for consultation with every passing year. The Canadian Council of Resource and Environment Ministers' National Task Force on Environment and Economy; the federal Energy Options Review; the Canadian Environmental Protection Act; the Environmental Assessment and Review Process; the Organisation for Economic Co-operation and Development (OECD) review of Canada's environment and energy policy; the Canadian Environmental Advisory Council; and of course the federally funded CEN and its regional parts – the list of round tables would have surpassed the dreams of twenty King Arthurs, though with rather less than a Camelot atmosphere of equality.[32] The flurry of consultations produced disappointing results: neither the federal gatherings nor their provincial counterparts (Voluntary Planning, the Nature Reserves Liaison Committee, and consultation on new legislation) ever diminished the speed with which new problems produced controversy at the local level. The EAC celebrated "politicians finally [realizing] ... that their constituents really care about the state of the environment," but at the same time found itself further away than ever from those constituents, who could not match the financial contributions on offer from Ottawa and Halifax.[33]

The not-so-secret ingredient that sweetened government consultation was participant funding. In 1981, the EAC admitted that it could not "exist financially solely on its membership," and it became progressively less self-conscious about reaching for other sources of money as the decade wore on.[34] Publication grants from Environment Canada supplemented payments for travel and for contribution to various consultative panels, encouraging further applications for carefully screened "public awareness lecture" grants, "job strategy" grants, student employment grants, and more.[35] Funding applications took up activist time (another reason to avoid topics likely to be rejected), but they represented a safer source of money in one significant way. After an audit by Revenue Canada following the herbicide trial, the EAC's directors became concerned with the security of the centre's tax-exempt charitable status and debated the legality of its actions: under the law, they found, charities were enjoined from attempting "to influence the policy making process [or] promote a change in the law," from lobbying politicians, and from demonstrating with the intent to embarrass or pressure a government.[36] Officially sanctioned processes were legitimate under their charitable status, offering an apparent route to influence without the legal liability. Thus, both the carrot and the stick encouraged mainstream environmentalists to pursue consultation and funding from government in the 1980s. The same activity saw more Nova Scotian environmentalists step onto a wider world stage as well, more often. Early participation by May and Holtz in a Canada-USA environmental council brought the EAC into global campaigns against whaling, ozone depletion, and transboundary pollution, especially acid rain. By the end of the 1980s, it was fully integrated into global networks with the World Wildlife Fund, Friends of the Earth, the Canada–United States Acid Rain Project, the New England Environmental Network, and the Fate of the Earth conferences, all of which increased its profile and reputation as the main Nova Scotian activist group, but none of which brought them any closer to those who remained in the province.[37]

In 1988, EAC coordinator Lois Corbett claimed that the environmental movement had matured from its antagonistic youth in the 1970s and now addressed itself to "two publics": the "grassroots supporters who may sometimes challenge the status quo, and bureaucrats and professionals whose interest may lie in a more mainstream image for the group."[38] Its radical critics, however, recognized that the EAC leaned far more towards the latter group, and deliberately so. "There are various tendencies which are essentially in contention for the soul of the movement," wrote Orton, and for those who would indeed challenge the status quo, "government lobbying or appeals to industry are seen as a waste of time" and a loss of power.[39] How could anyone celebrate concessions from above when they had so often turned out to be hollow? Activists who kept a close eye on the provincial government recognized the weakness of the "two publics" strategy at work in the EAC's cheerful announcement in 1986 that the environment minister had finally agreed to cease issuing permits for 2,4-D in the province, followed by a quiet resumption of its use on the power corporation's rights-of-way.[40] As Ian Sherman, one of the earliest opponents of Cape Breton insecticide spraying in the 1970s, wrote in the early years of the following decade:

The last battle to stop chemical spraying back in 1976 was won *not* by environmental group pressure or media events but because all kinds of people in communities throughout Cape Breton stood up to voice their opposition to chemical spraying. It was a door to door, face to face, grassroots petition campaign ... ultimately, only a similar grassroots movement of local people, especially those whose livelihoods depend directly on the forestry industry, will prevail to stop the spraying and regain control of local forest management.[41]

The myth of the neutral regulator held least sway over self-described "Greens," who insisted on the need for wholesale social change, beginning with the demise of industrial capitalism. A socialist strand in environmental thought was certainly nothing new. It had been around long enough to earn its proponents a nickname: "watermelons," green on the outside and red on the inside. In contrast to the mainstream's commitment to co-operation with government and industry, however, the fringe's antagonism towards both grew more intense in the 1980s. In 1981, Michael Clow argued that "it is very unlikely that an attempt to fuse a liberal understanding of capitalist society with an ecological awareness will be able to grapple with the dynamics of capitalism as a social system [that] requires growth to continue."[42] Six years later, after the herbicide trial, the uranium inquiry, and the associated activist schism, CAP's Charlie Restino observed in less academic terms that "when it comes to corporate profits, more is always better, even if it should mean the destruction of a forest ecosystem developed over thousands of years."[43] And there was nothing unintended about the destructive consequences of economic growth, he added.

Though the network of Greens centred on the north shore was determined to remain primarily concerned with local bioregional politics, they were equally committed internationalists and coalition builders, "part of a worldwide ecological movement."[44] The "informed consent or informed rejection" concept originating with the NSEW spread quickly into the rest of the world in 1987 and 1988, and the members of the NSEW and its successor organization, the Greenweb, participated in a truly global discussion around the theory and politics of "socialist biocentrism" or "left biocentrism."[45] In 1990, they joined as well in forming a new provincial coalition, the Nova Scotia Environment Alliance (NSEA), which made its philosophical foundations (and distinction from the mainstream) clear: the NSEA, they wrote,

> believes in the fundamental right of all living beings to clean air, clean water, and clean soil. The natural world has a right to exist as an entity unto itself,

independent of its utility to humans. We believe it is not possible to have infinite growth in a finite world. In questions of economic development versus the environment, the earth comes first.[46]

The NSEA statement was indeed a far cry from Holtz's complaint that talk of nature's rights "is a distraction from the main human issues facing us," but then it was meant to be.[47] The Greens were contemptuous of the "belief that the existing political and economic system can be reformed – if only the 'political will' can be summoned."[48] In their view, such attempts led to the kind of craven compromise that turned Elizabeth May and the EAC into advocates of *Btk* spraying and, by extension, defenders of the industrial forestry system.[49]

This conflict between the environmental mainstream and fringe was not, like so much else examined in previous chapters of this work, a factor in the shaping of the provincial movement. It was itself the shape of the movement, and would remain so for long after the events described herein. It should be noted that the factions did not persist in isolation. Cooperation was the norm, if not always the rule.[50] Ironically, the EAC and NSEW together comprised the entire Nova Scotian component of the International Uranium Congress in 1988, for example.[51] Theoretical differences might be left off the agenda in mixed company, yet the differences between the two sides were so profound that never could anyone speak honestly about a single movement, and never could any attempt at collaboration pass without debate over consultation versus confrontation – the tactics of the expert or of the citizen – as the proper stance towards those in power.

CONCLUSION

The initial motive for investigating the history of environmentalism in Nova Scotia – one province among ten possible subjects and a great many more possible combinations thereof – was unabashedly grounded in present-day observation of an environmental movement seemingly uncomfortable with acknowledging the clear divisions within itself: between, for example, those who would resist the further industrialization of the rural countryside and those who believe that the stabilization of the global climate depends somehow on the construction of wind turbine arrays. It was obvious early in the process that the variety and geographic distribution of environmental organizations in Nova Scotia warranted the focus on a single province; the wider the scope of investigation, the more small groups would necessarily be overlooked or omitted in the final account, and those small groups clearly showed the greatest vitality in the movement. They also presented the greatest contrast with the peripatetic, professional global environmentalism that forms such an insistent public face of environmental concern in the early twenty-first century. That contrast provided the central fact of the story and came to explain most clearly both the present-day divisions within environmentalism and the history of their development: environmental activism in Nova Scotia has always been essentially local in its inception, in its organization, and in its reason for being. The modernization of one segment of the movement marks the greatest change in its history. Each issue examined in this book has become the account of a different phase or aspect of the struggle between the place-loving soul of the movement and the temptations of a placeless modernity.

The essentially local nature of environmental activism is concealed not only by its rejection by some present-day modernist environmentalists but also by the direction of earlier activism towards the appropriate jurisdiction, which was not often the local municipal level. The Canadian Constitution places responsibility for natural resources at the provincial level, and activists attempting to influence the course of environmental policy most often cooperated on that level, forming issue-based coalitions or common fronts like CAP or the Uranium Committee of the EAC. Extraordinary cooperation among provinces can and did pull activist cooperation towards the same level, as when the Maritime Energy Corporation spawned the Maritime Energy Coalition. Once the immediate exigency had passed, however, the activist MEC dispersed back into mainly provincial networks. Federal-level coalitions proved more lasting, but those too simply followed jurisdiction; responsibility for atomic energy regulation or for the negotiation of international agreements dealing with acid rain belonged to Ottawa, for example, and the Canadian Coalition for Nuclear Responsibility or Canadian Coalition on Acid Rain formed to address that responsibility.

The nature of state power in action also goes some way towards concealing the local essence of environmentalism. One of the implicit arguments of the preceding chapters is that in situations where novelty or lack of firm direction from above allows bureaucrats to act on their differences of opinion, state actors may come to appear as issue-based activists first and guardians of bureaucratic prerogative second. This occurred with some professional foresters and federal energy bureaucrats in the late 1970s. But those liberties can be swiftly swept away by determined leadership, as Premier Buchanan demonstrated upon taking power in Nova Scotia in 1978.

In the final analysis, state power and state modernism are constant formative factors in environmental activism. The model of state/industry/activist relations presented in this book, including the centrality of the local experience, is entirely consistent with the history of other Canadian environmentalisms and might be profitably applied to more of them.[52]

Environmentalist cooperation at the higher levels of geographic integration – the provincial and federal levels – was sustained by the political structure of the Canadian state, but it never diminished the centrality or energy of the local. Every Nova Scotian group discussed in this book had its roots in a local reaction to environmental harm, either actual or prospective. Even the EAC, eventually the staunchest champion of modernist environmentalism, began as a small group at Dalhousie University concerned with recycling, urban air quality and sanitation, and municipal planning, local issues that earned it enough support among Haligonians to survive the end of full government funding in 1974. It is worth noting as well that localism is not a quality exclusive to environmental activist organizations; in contrast to the US experience, where unitary national groups have existed from the early days of many social movements, Canadian social movement organizations as a rule remained subnational in the 1970s. Logistical difficulties that hobbled communication – "no electronic mail and a costly long-distance telephone service" – have been singled out as an explanation, along with unequal access to financial resources across regions, leading to imbalance and resentment against the heartland of activism in Ontario. This is not obviously false, but it does take national organization as the norm, its absence to be explained.[53] As suggested above, Nova Scotia's environmentalist history demonstrates the importance of local, lived reality as a driver of activist recruitment. It is likely that social movement activism of any type that questions systems of modernity is inherently and normally local, and other explanations (from political culture and legal history, for instance) should be provided to account for national or provincial unity, rather than for its absence.

More than other kinds of activists, environmentalists have a particular attachment to the local level, due to their movement's origin in a reaction to industrial modernity's destructive effects. The modernist ethos is "a strategy of conceptual encompassment" of identities defined in relation to specific places and communities.[54] That is, it forces people to speak and think in the language of a universally applied scientific and technological idiom that makes any place interchangeable with any other. Those standing against it and defending specific places intuitively understand that an assertion of the irreducible local experience must necessarily end up in "some kind of boundary-drawing between the local and the global," implying a challenge to the combined forces of modernity: global capitalism, industrialism, normal science, and the rules of governmentality.[55] The story of Nova Scotian environmentalism set out in the previous chapters offers clear proof of the continuity of non-modern argument: from the south shore fishermen who in opposing the Stoddard Island nuclear plant defined their community as a fishing community and defied the language of cost-benefit analysis that suggested they might more profitably become a high-technology community, to the stubborn insistence of woodlot owners that local industry was preferable to multinational pulp and paper forestry and not readily compatible with it, to the many arguments presented against uranium mining in 1982 (and aggregate quarrying a decade later) that relied not on science alone but also on the meaningfulness of the provincial environment and the idea that a project might be legitimately resisted in order that a region or a mountain might continue to "be seen to be beautiful" or sacred.[56] The argument only gains from the move towards explicitly formulated localism by the most radical groups in the 1980s, such as the Greenweb's "informed consent or informed rejection" proposal, a profoundly subversive doctrine of extreme local democracy that effectively attacked every one of the modernist systems listed above and repudiated the image of environmentalist as expert manager.

Initially, in the early 1970s, activists with more and less radical views worked side by side in the same groups, defending harbours from destructive development, using rhetorical ammunition based on the language of environmental justice, biological science, traditional moral economies, precautionary principles, economic theory, and violent resistance. The non-modernist strand within early activism could not be eradicated, and finding a way to separate its most committed advocates from their more modernist peers was therefore essential for governments wishing to defuse the challenge. Eventually, they did just that: by the end of the story related in these chapters, the movement had failed decisively as a challenge to modernity. Activists in general never achieved the power to subvert modernity itself. Rather, large segments of the movement, large enough to define themselves as its mainstream, were subsumed into the modern, seeking expert status and accepting the sanctity of economic growth, capitalism, industry, science, and political liberalism. Government and industry cooperated in supporting the activists most likely to form a mainstream, and vilifying those who resisted. Consultation and red-baiting were the two most common tactics used to achieve those ends in the 1970s, but they were not alone, and the process continues in the twenty-first century

with wilderness areas and "green energy" megaprojects to tempt the bid-
dable activists and charges of "ecoterrorism" to marginalize the rest. Since
the end of the 1970s, the radical remainder relegated to fringe status has
enjoyed only enough power to mount occasionally successful challenges
under the most favourable circumstances, as the Mi'kmaq Warrior Society did by capitalizing on the popular notion of Native people's ecological
spirituality in order to advance a non-modern sanctity argument in defence
of Kelly's Mountain in 1990.

To explain this difference between the mainstream and the radical, the
balance of evidence from the history of Nova Scotian activism suggests that
urban activists, closer to the physical seat of bureaucratic power as well as
to the sources of funding in government and major industry, more readily
adopted modernist assumptions (or more often came with such assumptions already in place). Possibly as well, activists whose first campaigns
deal with urban planning and sanitation, areas of interest in which some
form of managerial control is unavoidable and debate centres on which
planning regime is best, are on track towards a universal, modernist sort
of activism from the beginning. That the same groups tend to be populated
by middle-class professionals, especially academics, could be a piece of
demographic coincidence owing to their concentration in urban environ-
ments, but for the fact that the same class of activists has displayed at every
location a greater level of comfort with the jargon of expertise as well as
with the bureaucratic system in which facility with that language functions
as a passport to greater access. For example, the relationship between the
academic Acadia Nuclear Power Study Group and the much more working-
class South Shore Environmental Protection Association – the former
abstractly scientific and the latter viscerally political (and successful) – finds
a parallel three chapters and nearly twenty years later in the tension between
the Save Kelly's Mountain Society and the Mi'kmaq Warrior Society.
Out-of-province origins account for no apparent difference in this regard
(though there does appear to have been a larger proportion of immigrants
among activists than in the general population), and neither does gender
(with no clear overrepresentation of either men or women in the movement): for every Susan Holtz, there was a Ralph Loomer, immigrant and
native modernists, respectively, and for every David Orton a Judy Davis,
their radical equivalents.[57] The geography and demography of dissent by
which those closer to the city and higher on the economic scale are faster
to abandon antagonism for conciliation is a tendency, not a rule, but as an
exemplar few can match Elizabeth May, whose move from Cape Breton

to Halifax and enrolment in law school in 1980 coincided with her shift in tactical choices.

The solidification of the mainstream's dominance required a rewriting of the history of the movement in the late 1980s – thus May's insistence that the herbicide trial had, by forestalling aerial spraying, prevented the use of Agent Orange in Nova Scotia, or that the better natures of Gerald Regan and Vince MacLean had been awakened in time to prevent insecticide spraying in the 1970s;[58] thus, as well, the suggestion that Judge McCleave's recommendations in 1985 constituted a rejection of uranium mining on terms articulated by environmentalists. In truth, however, the victories of environmental activists in Nova Scotia were invariably built on pressure politics and appeals to the interests of the local area, quite contrary to modernist claims to represent a wider society or expert perspective. The fishermen of the Yarmouth and Shelburne areas who cowed Premier Regan into shelving the Stoddard Island plan explicitly rejected the blithe assurances of the federal fisheries scientists and atomic energy experts who cooperated in the Canadian government's nuclear boosterism. The budworm battlers of Cape Breton Island knew enough to present themselves as the defenders of small lowland woodlot owners against the depredations of a foreign multinational, Stora. And McCleave's antagonists during the Royal Commission on Uranium Mining saw clearly the fallacy of public consultation and the utility of political embarrassment. Every one of them sought to mobilize the public en masse as well, and made frequent reference to the failure of the government in Halifax to uphold the interests of the hinterland.

The radicals (for that is what an insistence on non-modern localism made them) did not operate alone at any phase in their development; the organizational resources of the mainstream or those who would later form it created the conditions in which pressure politics could function, and armed all segments of the movement with the most compelling scientific arguments. Indeed, the radical approach did not ever function without a more rhetorically respectable counterpart, often voiced by the same people. The two strands of the movement diverged but remained intertwined, even within individuals. Every anti-nuclear campaigner in the province leaned gratefully on the research of the Acadia NPSG for instance, every anti-uranium campaigner on reports of the British Columbian experience circulated by the EAC. The Mi'kmaq Warrior Society readily acknowledged the value of its partnership with the research-heavy advocacy of the SKMS. May herself, who helped lead the greatest political pressure campaign in this story during the budworm spray controversy, frequently returned to praising the virtues of populist activism in later years, even as she pursued the lobbyist style. It was when the modernist tendency within the movement completely lost sight of its topophilic roots and contrived to act alone, excluding the radicals or softening the impact of their mass movement politics, that environmental activism failed. The herbicide trial, which compelled submission to the rules and procedures and evidentiary standards of the court, demonstrated the impotence of the method. So did the later Sydney tar ponds battle with its duly constituted but ineffective consultative bodies, and the fight over Point Aconi's power station, which brought yet another doomed legal challenge to court.

A lasting environmental movement in Nova Scotia began as an undifferentiated mixture of modern and non-modern activists. Conservationists, planners, and scientists worked alongside back-to-the-landers, student radicals, and the defenders of traditional economies. An eventual organizational distinction was predictable and probably innocuous, but the imbalance of political influence was not; it required a combination of encouragement for the modernists from two levels of government that wished to marginalize the radicals, willing participation by the modernists in the marginalization of their allies, and a global modernist environmentalism for the chosen few to participate in. What the creation of a mainstream could not do, however, was abolish the entirely local experience of environmental harm. Few environmentalists in the 1980s came to their activism out of concern for issues in the abstract; rather, most environmentalism in Nova Scotia remained an expression of love of place and a determination to defend it.

Notes

FOREWORD: ENVIRONMENTAL ACTION AND THE QUESTION OF SCALE

1 For Dubos's use of the term in 1972, at the United Nations Conference on the Human
   Environment in Stockholm, see Ralph Keyes, *The Quote Verifier: Who Said What, Where,
   and When* (New York: St Martin's Griffin, 2006), 79.
2 Denis E. Cosgrove, *Apollo's Eye: A Cartographic Genealogy of the Earth in the Western Imagination* (Baltimore and London: Johns Hopkins University Press, 2001); R. Buckminster
   Fuller, *An Operating Manual for Spaceship Earth* (Washington, DC: n.p., 1967); Kenneth
   E. Boulding, "The Economics of the Coming Spaceship Earth," in H. Jarrett, ed., *Environ-
   mental Quality in a Growing Economy: Essays from the Sixth RFF Forum* (Baltimore: Johns
   Hopkins University Press, 1966), 3–14.
3 John Muir, *My First Summer in the Sierra* (Boston: Houghton Mifflin, 1911; San Francisco:
   Sierra Club Books, 1988), 110 (citations are to the 1988 edition); Aldo Leopold, *A Sand
   County Almanac, and Sketches Here and There* (New York: Oxford University Press, 1949);
   Rachel Carson, *Silent Spring* (Boston: Houghton Mifflin, 1962); Paul R. Ehrlich, *The Popu-
   lation Bomb* (New York: Ballantine Books, 1968); Donnella H. Meadows, Dennis L.
   Meadows, Jørgen Randers, and William W. Behrens III, *The Limits to Growth* (New York:
   Universe Books, 1972); Andrew Kirk, *Counterculture Green* (Lawrence: University Press of
   Kansas, 2007). Ursula K. Heise offers a smart, wide-ranging, and important discussion of
   the relations between ways of imagining the global and ethical commitments to the local
   (upon which these opening paragraphs broadly rest) from the perspective of literary ecocriticism in *Sense of Place and Sense of Planet: The Environmental Imagination of the Global*
   (New York: Oxford University Press, 2008), where she pays particular attention to global-
   scale representations of ecological crisis.
4 Scott Russell Sanders, *Staying Put: Making a Home in a Restless World* (Boston: Beacon
   Press, 1993), xvi (cited by Heise, *Sense of Place*, 38).
5 Yi-fu Tuan, *Topophilia: A Study of Environmental Perception, Attitudes and Values* (Englewood
   Cliffs, NJ: Prentice Hall, 1974), 4. At the University of Toronto, Edward C. (Ted) Relph

submitted a PhD dissertation titled "The Phenomenon of Place" in 1973. Revised and published as *Place and Placelessness* (London: Pion, 1976), it became a "classic of human geography" (see *Progress in Human Geography* 24, 4 [2000]). Relph recalls that his search of library card catalogues ca. 1970 revealed that almost nothing had been written about place (see his website, Placeness, Place, Placelessness, http://www.placeness.com). In his discussion of Tuan's influential book on his website, Relph points out that both W.H. Auden and Gaston Bachelard had earlier used variants of the term.

6   Paul Shepard, "Place in American Culture," *North American Review* 262, 3 (Fall 1977): 32; Wendell Berry, *A Continuous Harmony: Essays Cultural and Agricultural* (New York: Harcourt Brace Jovanovich, 1972), 68–69; Sanders, *Staying Put*, xiii–xv (Shepard, Berry, and Sanders are cited in Heise, *A Sense of Place*, 29–31); Robert Fulford and John Sewell, *A Sense of Time and Place* (Toronto: City Pamphlets, [1971]); Northrop Frye, "Conclusion," in *Literary History of Canada: Canadian Literature in English*, ed. Carl F. Klinck (Toronto: University of Toronto Press, 1965); Neil Evernden, "Beyond Ecology: Self, Place and the Pathetic Fallacy," in *The Ecocriticism Reader: Landmarks in Literary Ecology*, ed. Cheryll Glotfelty and Harold Fromm (Athens: University of Georgia Press, 1996), 92–104; Philip Buckner, "'Limited Identities' Revisited: Regionalism and Nationalism in Canadian History," *Acadiensis* 30, 1 (Autumn 2000): 4–15, and J.M.S. Careless, "'Limited Identities' in Canada," *Canadian Historical Review* 50, 1 (March 1969): 1–10.

7   This paragraph distills much of the substance of Heise, *Sense of Place*, ch. 1, "From the Blue Planet to Google Earth: Environmentalism, Ecocriticism, and the Imagination of the Global." See also Arne Naess, "Identification as a Source of Deep Ecological Attitudes," in *Deep Ecology*, ed. Michael Tobias (San Diego: Avant Books, 1985), 268 (and in Heise, *Sense of Place*, 34).

8   T.W. Acheson, "The National Policy and the Industrialization of the Maritimes, 1880–1910," *Acadiensis* 1, 2 (1972): 3–28.

9   *Evidences of the Industrial Ascendancy of Nova Scotia* (Halifax: Canadian Manufacturers' Association, Publicity Committee of the Nova Scotia Branch, 1913).

10 E.R. Forbes, "Misguided Symmetry: The Destruction of a Regional Transportation Policy for the Maritimes," in *Canada and the Burden of Unity*, ed. D.J. Bercuson (Toronto: Macmillan of Canada, 1977), 60–86; and E.R. Forbes, *The Maritime Rights Movement, 1919–1927* (Montreal and Kingston: McGill-Queen's University Press, 1979). But see K. Cruikshank, "The Intercolonial Railway, Freight Rates and the Maritime Economy," *Acadiensis* 22, 1 (Autumn 1992): 87–110 for a different view.

11 Roy E. George, *A Leader and a Laggard: Manufacturing Industry in Nova Scotia, Quebec and Ontario* (Toronto: University of Toronto Press, 1970). In 1957, the federal government of Canada introduced a fiscal equalization program to achieve a national standard in public services. Tax dollars collected by the federal government were redistributed according to need, to enable poorer provinces to provide a minimum level of health care, social programs, and educational services. This did little to support regional growth beyond the service sectors; to this end, beginning in 1960, firms and regions were offered a sometimes bewildering array of tax incentives and assistance from special programs identified by an alphabet soup of acronyms.

12 These developments are well summarized in Donald J. Savoie, "Reviewing Canada's Regional Development Efforts," in [Newfoundland] *Royal Commission on Renewing and Strengthening Our Place in Canada* (St. John's: Queen's Printer, 2003), 147–83. For more details, see Donald J. Savoie, *Regional Economic Expansion: Canada's Search for Solutions* (Toronto:

University of Toronto Press, 1992), and Ralph Matthews, *The Creation of Regional Dependency* (Toronto: University of Toronto Press, 1983). In 1981, federal transfers (of all types, including unemployment insurance), counted for more than half of provincial revenues in all four Atlantic provinces. For later reflection on the political economy of regional development, see Donald J. Savoie, *Visiting Grandchildren: Economic Development in the Maritimes* (Toronto: University of Toronto Press, 2006).

13 Jenny Higgins and Melanie Martin, "The Come by Chance Oil Refinery," http://www. heritage.nf.ca/articles/politics/come-by-chance.php; H.A. Fredericks and Allan Chambers, *Bricklin* (Fredericton: New Brunswick Books, 1977). See also the equally notorious but earlier failure of Clairtone in Stellarton in 1967, attributed in an internal company report to the failings of the workforce, but the consequence of many influences, including poor infrastructure, overreach, and hubris: Nina Munk and Rachel Gotlieb, *The Art of Clairtone: The Making of a Design Icon, 1958–1971* (Toronto: McClelland and Stewart, 2008).

14 For resettlement schemes, see George Withers, "Resettlement of Newfoundland Inshore Fishing Communities, 1954–1972: A High Modernist Project" (MA thesis, Memorial University of Newfoundland, 2009); for the Comprehensive Development Plan, see Wade MacLauchlan, *Alex B. Campbell: The Prince Edward Island Premier Who Rocked the Cradle* (Charlottetown: Prince Edward Island Museum and Heritage Foundation, 2014).

15 Carson, *Silent Spring;* Ryan O'Connor, *The First Green Wave: Pollution Probe and the Origins of Environmental Activism in Ontario* (Vancouver: UBC Press, 2014); Mark J. MacLaughlin, "Rise of the Eco-Comics: The State, Environmental Education, and Canadian Comic Books, 1971–1975," *Material Culture Review* 77/78 (Spring/Fall 2013 [August 2014]): 9–20. Alan A. MacEachern, *The Institute of Man and Resources: An Environmental Fable* (Charlottetown: Island Studies Press, 2003); E.F. Schumacher, *Small Is Beautiful: A Study of Economics as if People Mattered* (New York: Harper and Row, 1973).

16 The phrase is adapted from the opening lines of William Wordsworth's poem called forth in opposition to the proposed Kendal and Windermere Railway in the English Lake District in 1844; in the original, it reads: "Is then no nook of English ground secure / From rash assault?" It was used in the title of James Winter, *Secure from Rash Assault: Sustaining the Victorian Environment* (Berkeley and London: University of California Press, 1999).

17 Garth Jowett and Victoria O'Donnell, *Propaganda and Persuasion,* 4th ed. (Thousand Oaks, CA: Sage Publications, 2006), 7.

18 See James C. Scott, *Weapons of the Weak: Everyday Forms of Peasant Resistance* (New Haven, CT: Yale University Press, 1985).

19 These facets of Royal Commission proceedings are well discussed in Molly Clarkson, "Speaking for Sockeye, Speaking for Themselves: First Nations Engagement in the Cohen Commission (2009–2012)" (MA thesis, University of British Columbia, 2016), ch. 2.

20 Frank S. Zelko, *Make It a Green Peace! The Rise of Countercultural Environmentalism* (New York: Oxford University Press, 2013); Robert Wilson, "Making Tracks," Seeing the Woods: A Blog by the Rachel Carson Center, August 25, 2016, https://seeingthewoods. org/2016/08/25/making-tracks-robert-wilson/#more-4668; Justin Page, *Tracking the Great Bear: How Environmentalists Recreated British Columbia's Coastal Rainforest* (Vancouver: UBC Press, 2014); Juliet Eilperin and Steven Mufson, "Activists Arrested at White House Protesting Keystone Pipeline," *Washington Post,* February 13, 2013.

21 "Judith Davis," http://www.inmemoriam.ca/view-announcement-198741-judith-davis.html.

22 David Orton, "Judy Davis – Portrait of an Activist," http://home.ca.inter.net/%7Egreenweb/ Judy_Davis.pdf.

23   This discussion draws from Orton's own accounts of his life, available at Deep Green Web, http://deepgreenweb.blogspot.com.

24   David Orton, "The McCleave Uranium Inquiry in Nova Scotia," *Atlantic Socialist* 1, 2 (December 1982), http://home.ca.inter.net/%7Egreenweb/Uranium_Inquiry_NS.html, where items on other topics mentioned may also be found.

25   Mike Allen, "Portsmouth-Born Canadian Activist Reflects on Life," *The News* (Portsmouth), November 25, 1994, http://home.ca.inter.net/~greenweb/David_Orton_reflects_on_life.pdf.

26   David Orton, "Left Biocentrism," in *Encyclopedia of Religion and Nature*, vol. 2, *K–Z* (Bristol, UK: Thoemmes Continuum, 2005), 1003–5.

27   Orton's writings are collected at Green Web, http://home.ca.inter.net/~greenweb.

28   David Orton, "Climate Change Pollyannas," a review essay on Elizabeth May and Zoë Caron, *Global Warming for Dummies* (Mississauga, ON: John Wiley and Sons Canada, 2009); see in a similar vein David Orton's review of L. Anders Sandberg, *Trouble in the Woods: Forest Policy and Social Conflict in Nova Scotia and New Brunswick* (Fredericton: Acadiensis Press, 1992), both available at Green Web, http://home.ca.inter.net/~greenweb.

29   Orton, "Climate Change Pollyannas."

30   *Between the Issues* (October 1980), https://dalspace.library.dal.ca/xmlui/bitstream/handle/10222/14780/MS-11-13_31264026410238.pdf?sequence=1&isAllowed=y.

31   Amory B. Lovins, "Energy Strategy: The Road Not Taken?" *Foreign Affairs* (October 1976): 65–96. Many years later, Holtz's brief resume noted that she was "the founding Vice Chair of both the Nova Scotia and the now-disbanded National Round Table on the Environment and the Economy," and that she had served on numerous other advisory bodies and panels. In a 2013 article titled "Redirecting Anti-Wind Energy," the fundamental philosophical difference between her position and those of more radical environmentalists committed to oppositional politics (between Leeming's ecomodernist and non-modernist groups) was starkly exposed in her assertion that "some public stands are simply characterized as broad – and predictable – knee-jerk negativity: CAVE (Citizens Against Virtually Everything); BANANA (Build Absolutely Nothing Anywhere Near Anything); and NOPE (Not On Planet Earth)." In Holtz's mature view, adversarial processes, including Canada's legal and political systems, served to block progress on contentious public issues: Susan Holtz, "Redirecting Anti-Wind Energy: Individuals, Communities and Politicians Can Turn a Debate Stalemate into an Opportunity for Collaboration," *Alternatives Journal* 39, 5 (September/October 2013): 44–47.

32   Richard Grant, "Paul Watson: Sea Shepherd Eco-Warrior Fighting to Stop Whaling and Seal Hunts," *Daily Telegraph* (London), April 17, 2009; e.g., Mark S. Winfield, *Blue-Green Province: The Environment and the Political Economy of Ontario* (Vancouver: UBC Press, 2011).

33   Harald Welzer, *Climate Wars: What People Will Be Killed for in the 21st Century* (Cambridge: Polity Press, 2012); Michael F. Maniates, "Individualization: Plant a Tree, Buy a Bike, Save the World?" *Global Environmental Politics* 1, 3 (August 2001): 31–52.

34   Heise, *Sense of Place*, 21.

35   David Harvey, *The Condition of Post Modernity: An Enquiry into the Origins of Cultural Change* (Oxford, UK: Blackwell, 1989), 240.

36   Doreen Massey, *Space, Place and Gender* (Minneapolis: University of Minnesota Press, 1994), 147. For Orton, see Allen, "Portsmouth-Born."

37   Doreen Massey, "A Global Sense of Place," *Marxism Today* 38 (1991): 24–29, quote from p. 28; Tim Cresswell, *Geographic Thought: A Critical Introduction* (Chichester: Wiley

Blackwell, 2013), Chapter 11; Tim Cresswell, "Place," in John A. Agnew and James S. Duncan, eds., *The Wiley Blackwell Companion to Human Geography* (Chichester, Sussex: John Wiley and Sons, 2016), 238. See also Jamie Peck and Adam Tickell, "Neoliberalizing Space," *Antipode* 34 (2002): 380–404 and "Doreen Massey on Space," Social Science Bites at: http://www.socialsciencespace.com/2013/02/podcastdoreen-massey-on-space/.

INTRODUCTION

1 Ronald Inglehart, *The Silent Revolution: Changing Values and Political Styles among Western Publics* (Princeton, NJ: Princeton University Press, 1977). This is not actually a very new idea of environmentalism, especially if one adheres to a broad definition including the Romantic movement; it echoes what Aldous Huxley wrote in the essay "Wordsworth in the Tropics," in *Do What You Will* (London: Chatto and Windus, 1956 [1929]). See also Christopher Rootes, ed., *Environmental Movements: Local, National, and Global* (Portland, OR: Frank Cass, 1999); and Samuel Hays, *Beauty, Health, and Permanence: Environmental Politics in the United States, 1955–1985* (Cambridge: Cambridge University Press, 1987), 3.

2 Ramachandra Guha, *How Much Should a Person Consume? Environmentalism in India and the United States* (Los Angeles: University of California Press, 2006), 8. Guha credits the definition to G.M. Trevelyan in the 1931 Rickman Godlee Lecture, titled "The Calls and Claims of Natural Beauty." Similar ideas appear in Mahesh Rangarajan, *Fencing the Forest: Conservation and Ecological Change in India's Central Provinces 1860–1914* (Delhi: Oxford University Press, 1996); E.P. Thompson, *Customs in Common* (London: Merlin Press, 1991); Ramachandra Guha, *The Unquiet Woods: Ecological Change and Peasant Resistance in the Himalaya*, 2nd ed. (Oxford: Oxford University Press, 1989); Juan Martinez-Alier, *Ecological Economics: Energy, Environment, and Society* (Oxford: Basil Blackwell, 1990); Juan Martinez-Alier, *The Environmentalism of the Poor: A Study of Ecological Conflicts and Valuation* (Northhampton, UK: Edward Elgar, 2002); Guha and Martinez-Alier, *Varieties of Environmentalism: Essays North and South* (London: Earthscan, 1997); Jürgen Habermas, "New Social Movements," *Telos* 1981, no. 49 (1981): 33–37. Also, Nick Crossley and Jürgen Habermas, *Making Sense of Social Movements* (Buckingham, UK: Open University Press, 2002).

Unfortunately, much of the international history remains trapped in the post-colonialists' jaundiced view of the global North: with the exception of the environmental struggles of a racial underclass, post-materialist notions of privileged "amenity" or "full-stomach" environmentalism dominate the view of activists in Europe and North America. See, for example, Ramachandra Guha, "Radical American Environmentalism and Wilderness Preservation: A Third World Critique," *Environmental Ethics* 11, no. 1 (1989): 71–83.

3 Andrew Dobson, *Green Political Thought* (London: Routledge, 2000 [1990]), 8; Alf Hornborg, "Environmentalism, Ethnicity, and Sacred Places: Reflections on Modernity, Discourse and Power," *Canadian Review of Sociology and Anthropology* 31, no. 3 (1994): 258; Alf Hornborg, "Undermining Modernity: Protecting Landscapes and Meanings among the Mi'kmaq of Nova Scotia," in *Political Ecology across Spaces, Scales, and Social Groups,* ed. Susan Paulson and Lisa Gezon (New Brunswick, NJ: Rutgers University Press, 2004), 196–216; Anthony Giddens, *The Consequences of Modernity* (Stanford, CA: Stanford University Press, 1990), 4–6; Bruno Latour, *We Have Never Been Modern* (Cambridge, MA: Harvard University Press, 1993 [1991]). The idea owes much to an earlier theorist of similar ideas: Thomas Kuhn, *The Structure of Scientific Revolutions* (Chicago: University of

Chicago Press, 1962). Similar ideas can be found in the work of Arne Naess and David Pepper: Naess, *The Ecology of Wisdom: Writings by Arne Naess* (Berkeley: Counterpoint, 2008); Pepper, *Modern Environmentalism* (London: Routledge, 1996).

4 This is especially true of neighbouring jurisdictions in New Brunswick and Prince Edward Island, where similar debates over nuclear power or chemical forestry, for example, were conducted contemporaneously with Nova Scotia's controversies. The intra-regional differences of political economy and political culture that justify treating Nova Scotia apart from its Maritime peers, even when their environmental movements joined forces as they did over nuclear power, are readily apparent in comparing the present study with those presenting histories of nuclear power, other energy politics, or forestry in New Brunswick and Prince Edward Island. See, for example, Adrian Egbers, "Going Nuclear: The Origins of New Brunswick's Nuclear Industry, 1950–1983" (MA thesis, Dalhousie University, 2008); James Kenny and Andrew Secord, "Engineering Modernity: Hydroelectric Development in New Brunswick, 1945–1970," *Acadiensis* 39, no. 1 (Winter/Spring 2010): 3–26; Alan MacEachern, *The Institute of Man and Resources: An Environmental Fable* (Charlottetown: Island Studies Press, 2003); and Mark McLaughlin, "Green Shoots: Aerial Insecticide Spraying and the Growth of Environmental Consciousness in New Brunswick, 1952–1973," *Acadiensis* 40, no. 1 (Winter/Spring 2011).

5 This book makes relatively little attempt to explain federal policy making in all of its unquestionably fractious detail. Readers keen to examine the federal relationship are encouraged to pay close attention to the role of the Canadian state in Chapters 2 and 4, to get the flavour of federal power in action. Federal development policy and environmental reactions to it are a well-studied component of Canada's political history, and interested readers would do well to look to James C. Scott, *Seeing Like a State: How Certain Schemes to Improve the Human Condition Have Failed* (New Haven, CT: Yale University Press, 1998). Canadian examples include Miriam Wright, *A Fishery for Modern Times: The State and Industrialization of the Newfoundland Fishery, 1934–1968* (Don Mills, ON: Oxford, 2001); Donald Savoie and John Chenier, "The State and Development: The Politics of Regional Development Policy," in *Still Living Together: Recent Trends and Future Directions in Canadian Regional Development,* ed. William Coffey and Mario Polese (Montreal: Institute for Research on Public Policy, 1998); Jennifer Nelson, *Razing Africville: A Geography of Racism* (Toronto: University of Toronto Press, 2008). Especially useful for tying together policy and theory is Hornborg, "Environmentalism, Ethnicity, and Sacred Places," 245–67; Hornborg, "Undermining Modernity"; Matthew Evenden, *Fish versus Power: An Environmental History of the Fraser River* (Cambridge: Cambridge University Press, 2004); Tina Loo, "People in the Way: Modernity, Society, and Environment on the Arrow Lakes," *BC Studies* 142/143 (Summer/Autumn 2004): 161–96; Philip Van Huizen, "Flooding the Border: Development, Politics, and Environmental Controversy in the Canadian-U.S. Skagit Valley" (PhD dissertation, University of British Columbia, 2013).

CHAPTER 1: AT HOME AND ABROAD

1 Mersey Tobeatic Research Institute, "Mersey Messages – Old Lake Rossignol," March 10, 2009, http://www.merseytobeatic.ca/pdfs/Mersey%20Messages/Mersey%20Messages%20March%2010%202009.pdf.

2 William Herrington and George Rounsefell, "Restoration of the Atlantic Salmon in New England," *Transactions of the American Fisheries Society* 70, no. 1 (1941): 123–27.

3   Frank Sobey to Russell McInnes, July 18, 1961, Public Archives of Nova Scotia, McInnes fonds, RG44, vol. 22, no. 4.

4   Russell McInnes, *Report of the Royal Commission into the Nova Scotia Light and Power Company Ltd. Gold River Hydro Development* (Halifax: Government of Nova Scotia, 1961).

5   Ibid.

6   Ibid.

7   "NSRC" document, 1981, Dalhousie University Archives and Special Collections, Ecology Action Centre fonds, MS-11-13 [hereafter DAL-EAC], box 33.2.

8   McInnes, *Report of the Royal Commission.*

9   The national scene shared much the same development in the mid-twentieth century, according to Tina Loo, whose book on Canadian wildlife conservation traced the rise of groups using both elite status and popular pressure to exert influence on the state, especially in the west. Tina Loo, *States of Nature: Conserving Canada's Wildlife in the Twentieth Century* (Vancouver: UBC Press, 2006).

10 "Wildlife Conservation," n.d. [c. 1950s], Acadia University Esther Clark Wright Archives, Harrison Flint Lewis fonds, accession 2006.020-LEW/36.

11 "Organization of the Nova Scotia Bird Society," 1955, Acadia University Esther Clark Wright Archives, Harrison Flint Lewis fonds, accession 2006.020-LEW/24.

12 Martin Rudy Haase, interview with the author, October 9, 2011; Sterling Evans, *The Green Republic: A Conservation History of Costa Rica* (Austin: University of Texas Press, 1999), 62.

13 Martin Rudy Haase, interview with the author, October 9, 2011; "FON newsletter," n.d. [c. 1970s], Rudy Haase papers.

14 "DDT: Who It's Killing and Why," *Mysterious East,* December 1969, 19–26. See also Chapter 4. The story of New Brunswick's rivers and the effect of DDT on them appeared famously in Rachel Carson, *Silent Spring* (New York: Fawcett Crest, 1962).

15 Rust Associates, *A Review of the Boat Harbour Waste Treatment Facilities for Nova Scotia Water Resources Commission* (Montreal: Rust Associates, 1970).

16 "Special Report: The Death of Boat Harbour," *Mysterious East,* September 1970, 20–27.

17 Ibid., 22. The Pictou Landing Band did eventually win in court a recognition of the deception perpetrated in part by the federal government, and a settlement in 1993 that paid $35 million: Settlement agreement, July 20, 1993, http://boatharbour.kingsjournalism.com/wordpress/wp-content/uploads/pdfs/15.199335millionagreement.pdf, copy on file with the author.

18 Henry Ferguson to Rust Associates, March 24, 1970, http://boatharbour.kingsjournalism.com/wordpress/documents/, copy on file with the author.

19 "Special Report: The Death of Boat Harbour," 22.

20 Ibid., 26; Reverend D. Glass, Sharon-Saint John United Church Stellarton, to Premier G.I. Smith, August 16, 1970, http://boatharbour.kingsjournalism.com/wordpress/wp-content/uploads/pdfs/09.1970smithfromchurch.pdf, copy on file with the author; Dr. J.B. MacDonald to Rust Associates Consulting Engineers, March 22, 1970, http://boat-harbour.kingsjournalism.com/wordpress/wp-content/uploads/pdfs/07.1970macDonaldLetterComplete.pdf, copy on file with the author.

21 "Special Report: The Death of Boat Harbour," 23; Reverend D. Glass, Sharon-Saint John United Church Stellarton, to Premier G.I. Smith, August 16, 1970, http://boatharbour.kingsjournalism.com/wordpress/wp-content/uploads/pdfs/09.1970smithfromchurch.pdf, copy on file with the author.

22 Tom Murphy, "Why Don't You Talk about the East River and Shut-Up about Boat Harbour," *Mysterious East,* October 1970, 29–30.

23 "Report by J.A. Delaney and Associates on Pollution in Boat Harbour," Dalhousie University Archives and Special Collections, Dalhousie University Institute of Public Affairs/Henson College fonds, UA-26, box 116.6.

24 "Special Report: The Death of Boat Harbour," 22, 26.

25 Ibid., 22.

26 J.B. MacDonald to Premier Stanfield, March 19, 1966, http://boatharbour.kingsjournalism. com/wordpress/wp-content/uploads/pdfs/03.1966Macdonaldhammletter.pdf, copy on file with the author.

27 "Ecology Supplement," *4th Estate,* September 1972, 19.

28 "Special Report: The Death of Boat Harbour," 23.

29 A pipe.

30 Robert Martin, "Purcell's Cove: Look Quick a Sewage Treatment Plant," *Mysterious East,* June 1970), 11–13; J.J. Betlam, Bedford United Church Social Action Chairman, and R.G. McClung, United Church Women President, to Premier Regan, January 13, 1971, Public Archives of Nova Scotia, Gerald Regan fonds, RG100 [hereafter REGAN], vol. 78, no. 36–6b.

31 Bedford Basin Pollution Committee, *Report of the Bedford Basin Pollution Committee of the Council of the Bedford Service Commission* (Bedford: Bedford Service Commission, 1970).

32 S.R. Kerr, "The McLaren Report: A Treatment Plant at Purcell's Cove," *Mysterious East,* December 1970, 19–20; E.L.L. Rowe to D.R. MacDonald, Minister under the Water Act, August 14, 1970, REGAN, vol. 116, no. 1.

33 Major site proposals during the following years included the tip of Point Pleasant Park, McNab's Island, the area around York Redoubt, and the locations of the plants existing at the time of writing.

34 "Brief to Canadian Preparatory Committee for the UN Conference on the Human Environment," April 28, 1972, Dalhousie University Archives and Special Collections, Movement for Citizens Voice and Action fonds, MS-11-1, [hereafter MOVE] box 6.35.

35 "Pictou Area Successfully Combating Water Pollution at Boat Harbour," *Chronicle-Herald,* January 2, 1974, 25.

36 Donald Savoie, *Regional Economic Development: Canada's Search for Solutions* (Toronto: University of Toronto, 1992), 6–7.

37 Silver Donald Cameron, interview with the author, November 1, 2011.

38 *Report of the Task Force Operation Oil (Clean-up of the Arrow Oil Spill in Chedabucto Bay) to the Minister of Transport* (Ottawa: Information Canada, 1970), 9.

39 Ibid.

40 Ironically, the *Irving Whale* also sank with a load of Bunker C oil, north of Prince Edward Island on September 7, 1970, causing another major spill and necessitating a laborious recovery. Environment Canada, Emergencies Science and Technology Division, "Bunker C Fuel Oil (Irving Whale)," http://www.etc-cte.ec.gc.ca/databases/Oilproperties/pdf/ WEB_Bunker_C_Fuel_Oil_(Irving_Whale).pdf.

41 Silver Donald Cameron, interview with the author, November 1, 2011; *Report of the Task Force Operation Oil;* "Chedabucto Bay: Waiting for the End," *Mysterious East,* July 1971, 34.

42 "Chedabucto Bay: Waiting for the End," 34. The answer took eight more years to arrive, with the wreck of the *Kurdistan* on March 15, 1979. "Oil Clean-Up Continues on Cape Breton Coast," *Mail-Star,* April 18, 1979, 2; J.H. Vandermeulen and D.E. Buckley, "The

Kurdistan Oil Spill of March 16–17, 1979: Activities and Observations of the Bedford Institute of Oceanography Response Team," Canadian Technical Report of Hydrography and Ocean Sciences No. 35 (Ottawa, January 1985), http://www.dfo-mpo.gc.ca/Library/90618.pdf. However, spills from the Gulf refinery itself were frequent enough that the management called a 12,000-gallon spill in 1972 "one of the mildest ones we've had." David Bentley, "Bunker C Spill: No Danger," *Chronicle-Herald*, June 22, 1972, 23.

43   Shelburne Harbour, Sydney Harbour, and Cole Harbour were notable others.

44   Silver Donald Cameron, interview with the author, November 1, 2011; Alan Ruffman, interview with the author, February 21, 2012. The Bedford Basin group listed ninety-one members in its report, about half to each gender. Bedford Basin Pollution Committee, *Report of the Bedford Basin Pollution Committee*.

45   Silver Donald Cameron, interview with the author, November 1, 2011.

46   Donald Worster argues that the "age of ecology" began with the explosion of the first atomic bomb in 1945. Donald Worster, *Nature's Economy* (Cambridge: Cambridge University Press, 1998), 342.

47   Robert Gottlieb, *Forcing the Spring: The Transformation of the American Environmental Movement* (Washington, DC: Island Press, 1993); Martinez-Alier, *Environmentalism of the Poor;* Guha, *How Much Should a Person Consume?* Hays, *Beauty, Health, and Permanence.*

48   Carson, *Silent Spring;* Garret Hardin, "The Tragedy of the Commons," *Science* 162, no. 3859 (December 13, 1968): 1243–48; Donella Meadows et al., *The Limits to Growth* (New York: Universe, 1972); E.F. Schumacher, *Small Is Beautiful* (London: Blond and Briggs, 1973). For an overview, see Gary Haq and Alistair Paul, *Environmentalism since 1945* (London: Routledge, 2012).

49   Ken Hartnett, "Encounter on the Urban Environment: Historian's Report," MOVE, box 25.13.

50   "Encounter on Metro Area," MOVE, box 25.10.

51   "Kentville Meeting minutes," MOVE, box 25.8.

52   "Kentville Meeting minutes," MOVE, box 25.8; Brenda Large, "Kentville Huddle Huge Success," *4th Estate,* March 4, 1971, 1.

53   Africville was a Black community in Halifax demolished in the 1960s, leaving a lasting feeling of anger among many of its former residents. The Heritage Trust group simply wished to curb the city's habit of demolishing many other venerable neighbourhoods and buildings. See Nelson, *Razing Africville;* Heritage Trust of Nova Scotia, *Annual Report 1970–1971* (Halifax: The Trust, 1971).

54   Carla Laufer, "Information Must Be Taken to the People: Where Is the Real Power behind Metro Planning?" *4th Estate,* January 14, 1971, 3.

55   "Encounter on Metro Area," MOVE, box 25.10.

56   "ECO Newsletter," March 1970, Public Archives of Nova Scotia, Ecology Action Centre fonds, MG20 [hereafter PANS-EAC], vol. 3434, file 28.

57   "Kentville Meeting minutes," MOVE, box 25.8; Large, "Kentville Huddle Huge Success," 1; *MOVE Bulletin* 1, no. 1 (September 1971), MOVE, box 6.31.

58   Brian Gifford, interview with the author, February 22, 2013; "Experimental Ecology 300000: A Resume of the First Term," Brian Gifford papers.

59   Brian Gifford to Hal Blackadar, CHNS Radio, April 17, 1974, DAL-EAC, box 42.3.

60   *Fine Print,* 1974, DAL-EAC, box 38.1.

61   Brian Gifford, interview with the author, February 22, 2013; "Ecology Action Centre – L.I.P. Project & MOVE," October 1972, Brian Gifford papers.

62 Brian Gifford to "Ian [MacDougall], Linda [Ruffman], Bernie [Hart], and Dennis [Patterson]," October 31, 1973, PANS-EAC, vol. 3420, no. 17.

63 The limits theory held uncommon currency in 1972 and 1973, attracting support from a visiting Roman Catholic archbishop and a Universalist Unitarian minister in the city, for example, in addition to the more expected enthusiasts like Gifford at the EAC. "Society Must Change or Collapse – Bishop," *Chronicle-Herald*, June 8, 1972, 21; "Universalist Unitarian Church newsletter," 7, no. 23 (March 27, 1972), Public Archives of Nova Scotia, Universalist Unitarian Church fonds, MG4, vol. 347, no. 2. For more on limits thinking, see Chapter 3.

64 "EAC Brief on Environmental Protection Act," March 3, 1973, PANS-EAC, vol. 3432, no. 18.

65 Alan MacEachern, *Natural Selections: National Parks in Atlantic Canada, 1935–1970* (Montreal and Kingston: McGill-Queen's University Press, 2001).

66 Claire Campbell, ed., *A Century of Parks Canada, 1911–2011* (Calgary: University of Calgary, 2011).

67 Alison Froese-Stoddard, "Ship Harbour National Park: The Breakdown between National Agendas and Local Interests," unpublished manuscript (2011–12). Adapted to Alison Froese-Stoddard, "A Conservation 'Could Have Been': Ship Harbour National Park," NiCHE Canada, *The Otter* blog, http://niche-canada.org/node/10446.

68 Danielle Robinson, "Modernism at a Crossroad: The Spadina Expressway Controversy in Toronto, Ontario ca. 1960–1971," *Canadian Historical Review* 92, no. 2 (June 2011): 295–322.

69 Editorial, *Dartmouth Free Press,* July 12, 1973, clipping file, REGAN, vol. 84, no. 38; "March of the 'Kooks,'" *Mail-Star,* May 15, 1973, 6.

70 APES to Jean Chrétien, July 9, 1973, REGAN, vol. 84, no. 38.

71 "Rear Door Regan Ducks Park Protestors," *Dartmouth Free Press,* May 16, 1973, 1; APES to Jean Chrétien, July 9, 1973, REGAN, vol. 84, no. 38.

72 "Kooks Win! Regan Dumps Federal Park Plan," *Dartmouth Free Press,* December 26, 1973, clipping file, REGAN, vol. 84, no. 38; *Evening News,* May 11, 1973, clipping file, REGAN, vol. 84, no. 38; Gordon Hammond, "Government Should Withdraw Its Proposals," *Chronicle-Herald,* March 12, 1973, 7.

73 *MOVE Bulletin,* December 13, 1972, MOVE, box 6.23; "Kooks Win! Regan Dumps Federal Park Plan," ibid.; Hammond, ibid.

74 P. Thomas, "The Kouchibouguac National Park Controversy: Over a Decade Strong," *Park News* 17, no. 1 (1981): 11–13.

75 Wilfrid Creighton, and Kenneth Donovan, "Wilfrid Creighton & the Expropriations: Clearing Land for the National Park, 1936," *Cape Breton's Magazine* 69 (August 1995): 1–20; "Regan Government Regenerates Interest in Wreck Cove Hydro-Electric Development," *Chronicle-Herald,* April 9, 1974, 25.

76 "Park Controversy Ended?" *Mail-Star,* December 21, 1973, clipping file, REGAN, vol. 84, no. 38; "Kooks Win! Regan Dumps Federal Park Plan," *Dartmouth Free Press,* December 26, 1973, clipping file, REGAN, vol. 84, no. 38.

77 Irene Edwards to Premier Regan, July 6, 1973, REGAN, vol. 84, no. 38.

78 Carson, *Silent Spring.*

79 W.P. Kerr, Deputy Minister of Transportation, to Alan Steel, coordinator of the Royal Commission on Forestry, August 3, 1982, Public Archives of Nova Scotia, Nova Scotia Royal Commission on Forestry fonds RG44, [hereafter RCOF], vol. 186, no. 5.

80 Bill Templeman, "The Soft Spray Job," *Mysterious East,* October 1971, 7–14; "The Warren Story," *Queens/Lunenburg SSEPA News* [hereafter *Q/L SSEPA News*] 2, no. 3 (Summer 1983): 24–26; Brenda Large, "2,4,5-T Leaves Path of Destruction," *4th Estate,* June 17, 1971, 14–16.

81 Templeman, "The Soft Spray Job," 8.

82 Ibid., 8.

83 Ibid., 12.

84 Ibid., 8; Nick Fillmore, "A Long Nightmare Follows Defoliant," *Globe and Mail,* April 10, 1971, 8; Brenda Large, "Chemical Kills N.S. Animals: No Action on Warren Farm Case," *4th Estate,* June 17, 1971, 1, 18; Large, "2,4,5-T Leaves Path of Destruction," 14–16.

85 Templeman, "The Soft Spray Job," 12.

86 Ibid., 13.

87 Letter from Rosemary Eaton, Cole Harbour Environment Committee, to J.E. Hutchinson, NSRF, April 6, 1972, DAL-EAC, MS-11-13, box 24.5; *MOVE Bulletin,* January 11, 1973, MOVE, DAL, MS-11-1, box 6.21; Roger Bacon, MLA Cumberland East, to Premier Regan, regarding Amherst Pollution Committee, n.d., REGAN, vol. 78, no. 36–6b; Province of Nova Scotia, *Annual Report: Environmental Control Council: For the Year Ending Dec. 31 1974,* Department of Environment Library, reference number 354.33, 14–15.

88 Letter from Glen Bagnell to Rosemary Eaton, December 6, 1972, DAL-EAC, MS-11-13, box 24.5; *Chronicle-Herald,* October 19, 1972, clipping file, REGAN, vol. 94, no. 3.

89 Templeman, "The Soft Spray Job," 11.

90 Ibid., 13.

91 J.L. Kirby to David Watts, US Department of the Interior, January 15, 1971, REGAN, vol. 78, no. 36–6b.

92 Memo on "Possibilities of co-ordination and integration of effort in the field of environmental affairs for discussion at the forthcoming meeting of the Premiers of the three Maritime Provinces," May 1971, REGAN, vol. 78, no. 36–6b.

93 Kirby to Rowe, March 26, 1973, REGAN, vol. 83, no. 10.

94 E.L.L. Rowe, Chairman of Water Resources Commission, to Kirby, April 17, 1973, REGAN, vol. 84, no. 37; Rowe to Bagnell, March 22, 1973, REGAN, vol. 83, no. 10.

95 J.L. Kirby to David Watts, US Department of the Interior, January 15, 1971, REGAN, vol. 78, no. 36–6b.

96 Summary of points on citizen input, Glen Bagnell, Minister of Environment, 1973, Public Archives of Nova Scotia, Man and Resources Program fonds, MG20, vol. 891; E.L.L. Rowe, "Brief on Pollution for Premier," January 19, 1970, REGAN, vol. 78, no. 36–6b.

97 Memo, "Environmental Conservation Council," REGAN, vol. 78, no. 36–6b.

98 Joan Fraser, "New Hardboard Plant Opens in Nova Scotia," *Montreal Gazette,* July 5, 1967, 23; William Chanclor and Pat Murphy, "Robert Whiting: What One Man Can Do," *Axiom* 2, no. 4 (May 1976): 9.

99 Brief to ECC [Environmental Control Council] on "Potential Effects of Anil Effluent That Could Not Have Been Detected in Prior Surveys," by Norman Dale, Dalhousie University Institute for Environment Studies, 1974, PANS-EAC, vol. 3432, no. 19.

100 Environmental Control Council (C.A. Campbell, Malcolm Moores, and Dr. J.G. Ogden) to G.M. Bagnell, Minister of Environment, January 31, 1975, Department of Environment Library, reference no. L778 75/01.

101 Chanclor and Murphy, "Robert Whiting," 9.

102 Martin Hunt, "The Brave New World of the Canada Water Act," *Mysterious East,* November 1969, 10.

103 "Anil Complies with Cleanup," *Chronicle-Herald,* June 1, 1972, 4.

104 Chanclor and Murphy, "Robert Whiting," 6–9, 21; Martin Haase, interview with the author, October 9, 2011.

105 Brief to ECC on "Potential Effects of Anil Effluent That Could Not Have Been Detected in Prior Surveys," by Norman Dale, Dalhousie University Institute for Environment Studies, PANS-EAC, vol. 3432, no. 19; Martin Haase, interview with the author, October 9, 2011; Alan Ruffman, interview with the author, February 21, 2012; Chanclor and Murphy, "Robert Whiting," 6–9, 21.

106 Chanclor and Murphy, ibid.; ECC (C.A. Campbell, Malcolm Moores, and Dr. J.G. Ogden) to G.M. Bagnell, Minister of Environment, January 31, 1975, Department of Environment Library, reference no. L778 75/01.

107 Province of Nova Scotia, *Annual Report – Environmental Control Council: For the Year Ending Dec. 31 1975,* DAL-EAC, box 41.20; Alan Ruffman, interview with the author, February 21, 2012.

108 Chanclor and Murphy, "Robert Whiting," 9. The Nova Scotia government also participated in a national consultative process called the "Man and Resources" program in 1971–73, which once again left activists disappointed with the results. *Bulletin of the Man and Resources Conference Program* 2, no. 2 (November 1972), Public Archives of Nova Scotia, Man and Resources Program fonds, MG20, vol. 891; *Bulletin of the Man and Resources Conference Program* 2, no. 6 (April 1973), Public Archives of Nova Scotia, Man and Resources Program fonds, MG20, vol. 891; "Environmental Improvement Committee – notes of first meeting," February 2, 1973, MOVE, box 11.12.

109 There was one other notable public hearing by the ECC, into a landfill siting process in Halifax County, but the minister refused to release the council's report for publication. Alan Ruffman, interview with the author, February 21, 2012; Gordon Black, "Jack Lake – 'Interference at the Highest Level,'" *Chronicle-Herald,* March 10, 1976, 7.

110 Irene Edwards to Premier Regan, July 6, 1973, REGAN, vol. 84, no. 38.

Chapter 2: The Two MECs

1 "Air of Secrecy Surrounds Talks," *Chronicle-Herald,* June 6, 1972, 1.

2 Alan Ruffman, interview with the author, February 21, 2012.

3 Silver Donald Cameron, *The Education of Everett Richardson: The Nova Scotia Fishermen's Strike 1970–71* (Toronto: McLelland and Stewart, 1977).

4 Sales slowed even further in the mid-1970s, after India's first nuclear weapons test in 1974 using plutonium created in its Canadian reactor; stricter safeguards against the diversion of weapons-grade material blunted the appeal of a reactor that, civilian or not, had always been advertised as the world's most efficient plutonium maker.

5 Gordon Edwards, "Canada's Nuclear Industry and the Myth of the Peaceful Atom," in *Canada and the Nuclear Arms Race,* ed. Ernie Regehr and Simon Rosenblum (Toronto: James Lorimer, 1983), 122–70; Robert Bothwell, *Nucleus: The History of Atomic Energy of Canada Limited* (Toronto: University of Toronto Press, 1988).

6 "Regan Denies Talks," *Chronicle-Herald,* August 8, 1972, 3.

7 "Nuclear Danger Feared," *Chronicle-Herald,* June 13, 1972, 17.

8 "Federal Assistance for Proposed Nuclear Plant 'Not Likely Unless ...,'" *Chronicle-Herald,* June 10, 1972, 2; Ralph Surette, *Montreal Star,* September 22, 1973, clipping file, PANS-EAC, vol. 3434, no. 2.

9   Ralph Surette, ibid.; "N.S. Residents Should Demand Answers – Doane," *Chronicle-Herald*, June 7, 1972, 4; "Former Resources Official Concerned by Nuclear Plan," *Chronicle-Herald*, June 7, 1972, 4; Ralph Surette, "What Is Public, What Is Secret?" *4th Estate*, October 15, 1975, 7.

10 Nuclear Power Plant Sub-Committee Meeting minutes, MOVE, box 11.16; Letter from S. Baskwill, MOVE, to the Editor, *Chronicle-Herald*, n.d., MOVE, box 11.16.

11 Perhaps unsurprising, given that physics professor Roy Bishop, who was largely responsible for its lengthy explanations of the science of nuclear fission, later went on to produce pro-nuclear material for AECL. Dr. Roy Bishop, interview with the author, January 16, 2012.

12 Information packet on Stoddard Island, n.d., DAL-EAC, box 37.3.

13 "Some Facts on the Problems and Dangers of Atomic Energy," December 1972, PANS-EAC, vol. 3421, no. 20.

14 "Policy Statement on the Proposed Stoddard Island Nuclear Power Plant," March 20, 1973, DAL-EAC, box 37.3; "Some Facts on the Problems and Dangers of Atomic Energy," December 1972, PANS-EAC, vol. 3421, no. 20.

15 "Participate in Energy Policy," EAC application to OFY, 1973, DAL-EAC, box 39.6; Brian Gifford to Ian MacLaren, CNF Halifax, November 16, 1973, DAL-EAC, box 42.3.

16 "Lobster Fishermen Would Fight Plant," *Chronicle-Herald*, June 17, 1972, 4; "Some Facts on the Problems and Dangers of Atomic Energy," December 1972, PANS-EAC, vol. 3421, no. 20; "Necessary to Get All the Facts, Says Regan," *Chronicle-Herald*, October 25, 1973, 10; "Participate in Energy Policy," EAC application to OFY, 1973, DAL-EAC, box 39.6.

17 "Necessary to Get All the Facts, Says Regan," *Chronicle-Herald*, 10.

18 Bruce Little, "Glace Bay Plant: Trying to Fix Costly Blunder," *Montreal Gazette*, May 16, 1973, 33; AECL, *Canada Enters the Nuclear Age* (Montreal and Kingston: McGill-Queen's University Press, 1997), 337; Robert Campbell, "Heavy Water: Jewel to Millstone," *Mysterious East*, August 1970, 11–13. The Glace Bay plant was officially opened in 1967 but did not function until 1975, while the Port Hawkesbury plant began operations in 1970 but operated at far less than full capacity until refurbished in 1974.

19 The risks posed by exposure to low-level radiation are a well-known and bitterly contested point of debate among activists, nuclear scientists, and medical researchers, as they have been since the famous Russell-Einstein Manifesto on radioactive fallout in 1955.

20 ECC meeting report, November 26, 1973, DAL-EAC, box 41.20.

21 Egbers, "Going Nuclear."

22 "Nuclear Route Likely for N.S.," *Mail-Star*, October 2, 1974, 1.

23 EAC Board of Directors Meeting minutes, October 7, 1974, PANS-EAC, vol. 3420, no. 18; Brian Gifford to Bill Zimmerman, November 13, 1974, PANS-EAC, vol. 3420, no. 17.

24 Francis Early, "'A Grandly Subversive Time': The Halifax Branch of the Voice of Women in the 1960s," in *Mothers of the Municipality*, ed. Judith Fingard and Janet Guildford (Toronto: University of Toronto Press, 2005), 258.

25 *VOW National Newsletter* 9, no. 3, November 1972, PANS-EAC, vol. 3434, no. 28; "MOVE bulletin," December 13, 1972, MOVE, box 6.23.

26 Early, "'A Grandly Subversive Time,'" 263.

27 Susan Holtz to Doris Calder, November 1, 1974, DAL-EAC, box 41.7.

28 Ibid.

29 Alan Ruffman, interview with the author, February 21, 2012.

30 Susan Holtz to Anne [Wickens], February 14, 1975, DAL-EAC, box 41.7.

31 Dorothy Norvell to Donna Elliott, VOW Ontario, n.d., DAL-EAC, box 42.3; Dorothy Norvell to Orville Erickson, CWF, December 11, 1974, DAL-EAC, box 42.3; Lille d'Easum to Dorothy Norvell, December 28, 1974, DAL-EAC, box 42.3; Susan Holtz to Dick Lurie, December 9, 1974, DAL-EAC, box 42.3; Susan Holtz to Karen Alcock, Energy Probe, May 12, 1975, DAL-EAC, box 38.16; EAC Board of Directors Meeting minutes, January 9, 1975, PANS-EAC, vol. 3420, no. 19.

32 Anne Wickens to Susan Holtz, October 4, 1974, October 25, 1974, PANS-EAC, vol. 3423, no. 30.

33 SSEPA press release, October 7, 1974, Public Archives of Nova Scotia, South Shore Environmental Protection Association fonds, MG20 [hereafter PANS-SSEPA], vol. 1016, no. 27–27j; "Nuclear Route Likely for N.S.," *Mail-Star,* October 2, 1974, 1.

34 "Nuclear Power in Eastern Canada," Hattie Perry, n.d., PANS-SSEPA, vol. 1016, no. 27–27j.

35 "Group Formed to Oppose N.B. Plant," *Chronicle-Herald,* April 8, 1974, 2.

36 "Maritime Coalition of Environmental Protection Associations," document, n.d. [1974], PANS-SSEPA, vol. 1016, no. 27–27j. Participation from Prince Edward Island was small, rather like its participation in the proposed energy corporation. Though the Institute of Man and Resources was widely admired, it did not join in activist activity and was generally seen as a government agency. Only one group from PEI in the late 1970s, Help Our Provincial Environment (HOPE), is recorded to have participated in the MEC.

37 "CCNR newsletter," August 1976, PANS-EAC, vol. 3422, no. 1; EAC Board of Directors Meeting minutes, April 1, 1976, PANS-EAC, vol. 3420, no. 20; EAC Board of Directors Meeting minutes, March 4, 1976, PANS-EAC, vol. 3420, no. 20.

38 EAC Board of Directors Meeting minutes, June 25, 1975, PANS-EAC, vol. 3420, no. 19; Susan Holtz to Joe and Helen Bongiovanni, February 5, 1975, DAL-EAC, box 41.7. The CSG presence within the EAC lasted for many years, long enough to remake the organization entirely, especially during the "two Susans" era, from 1975 to 1980, when Susan Mayo as coordinator and Susan Holtz as energy researcher put their stamp on every aspect of the centre's activity. For some examples, see Board of Directors membership lists, PANS-EAC, vol. 3420, no. 23–24.

39 Donald Hamilton, NORDA, to Susan Mayo, July 29, 1975, DAL-EAC, box 42.4.

40 Susan Holtz to Liberty Pease, AECL, May 5, 1975, PANS-EAC, vol. 3421, no. 20; Susan Holtz to J. Blair Seaborn, Deputy Minister Environment Canada, June 8, 1975, PANS-EAC, vol. 3423, no. 7.

41 Susan Holtz to Anne Wickens, November 25, 1974, DAL-EAC, box 42.3.

42 "Dorothy" to "Carla," November 1974, DAL-EAC, box 41.7; Susan Holtz to Anne Wickens, November 25, 1974, DAL-EAC, box 42.3.

43 World oil prices had tripled by the end of that year, and would continue to rise through the rest of the decade, to the point that a barrel of oil that had cost $2 before the crisis cost an unprecedented $35 in 1981. Francisco Parra, *Oil Politics: A Modern History of Petroleum* (London: I.B. Tauris, 2004); MacEachern, *The Institute of Man and Resources,* 12–13.

44 *Energy and People Conference Proceedings,* October 1975, MOVE, box 22.1.

45 The term achieved unexpected popularity following the SCC report, and the council issued three follow-up reports over the next ten years, including one in 1977 written under the chairmanship of Ursula Franklin, then a renowned scientist, anti-nuclear activist, Voice of Women member, and Quaker. Science Council of Canada, *Natural Resource Policy Issues in Canada,* Report No. 19 (Ottawa: SCC, 1973); Science Council of Canada, *Canada as a*

Conserver Society: Resource Uncertainties and the Need for New Technologies, Report No. 27 (Ottawa: SCC, 1977).

46 *Energy and People Conference Proceedings,* October, 1975, MOVE, box 22.1.

47 See for example, Doris McMullan, Probe Ottawa, to Susan Holtz, August 11, 1975, PANS-EAC, vol. 3422, no. 1. McMullan was on CCNR's steering committee, and Holtz was on its policy committee. Also, describing the group's "rather conservative approach" as a positive feature: Susan Holtz to CCNR, March 14, 1979, DAL-EAC, box 44.1.

48 "Keynote – Dr. Gordon Edwards," *Energy and People Conference Proceedings,* October 1975, MOVE, box 22.1.

49 "Energy Policy Panel," *Energy and People Conference Proceedings,* October 1975, MOVE, box 22.1.

50 *Energy and People Conference Proceedings,* October 1975, MOVE, box 22.1. An account of the resolutions debate was also printed in the activist paper *Nuclear Reaction,* Winter 1975–76, DAL-EAC, box 41.7.

51 For example, "Some Energy Proposals 'Irresponsible,'" *Mail-Star,* September 22, 1975, 5.

52 "Follow-up Notes from Energy and People Conference," October 30, 1975, PANS-EAC, vol. 3422, no. 21.

53 J.R. Helliwell to Susan Holtz, March 3, 1976, DAL-EAC, box 42.4.

54 EAC Board of Directors Meeting minutes, May 6, 1976, PANS-EAC, vol. 3420, no. 20.

55 Notes from APEC energy seminar, January 21, 1976, PANS-EAC, vol. 3421, no. 18; Energy Options Committee Meeting minutes, January 1976, DAL-EAC, box 32.32.

56 Energy Options Committee minutes, November 29, 1975, DAL-EAC, box 32.32; Surette, "What Is Public, What Is Secret?" 7.

57 Susan Holtz to CCNR, March 14, 1979, DAL-EAC, box 44.1.

58 "Discussion on the Nuclear Option – Some Impressions," EMR planning and evaluation note, November 21, 1975, DAL-EAC, box 42.4; Gordon Edwards, "Nuclear Wastes: What, Me Worry?" 1978, http://www.ccnr.org/me_worry.html.

59 Call transcript, Susan Mayo and Ray Bouchard, August 12, 1977, PANS-EAC, vol. 3424, no. 5.

60 In New Brunswick, activists complained that "the federal government is buying off opposition to its policies" with empty consultation: *Nuclear Reaction,* June 9–11, 1978. The same journal had noted the previous year that "renewable energy is receiving attention mainly through the political expedient of keeping a vocal (eg: anti-nuclear) group quiet": *Nuclear Reaction,* April 30, 1977. Even one of Susan Holtz's friends at EMR told her that "Alastair [Gillespie of EMR] may be trading off renewables and conservation": John [MacEwan] to Susan [Holtz], n.d., PANS-EAC, vol. 3422, no. 38.

61 Notes from CEAC meeting, March 15, 1977, DAL-EAC, box 39.1.

62 Notes from CEAC meeting, November 21/22, 1977, DAL-EAC, box 39.1.

63 EAC Board of Directors Meeting minutes, June 1, 1978, PANS-EAC, vol. 3420, no. 22.

64 Robert Bott, David Brooks, and John Robinson, *Life after Oil* (Edmonton: Hurtig, 1983), 9; "FOE Workshop, October 8–10, 1978," DAL-EAC, box 28.15.

65 "A Soft Energy Path for Nova Scotia," EAC press release, November 24, 1977, DAL-EAC, box 28.14. Even the press noted the elite status of the audience for the soft path effort. Michael Shea at the CBC called the Halifax event a "bauble of the rich" and pointed out that nearly all of the attendees earned $20,000 or more annually: Sylvia Mangalam to Michael Shea, December 1977, DAL-EAC, box 42.9.

66 Amory Lovins and Hunter Lovins, "Introduction," in Bott, Brooks, and Robinson, *Life after Oil*, 4 [emphasis in original].

67 Ibid., 15–21.

68 "Special Report: A Soft Energy Path for Canada," *Alternatives* 12, no. 1 (Fall 1984).

69 Susan Holtz, *2025: Soft Energy Futures for Canada*, vol. 3, *A Soft Energy Path for Nova Scotia* (Ottawa: Energy, Mines and Resources, 1983). The population of the province in fact grew approximately 8.7 percent from 1981 to 2011. Statistics Canada, *Census Divisions and Subdivisions, Population, Occupied Private Dwellings, Private Households and Census and Economic Families in Private Households, Selected Social and Economic Characteristics, Nova Scotia* (Toronto: Statistics Canada, 1983), http://archive.org/details/1981959851983engfra.

70 "Interview with Susan Mayo and Susan Holtz," *Dartmouth Free Press*, January 31, 1979, DAL-EAC, box 39.7.

71 "Energy Corporation Urged for Maritimes," *Chronicle-Herald*, October 20, 1976, 1.

72 EAC Board of Directors Meeting minutes, April 14, 1977, PANS-EAC, vol. 3420, no. 21; EAC press release, June 11, 1976, PANS-EAC, vol. 3432, no. 19.

73 *Jusun* 5, no. 5 (November 1977), DAL-EAC, box 28.14.

74 *Nuclear Reaction*, June 9–11, 1978. Many directed the same critique at EMR's Committee on Nuclear Issues in the Community, created in 1978 "to ease fears" among the public. An ecologist among its founding members promptly resigned from the panel of nuclear apologists, but FOE's David Brooks did later join, along with Greenpeace's Patrick Moore: "Committee on Nuclear Issues in the Community," March 1978, PANS-EAC, vol. 3422, no. 1.

75 Paul Armstrong to unknown recipient, May 5, 1978, DAL-EAC, box 28.1.

76 Tricia O'Brien, AVEC, to "Susan(s)," EAC, April 17, 1978, PANS-EAC, vol. 3421, no. 19; Hattie Perry to Tony Reddin, HOPE (PEI), December 21, 1977, PANS-EAC, vol. 3424, no. 1. There was also by 1978 a group in Antigonish, the "alternative energy group," that followed a similar path without creating a "centre" of any sort, and a Cape Breton Alternate Energy Society, a Fundy Solar Research group, and other smaller congregations: Sister Donna Brady to Susan Holtz, January 12, 1978, DAL-EAC, box 42.9; Notes from EMR Office of Energy Conservation Atlantic Group Workshop, February 23–25, 1978, PANS-EAC, vol. 3422, no. 27.

77 Barb Taylor to Susan Holtz, March 31, 1979, DAL-EAC, box 41.3; Barb Taylor to Ian MacPherson (federal candidate), April 10, 1979, DAL-EAC, box 41.3; FACT committee to Premier Buchanan and all MLAs, April 1979, DAL-EAC, box 41.3; FACT (David Simon) to all Councilors, Commissioners, and planning advisors in Annapolis County and the towns of Annapolis Royal, Bridgetown, Digby, Lawrencetown, Kingston, and Middleton, n.d. [April-May 1979], DAL-EAC, box 41.3; George deAlth to Susan Holtz, May/June 1979, DAL-EAC, box 41.3. The group reported sixteen core members and strong public support in 1979, enough that they could later split into eastern and western branches: "FACT Newsletter," October 1979, DAL-EAC, box 41.3.

78 "MEC (NS)," PANS-EAC, vol. 3423, no. 29; "HOPE of Colchester County brochure," 1979, PANS-EAC, vol. 3424, no. 21.

79 John Morrison, "NS Energy Awards Application for CBAES," 1978/79, DAL-EAC, box 42.9.

80 Dr. Ron Loucks to Premier Buchanan, April 7, 1979, PANS-EAC, vol. 3421, no. 14.

81 *It Can Happen Here*, leaflet, May 1979, PANS-EAC, vol. 3421, no. 16; Hattie Perry to the premier and all MLAs, April 11, 1979, DAL-EAC, box 41.3.

82 Multiple newspaper clippings, PANS-EAC, vol. 3421, no. 16.

83 Dana Silk represented New Brunswick and Tom Reddin Prince Edward Island. *The Eastern Graphic,* clipping file, PANS-EAC, vol. 3421, no. 16.

84 EAC Board of Directors Meeting minutes, June 13, 1979, PANS-EAC, vol. 3420, no. 23.

85 J. Wilson Fitt to Susan Holtz, April 27, 1979, PANS-EAC, vol. 3421, no. 14.

86 Susan Holtz to Ursula Franklin, SCC, January 9, 1978, DAL-EAC, box 32.7; Susan Holtz to Premier Buchanan, June 18, 1979, DAL-EAC, box 44.1; Susan Holtz to Premier Buchanan, May 24, 1979, PANS-EAC, vol. 3421, no. 16.

87 Brief to the Premiers at Brudenell, June 4, 1979, PANS-EAC, vol. 3421, no. 16. The petition they offered accumulated fifteen thousand names by early 1980: EAC Board of Directors Meeting minutes, March 12, 1980, PANS-EAC, vol. 3420, no. 4.

88 David Folster, "Double Trouble – Power Bubble," *Maclean's,* October 6, 1980, 38–39.

89 EAC Board of Directors Meeting minutes, June 13, 1979, PANS-EAC, vol. 3420, no. 23.

90 Egbers, "Going Nuclear."

91 The warning came from Walt Patterson, in a letter to Susan Mayo, November 12, 1975, PANS-EAC, vol. 3422, no. 29.

92 Amy Zierler, "Laws to Protect Our Environment Are Feeble. They Just Don't Work," *Atlantic Insight* 1, no. 10 (December 1979): 44–49.

93 Notes from interview with minister Bill Gillis, by Susan Holtz, October 29, 1977, PANS-EAC, vol. 3424, no. 11.

94 Personal Report, Susan Holtz, January 6, 1977, PANS-EAC, vol. 3422, no. 34. The board of directors explicitly validated the strategy of "affecting policy decisions" by building the centre's "credible and respectable image and develop[ing] a sound basis for the policy options it presents." EAC, "Ecology Action Centre: A Public Interest Group Using Conservation and Renewable Energy," n.d. [c. 1979], PANS-EAC, vol. 3420, no. 4.

95 Solar Energy Research Institute symposium, September 12–13, 1978, DAL-EAC, box 28.13.

96 "Workshop on Energy Conservation and Community Economic Development," May 24–26, 1979, DAL-EAC, box 32.14.

CHAPTER 3: POWER FROM THE PEOPLE

1 Elizabeth May, *Budworm Battles* (Halifax: Four East, 1982), 8.

2 *Halifax Field Naturalists Newsletter* 3 (January-February 1976): 11–14.

3 Scott Cunningham, "Aerial Spraying Plan Dangerous," *Chronicle-Herald,* March 1, 1976, 7; Susan Mayo, April 12, 1976, DAL-EAC, box 42.5; "The Spruce Budworm Problem," April 1976, DAL-EAC, box 24.5; EAC Board of Directors Meeting minutes, December 17, 1975, PANS-EAC, vol. 3420, no. 19.

4 "Cabinet Approves Budworm Spraying Request," *Chronicle-Herald,* March 27, 1976, 1; "The Spruce Budworm Problem," April 1976, DAL-EAC, box 24.5; Lloyd Hawboldt to Burgess, December 29, 1975, Public Archives of Nova Scotia, Department of Lands and Forests fonds, MG20 [hereafter DLF], vol. 890, no. 1.

5 May, *Budworm Battles,* 16, 28–29.

6 Parker B. Donham, "Fatal to Children: Disease May Be Linked to Budworm Spray," *Cape Breton Post,* March 31, 1976, 1; May, *Budworm Battles,* 19.

7 May, *Budworm Battles,* 12.

8 Ian McLaren, NSRC, "Spruce Budworm Spraying – Human Health Hazard," *Mail-Star,* April 2, 1976, 7; David Folster, "The Agonizing Fight over Budworm Spray," *Atlantic Insight* 1, no. 3 (June 1979): 34–36.

9 Proceedings of Regional Meeting "Forest Protection Against Spruce Budworm in Maine, Quebec, and New Brunswick," November 2, 1976, DLF, vol. 890, no. 2.

10 Lloyd Hawboldt to Gary Saunders, May 14, 1976, DLF, vol. 890, no. 1; R.M. Bulmer to E.S. Atkins, November 16, 1976, DLF, vol. 890, no. 2. The anti-spray group included Gary Saunders and N.A. Wiksten; the pro-spray group included Ed Cloney and E.S. Atkins, Planning Services Coordinator.

11 L. Anders Sandberg, "Forest Policy in Nova Scotia: The Big Lease, Cape Breton Island, 1899–1960," *Acadiensis* 20, no. 2 (Spring 1991): 124, n. 86; Memo, N.A. Wiksten to E.S. Atkins, November 16, 1976, DLF, vol. 890, no. 2. Wiksten was blunt, insisting that "the company knew what they bought." Department of Lands and Forests, *Nova Scotia Forest Inventory: Cape Breton Island Subdivision 1970* (Halifax: Lands and Forests, 1970), 17, 25.

The values underpinning chemical forestry were as well established as chemical forestry, for example, in New Brunswick. See McLaughlin, "Green Shoots." The wider story of Nova Scotia's forest policy can be found in Nova Scotia, *House of Assembly Debates* (1960), 73–74. Cited in Sandberg, "Forest Policy in Nova Scotia," 105–28. *Statutes of Nova Scotia*, c.6, 1942; *Statutes of Nova Scotia*, c.5, 1962; Harry Thurston, "Prest's Last Stand," in Harry Thurston, *The Sea among the Rocks* (East Lawrencetown, NS: Pottersfield Press, 2002), 184–220; Sandberg, "Forest Policy in Nova Scotia"; Memo, Lloyd Hawboldt to Burgess, December 29, 1975, DLF, vol. 890, no. 1; Memo, N.A. Wiksten to E.S. Atkins, November 16, 1976, DLF, vol. 890, no. 2; Susan Mayo to Lloyd Hawboldt, October 15, 1976, DAL-EAC, box 42.5; L.S. Hawboldt, "Toward 'Budworm-Proofing' the Forests of Nova Scotia," 1976, DLF, vol. 890, no. 2.

12 Lloyd Hawboldt, "Toward 'Budworm-Proofing' the Forests of Nova Scotia," ibid.; R.M. Bulmer to Hollis Routledge, NSFI, November 16, 1976, DLF, vol. 890, no. 2; Proceedings of Regional Meeting "Forest Protection Against Spruce Budworm in Maine, Quebec, and New Brunswick," November 2, 1976, DLF, vol. 890, no. 2. The other jurisdictions' spray programs were established since 1954 (Maine), 1952 (New Brunswick), and 1970 (Quebec).

13 Lloyd Hawboldt to Gary Saunders, May 14, 1976, DLF, vol. 890, no. 1.

14 May, *Budworm Battles*, 27. Budworm forecasts are accomplished by counting the number of egg masses on conifer branches in the fall; the eggs will provide the following year's budworm population.

15 Editorial, *Evening News*, n.d., clipping file, Public Archives of Nova Scotia, Betty Peterson fonds, MG1 [hereafter PANS-BP], vol. 3469, no. 8.

16 Proceedings of Regional Meeting "Forest Protection Against Spruce Budworm in Maine, Quebec, and New Brunswick," November 2, 1976, DLF, vol. 890, no. 2.

17 Scott Paper, Bowater Mersey, Minas Basin Pulp and Power Company Limited, McLellan Lumber Company, Cobequid Lumber Company, to Vincent MacLean, Minister of Environment, December 8, 1976, DLF, vol. 890, no. 3.

18 "Budworm Politics: While Larvae Sleep, Political Forces Clash over Spraying," *4th Estate*, October 13, 1976, 4.

19 Miss Lettice Edwards, Shelburne, to Lands and Forests, December 6, 1976, DLF, vol. 890, no. 3; Susan Mayo to Norma Mosher, Women's Institutes of Nova Scotia, December 20, 1976, DAL-EAC, box 24.5; Susan Mayo to David Steadman, Association of Outdoor Nova Scotians, December 23, 1976, DAL-EAC, box 24.5; Anne Wickens, SSEPA, to all Cabinet members, December 2, 1976, DAL-EAC, box 24.5; Martin Haase to Ministers of Lands and Forests, Recreation, and Public Health, and the Premier, December 3, 1976, DAL-EAC, box 24.5.

At the intended date of decision, the Department of Lands and Forests had logged 899 letters and signatures received in opposition to the 1977 spray request, including the above as well as the Inverness/Guysborough Presbytery of the United Church, the Cape Breton Metropolitan Alliance for Development, and DEVCO's Marine Farming Research Branch at Baddeck. There were only 7 in favour: "Spruce Budworm Spray Program – 1976," December 15, 1976, DLF, vol. 890, no. 1.

20 May, *Budworm Battles,* 33, 45–46.

21 CBLAS poster, n.d., DAL-EAC, box 28.14.

22 Memo on CBLAS handbills, DLF, vol. 890, no. 4.

23 Jon Everett, "More Scary Questions in the Spray Debate," *Atlantic Insight* 4, no. 7 (July 1982): 12; May, *Budworm Battles,* 57–59.

24 Betty Peterson to Dorothy Norvell, February 7, 1977, PANS-BP, vol. 3469, no. 8; May, *Budworm Battles,* 74. Betty Peterson described the audience, which she put at over five hundred and decidedly anti-spray, as "organic food growers, beekeepers, oystermen, owners of lobster pounds, mothers with children, small woodlot owners, [and] rugged oldsters."

25 May, *Budworm Battles,* 76–77; "Spray Program Turned Down," *Chronicle-Herald,* February 4, 1977, 1.

26 May reported that information from Vince MacLean put the final number of supporting names at more than seven thousand (versus eighteen in favour of spraying): *Budworm Battles,* 78.

27 Ibid., 107–20.

28 Ibid., 116.

29 Ralph Surette, "Effort Made to End Abuse of Forests," *Globe and Mail,* August 5, 1978, 8. There was pressure within Lands and Forests to access even more federal money available to provinces with spray programs, such as the $7 million in additional funds granted to New Brunswick in 1976: Richard Butler, Administrative Assistant to the Deputy Minister of Environment, to Lloyd Hawboldt, April 6, 1976, DLF, vol. 890, no. 1.

30 Bruce Doern and Thomas Conway, *The Greening of Canada: Federal Institutions and Decisions* (Toronto: University of Toronto Press, 1994), 104–6. The Department of Energy, Mines and Resources did likewise in 1975, but soon lost interest: "Discussion on the Nuclear Option – Some Impressions," EMR planning and evaluation note, November 21, 1975, DAL-EAC, box 42.4.

31 The EAC met with the Atlantic Regional Board in 1976 and 1977: EAC Board of Directors Meeting minutes, July 8, 1976, PANS-EAC, vol. 3420, no. 20; EAC to Environment Canada Atlantic Regional Board, April 13, 1977, DAL-EAC, box 41.11.

32 EAC Board of Directors Meeting minutes, June 1, 1978, PANS-EAC, vol. 3420, no. 22.

33 Environment Canada, "Announcement: Public Consultation Transportation Expenses Assistance," 1984, DAL-EAC, box 43.5.

34 Joanne Lamey, Community Planning Association of Canada, "Notice of CEAC Meeting, Ottawa, 25–29 May, 1980," April 18, 1980, DAL-EAC, box 44.2. The threat of "co-optation" was consistently misunderstood by those who accepted such funding, even warily; there is little or no evidence that the money ever changed anyone's opinions, only that those already holding the desired opinions were selected (and self-selected) to receive the money. This is another case where blindness to the diversity of the environmental movement has created the illusion of novelty out of simple changes in the internal balance of power.

35 EAC Board of Directors Meeting minutes, November 14, 1979, PANS-EAC, vol. 3420, no. 23; Gilbert Savard, Citizens' Group Liaison, Department of Fisheries and Environment, to Susan Mayo, June 14, 1979, DAL-EAC, box 43.1.

36 Brian Gifford to Vince MacLean, April 14, 1977, DAL-EAC, box 24.5.

37 Memo, "Pete Ogden: Saturday March 9," DAL-EAC, box 41.20.

38 Vincent MacLean, n.d./n.s., clipping file, PANS-BP, vol. 3469, no. 8.

39 As an example of the use of concepts borrowed from industry, few can surpass the brief to the Task Force on Wood Allocation by the NSRC (and endorsed by the NSBS, HFN, and CNF). In it, these groups agreed on the need to "manage the threat of budworm," ideally with biological controls, to maximize the use of the forest resource, and to practise the most "intensive silviculture ... for the benefit of the total resources of Nova Scotia." DAL-EAC, box 24.5.

40 May, *Budworm Battles,* 132; Elizabeth May, "Qualified Approval Given Spray Test," n.d., PANS-BP, vol. 3469, no. 8.

41 EAC Board of Directors Meeting minutes, May 4, 1978, PANS-EAC, vol. 3420, no. 22; Vince MacLean to Brian Gifford, April 20, 1977, DAL-EAC, box 24.5; Vince MacLean to Gary Harris, Halifax, December 6, 1976, DLF, vol. 890, no. 3.

It was also a false claim, as the ECC had requested, directly to the previous minister himself, permission to hold hearings into the budworm spray issue ten months earlier: "Points for information discussion about spruce budworm control in Nova Scotia from technical advisory sub-committee, Nova Scotia Environmental Control Council," January 27, 1976, DLF, vol. 890, no. 1; E.L.L. Rowe, ECC, to Bagnell, Minister of Environment, February 4, 1976, DLF, vol. 890, no. 1.

42 Eve Smith, BC, to the Editor, *Jusun* (EAC), n.d. [c. 1978], DAL-EAC, box 42.8. The Queens/Lunenburg SSEPA also warned Nova Scotian environmentalists to "approach with caution" the Atlantic ENGO meeting arranged by Environment Canada, quoting David Brooks on the "threat of co-optation ... any time you take money." *Q/L SSEPA News* 1, no. 9 (January 1983), PANS-BP, vol. 3470, no. 6.

43 Memo, "Pete Ogden: Saturday March 9," DAL-EAC, box 41.20. (The EAC staff member who spoke with Ogden was quite defensive about it and preferred to see Ogden's position as an "anti-action-group stance.")

44 Elizabeth May, "A Case History of Citizen Action Victory," *PEI Environeer* 6, no. 3 (1978): 23.

45 "Harmless Spray?" *Rural Delivery* 4, no. 7 (December 1979); "EAC Brief to Public Utilities Board," April 3, 1979, PANS-EAC, vol. 3424, no. 21.

46 *Rural Delivery* 5, no. 10 (March 1981); "Waste Farm Chemicals," *Rural Delivery* 6, no. 11 (April 1982); Chris Wood, "Crop Sprays: Sickness and Death Down on the Farm," *Atlantic Insight* 4, no. 2 (February 1982): 38–43.

47 The Royal Commission on Forestry eventually collected records from various departments and corporations, showing herbicide use (often 2,4-D/2,4,5-T) by the Department of Transportation back to 1964, Department of Agriculture back to 1960, and Nova Scotia Power Corporation back to 1970 (an incomplete record). "Memos on chemicals," Public Archives of Nova Scotia, Royal Commission on Forestry fonds [hereafter RCOF], vol. 186, no. 5.

For the wider story, see David Kinkela, *DDT and the American Century* (Chapel Hill: University of North Carolina Press, 2011).

48 Gale Peterson, "The Discovery and Development of 2,4-D," *Agricultural History* 41, no. 3 (July 1967): 253.

49 Chris Arsenault, *Blowback: A Canadian History of Agent Orange and the War at Home* (Halifax: Fernwood, 2009), 60–64. The total use of Agent Orange alone in Vietnam is estimated at about 45 million litres. Edwin Martini, *Agent Orange: History, Science, and the Politics of Uncertainty* (Boston: University of Massachusetts Press, 2012).

50 Elizabeth Blum, *Love Canal Revisited: Race, Class, and Gender in Environmental Activism* (Lawrence: University Press of Kansas, 2008); Martini, *Agent Orange*, 126–37.

Others included the 1976 dioxin explosion at Seveso, Italy, the ongoing revelations of mercury poisoning and cover-ups at Minamata, Japan, and among the Grassy Narrows First Nation in Ontario, for example. Bruna De Marchi, "Seveso: From Pollution to Regulation," *International Journal of Environment and Pollution* 7, no. 4 (September 1997): 526–37; Paul Almeida and Linda Brewster Stearns, "Political Opportunities and Local Grassroots Environmental Movements: The Case of Minamata," *Social Problems* 45, no. 1 (February 1998): 37–60; George Hutchison and Dick Wallace, *Grassy Narrows* (Scarborough, ON: Van Nostrand Reinhold, 1977).

51 Arsenault, *Blowback*, 91.

52 Herbicides were used in forestry in New Brunswick as early as 1970: "Monitor," *Mysterious East*, November 1971, 24.

53 "ECC Annual Report, 1978," DAL-EAC, box 41.20; Alan Ruffman to Roger Bacon, Minister of Environment, July 16, 1979, DAL-EAC, box 41.20.

54 Government of Nova Scotia, *Supplement to the Public Accounts of the Province of Nova Scotia for the Year Ended March 31, 1977* (Halifax: Queen's Printer, 1978), 67; N.A. Wiksten, forestry economist, to Earl Atkins, Lands and Forests, January 9, 1978, DLF, vol. 890, no. 6; Memo from N.A. Wiksten to R.H. Burgess, October 20, 1977, DLF, vol. 890, no. 5; Parker Donham, "Who's Winning the War Over Chemical Spraying?" *Atlantic Insight* 4, no. 1 (January 1982): 24.

55 Gary Baudoux, New Glasgow, to George Henley, August 30, 1979, DLF, vol. 887, no. 3; George Henley to Gary Baudoux, n.d., DLF, vol. 887, no. 3; A.A. Pearson, Stellarton Town Clerk, to Doug Carter, Deputy Minister of Environment, September 20, 1979, DLF, vol. 887, no. 3; George Henley to Frank Craig, Trenton, September 10, 1979, DLF, vol. 887, no. 3.

Eldridge himself represented the Nova Scotia Department of Lands and Forests at the Eastern Spruce Budworm Council (with members from Ontario, Quebec, Nova Scotia, New Brunswick, Newfoundland, Maine, and the Canadian Forestry Service [CFS]), where he worked with spray advocates like CFS's I.W. Varty, who in 1980 offered a novel rationalization of the safety of insecticide sprays: no spray onto uninhabited land could be pollutant by definition, since only upon reaching people could any substance be considered pollution. *CANUSA Newsletter* 8 (January 1980), DLF, vol. 604, no. 5.

56 "Forest Industry 'Needs' Informed Public," *Forest Times* 3, no. 2 (March 1981).

57 *CANUSA Newsletter* 8 (January 1980), DLF, vol. 604, no. 5; Nova Scotia Government press release, 1982, DAL-EAC, box 24.5.

58 Environment Canada press release, August 23, 1978, DAL-EAC, box 24.5.

59 Quoted from Dirk VanLoon, "Roadside Spraying," *Rural Delivery* 7, no. 2 (July 1982). On the Crowdis Coalition, see Elizabeth May to "Susans," n.d., DAL-EAC, box 44.1.

60 Val Blofeld, Tantallon, to Susan Holtz, February 21, 1980, DAL-EAC, box 43.1.

61 "80/81 Board of Directors," *Jusun* 8, no. 3 (December 1980), PANS-EAC, vol. 3420, no. 3.

62 Vincent MacLean to Susan Mayo, September 21, 1977, DAL-EAC, box 42.6.

63 George Butters, "Spray Wars, Part Two," *Atlantic Insight* 4, no. 10 (October 1982): 10–11. The government also issued permits for the 1982 season on the day after the Legislature finished its session: "After the Herbicide Trial" (draft), DAL-EAC, box 24.9.

64 The injunction and suit were settled the following January without going to court. EAC Board of Directors Meeting minutes, March 25, 1981, PANS-EAC, vol. 3420, no. 25; J.D. Smith, Lands and Forests, to D.L. Eldridge (marginal notes), August 18, 1980, DLF, vol. 608, no. 13; Sheila Jones, "Big Pond Goes After a Big Fish," *Atlantic Insight* 2, no. 11 (November 1980): 26–27.

65 Vicki Palmer, "A Report on the Lochaber Spray Situation, Summer 1981," DAL-EAC, box 29.10; Petition, 1981, DAL-EAC, box 29.10.

66 Palmer, ibid.

67 "N.B. Looking at Same Defoliants Planned for Lochaber Spray Area," *Evening News*, July 16, 1981, 3.

68 Ginny Point, EAC, to "friends," January 14, 1982, DAL-EAC, box 29.1; Forestry Management Committee Strategy Meeting minutes, April 20, 1982, DAL-EAC, box 28.25. The April 20 meeting had sixteen attendees, all from the mainland; within about two months, the committee had representatives from several Cape Breton groups. The committee also went through several name changes, from "Forestry Management Committee" initially, to "Forestry (Toxic Substances) Committee" while still mainly a mainland group, to simply the "Forestry Committee." EAC Board of Directors Meeting minutes, March 23, 1982, PANS-EAC, vol. 3421, no. 1.

69 J.D. Smith, Lands and Forests, to D.L. Eldridge (marginal notes), August 18, 1980, DLF, vol. 608, no. 13.

70 EAC Board of Directors Meeting minutes, May 24, 1982, PANS-EAC, vol. 3421, no. 2; Q/L SSEPA press release, April 30, 1982, DAL-EAC, box 29.9; Notice of Public Lecture "You and Me and 2,4-D" by Murray Prest, Vicki Palmer, and Dr. Cameron McQueen, April 20, 1982, DAL-EAC, box 29.1.

71 Adam Ashforth, "Reckoning Schemes of Legitimation: On Commissions of Inquiry as Power/Knowledge Forms," *Journal of Historical Sociology* 3, no. 1 (March 1990): 1–22.

72 Alexa McDonough to EAC, April 27, 1982, DAL-EAC, box 29.1. There was also the co-incidence of a resolution by the Canadian Institute of Foresters, asking Nova Scotia to repeal the Forest Improvement Act. EAC press release, March 24, 1982, DAL-EAC, box 29.9.

73 EAC Board of Directors Meeting minutes, May 24, 1982, PANS-EAC, vol. 3421, no. 2; Ginny Point, EAC, to Greg Kerr, Minister of Environment, June 2, 1982, DAL-EAC, box 29.1; Greg Kerr to Ginny Point, June 17, 1982, DAL-EAC, box 29.1.

74 EAC Memo on FACT meeting with John Sansom, Department of Environment, April 19, 1982, DAL- EAC, box 29.7. Laura Colpitts joined the Women's Health Education Network presentation at the Royal Commission on Forestry to tell of her experience with public announcements coming after spraying had already been done: Presentation by WHEN, March 24, 1983, RCOF, vol. 159, no. 4.

75 Alternative modes of argument were best represented, incongruously, among the rural Cape Breton activists who made up the strongest supporters of the seventeen plaintiffs in the herbicide trial. Presentation by FALASH, October 8, 1982, RCOF, vol. 158a, no. 2.

76 "SSEPA Fact Sheet," May 1982, DAL-EAC, box 28.28; EAC press release, July 2, 1982, DAL-EAC, box 28.28; "Forest Herbicide Trial – Background," PANS-BP, vol. 3469, no. 8; Peter Cumming, "The Herbicide Fight," *Rural Delivery* 7, no. 12 (May 1983): 32.

Disputes over terminology were numerous. Perhaps the best example came in the course of Murray Prest's testimony before the Royal Commission on Forestry, when challenged by Commissioner Rev. Greg MacKinnon:

> MacKinnon: I don't think it's fair. I think it's using scare tactics to talk about Agent Orange. You know, that conjures up all kinds of things from Vietnam, when in fact the solution they were using was in fact laced with dioxin. I've seen the figures, I can't remember but –
>
> Prest: Up to 70 parts per million, as compared to our levels now is 0.1 parts per million. But the thing is, it's still poison at parts per trillion so, you know –
>
> MacKinnon: Well, of course.
>
> Prest: You can only kill a fellow so dead, you know. The overkill doesn't matter."

Presentation by Murray Prest, Mooseland, April 22, 1983, RCOF, vol. 159, no. 9.

77 "MLA Supports Band's Efforts to Stop Spraying," *Chronicle-Herald,* July 8, 1982, 21; EAC Forestry Committee Meeting minutes, July 14, 1982, DAL-EAC, box 29.7.

78 "Forest Herbicide Trial – Background," PANS-BP, vol. 3469, no. 8; Peter Cumming, "The Herbicide Fight," *Rural Delivery* 7, no. 12 (May 1983): 32; EAC press release, July 8, 1982, DAL-EAC, box 29.9. It is important to note that May and the EAC were not criticizing Googoo or the people of Whycocomagh for their choice, only the fact that they should have had to make it.

79 George Butters, "Spray Wars, Part Two," *Atlantic Insight* 4, no. 10 (October 1982): 10–11.

80 Peter Cumming, "The Herbicide Case: Part I: Plaintiffs against the Spray," *Rural Delivery* 8, no. 1 (June 1983): 24.

81 "Publicity Sheet," [late] 1982, DAL-EAC, box 28.28; *Q/L SSEPA News Special Edition* 1, no. 5 (August 1982), PANS-BP, vol. 3469, no. 8. In fact, only fifteen of the "plaintiffs" were true plaintiffs. Elizabeth May had been rejected by Justice Burchell as a representative of all Nova Scotians, but she and Ruth Schneider of North River Bridge, Cape Breton County, kept their financial undertakings before the court in solidarity with the fifteen class-action representatives, making seventeen in total.

82 The total in the end was $14,465.17, and it was paid by Stephanie and John May after selling property near Baddeck. Peter Cumming, "The Herbicide Fight," *Rural Delivery* 7, no. 12 (May 1983); *Mail-Star,* April 27, 1983, clipping file, PANS-BP, vol. 3469, no. 8; Bruce Wildsmith to Peter Bessen, United States, December 8, 1983, DAL-EAC, box 29.6.

83 Elizabeth May to the plaintiffs, February 1, 1983, DAL-EAC, box 24.7.

84 Presentation by People for Environmental Protection (PEP), March 22, 1983, RCOF, vol. 159, no. 3; Rhonda Ryan, ed. "PEP TALK newsletter" 1, February 1983, DAL-EAC, box 40.13; Rhonda Ryan to EAC, n.d., DAL-EAC, box 28.25. New groups, small and local, continued to arrive throughout the approximately year and a half of high controversy, including those like PEP which jumped into the job of province-wide organization, and those like the Concerned Citizens Against 2,4-D in Yarmouth and Argyle, which spent most of their efforts on local proselytizing and left a very scant documentary record despite, in its case, successfully halting a roadside spray program in Yarmouth County: Veralyn Rogers to Roger Bacon, Minister of Agriculture and Marketing, June 24, 1983, DLF, vol. 882, no. 3.

85 Heather Laski, "A Costly Fight in Cape Breton," *Maclean's*, May 9, 1983, 20; "Sackville Environmental Protection Association" document, 1979, DAL-EAC, box 43.2.

86 Mailing List, July 1982, DAL-EAC, box 29.1; "Nova Scotia Environmental Network, 82-83" document, DAL-EAC, box 28.25.

87 The EAC, mired in perennial fundraising difficulties of its own, was happy to direct support toward the HFS and devote its own fundraising energies to finding its own funds. EAC Board of Directors Meeting minutes, February 16, 1983, PANS-EAC, vol. 3421, no. 3; EAC Communications Resource Group Meeting minutes, January 27, 1983, PANS-EAC, vol. 3421, no. 11.

88 Rhonda Ryan, ed., "PEP TALK newsletter" 1, February 1983, DAL-EAC, box 40.13.

89 McLaughlin, "Green Shoots," 22.

90 Pesticide Action Network, *Pesticide Digest* 2 (1983), PANS-EAC, vol. 3434, no. 3. The worldwide PAN was created in Malaysia on May 28, 1982, at an NGO workshop on the global trade in pesticides.

91 EAC Board of Directors Meeting minutes, March 23, 1983, PANS-EAC, vol. 3421, no. 3.

92 "HFS Public Relations Committee Note: Fund-Raising Tours," DLF, vol. 882, no. 3; Stephanie May, "Getting into PAN," *Between the Issues* 4, no. 1 (May-June 1984), on her trip to see the PAN–North America in Washington, DC, in November 1983. Support, financial and otherwise, did come from all over: Farley Mowat, Ralph Nader, the Ontario Federation of Labour, and similarly diverse sources. Elizabeth May to the plaintiffs, February 1, 1983, DAL-EAC, box 24.7; "Draft Motion from the Ontario Federation of Labour Health and Safety Committee, re: 2,4,5-T / 2,4-D Use in Nova Scotia," DAL-EAC, box 24.7.

93 Peter Cumming, "The Stink of Defeat (draft)," 5, DAL-EAC, box 24.8; Liz Calder, EAC, to Lars Moberg, Sweden, January 25, 1984, DAL-EAC, box 44.7.

94 David Folster, "The Agonizing Fight over Budworm Spray," *Atlantic Insight* 1, no. 3 (June 1979): 34–36.

95 *Between the Issues* 3, no. 2 (May-June 1983). Amusingly, NSFI's lawyer, George Cooper, said almost the same thing in May: *Chronicle-Herald*, May 6, 1983, clipping file, PANS-BP, vol. 3469, no. 8.

96 The nearest to open discussion was Peter Cumming's comment on the decision to go to court that "the issue seems to have taken on even more of a 'technical' and 'scientific' nature and less of a 'political' and 'social' and 'philosophical' and 'values' nature ... the change from a 'people's case' to an 'expert's case' may prove to be the most expensive few minutes of these 'ordinary people's' lives." *Between the Issues* 3, no. 2 (May-June 1983).

97 Bruce Wildsmith and Richard Murtha to plaintiffs, December 17, 1982, DAL-EAC, box 24.7. Nunn decided against a jury trial on account of the complexity of the evidence expected to be presented.

98 *Between the Issues* 3, no. 2 (May-June 1983).

99 Logan Norris, Oregon State University Forest Science Department, to the President, Dean, and Directors of the same, October 20, 1983, DAL-EAC, box 24.9.

100 Cumming, "The Herbicide Case: Part I," 26.

101 Ibid., 24–26; Peter Cumming, "Herbicide Case: Part II: Expert Dispute," *Rural Delivery* 8, no. 2 (July 1983): 24–27.

102 Fred McMahon, "Residents 'Guinea Pigs' in Spray Plan," *Chronicle-Herald*, June 7, 1983, 4.

103 Cumming, "Herbicide Case: Part II," 24–25.

104 Ibid., 22.

105 *Between the Issues* 3, no. 2 (May-June 1983).

106 Members of the EAC board of directors were quite worried that "the Judge does not appear to understand some of the very basic scientific principles involved." EAC Board of Directors Meeting minutes, May 18, 1983, PANS-EAC, vol. 3421, no. 3. Nunn himself asked the assembled lawyers and witnesses at trial how "can I possibly absorb all this stuff?" Cumming, "Herbicide Case: Part II," 26.

107 McMahon, "Residents 'Guinea Pigs' in Spray Plan," 4.

108 One witness for the plaintiffs, Theodore Sterling, statistician and epidemiologist at Simon Fraser University, was incensed at Nunn's attitude, asking why only Nova Scotia, of all jurisdictions in the world, still allowed 2,4,5-T aerial spraying: "Even the Russians don't use it now." Cumming, "Herbicide Case: Part II," 26–27.

109 McMahon, "Residents 'Guinea Pigs' in Spray Plan," 4.

110 Cumming, "Herbicide Case: Part II," 27.

111 Glen Wannamaker, "Spray Opponents Lick Their Wounds and Get Ready for Another Fight," *Atlantic Insight* 5, no. 11 (November 1983): 7. Anger among the witnesses as well: the Swedish researcher Mikael Eriksson complained that "the judge himself admitted that he had difficulties comprehending, yet he acquits the company and accuses me and other independent researchers of being partial." *Dala-Demokraten,* November 10, 1983, enclosed with Letter from Hollis Routledge, NSFI, to D.L. Eldridge, November 21, 1983, DLF, vol. 882, no. 3.

112 *Between the Issues* 3, no. 4 (October 1983).

113 Peter Cumming, "The Herbicide Fight," *Rural Delivery* 7, no. 12 (May 1983).

114 *Between the Issues* 3, no. 5 (December 1983).

115 Cumming, "The Stink of Defeat (draft)," 3.

116 Susan Murray, "Trouble in the Anti-Spray House," *Atlantic Insight* 6, no. 6 (June 1984): 7. At least one plaintiff, Bob Sampson, also told the CBC that he would have given up much sooner if he could have: "Transcript of CBC Inquiry," March 16, 1983, DLF, vol. 882, no. 3.

117 Cumming, "The Stink of Defeat (draft)," 4.

118 United Press Agency of the Swedish Press, December 13, 1983, clipping file, DAL-EAC, box 29.9. May had no right to appeal on her own, as she was not a true plaintiff. Stephanie May, "Getting into PAN," *Between the Issues* 4, no. 1 (May-June 1984); "Interview with Ryan Googoo," *Between the Issues* 3, no. 6 (February-March 1984).

119 Cumming, "The Stink of Defeat (draft)," 8–9. In the end, only $3,993.91 went to NSFI: "Details of Finalization of Settlement," DAL-EAC, box 24.8. The HFS formed a new Citizens Against Pesticides (CAP) group on December 14, 1983, initially under the leadership of John Shaw, Jeff Brownstein, Aaron Schneider, Peter Cumming, and John Roberts, with support from Margaree Environmental Association, FALASH, Victoria County Landowners, Mabou Support Group, Glendale Against Herbicide Spraying, Whycocomagh Against Herbicide Spraying, Antigonish Support Group, Baddeck–Middle River Support Group, Sydney–Big Pond Support Group: "Announcement: 1st AGM of CAP – 11 February 1984, Baddeck," n.d., DAL-EAC, box 24.9.

120 Cumming, "The Stink of Defeat (draft)," 6.

121 EAC Communications Resource Group Meeting minutes, January 27, 1983, PANS-EAC, vol. 3421, no. 11.

122 Elizabeth May to the Editor, *Chronicle-Herald,* February 25, 1983, clipping file, DAL-EAC, box 39.7; *Q/L SSEPA News* 1, no. 12 (May 1983).

123 Speech by George Henley, n.d., DAL-EAC, box 24.5. Connie Schnell in South Haven, Victoria County, soon began making "I'm an ENVIRONMENTAL SUBVERSIVE" buttons to sell for the HFS: Peter Cumming to EAC, DAL-EAC, box 24.5.

124 John Goodall, Stellarton, to the Editor, *Chronicle-Herald*, October 12, 1982, clipping file, RCOF, vol. 192, no. 2.

125 EAC Board of Directors Meeting minutes, May 24, 1982, PANS-EAC, vol. 3421, no. 2; EAC Board of Directors Meeting minutes, February 13, 1980, PANS-EAC, vol. 3420, no. 24. The EAC's leaders discussed the change themselves in 1978, noting the organization's "lack of contact with membership," "lack of outreach," and poor "relationship of centre to hinterlands." (The fact that they viewed the Centre as "the centre" is also quite telling, given the great vitality of environmentalism outside of Halifax.) Special Meeting of Board of Directors minutes, December 9, 1978, PANS-EAC, vol. 3420, no. 22.

126 Quoted in *Pesticide Action Network Newsletter* 2 (1983), PANS-EAC, vol. 3434, no. 3. It is worth noting that Nunn's ruling was against the plaintiffs, but not necessarily for the defence – the failure of one to make the case does not necessarily mean that the other's position is therefore correct – but that kind of nice distinction rarely comes across.

127 Department of Environment spokesperson Linda Laffin, quoted in *Between the Issues* 3, no. 4 (October 1983).

128 "Minutes of Joint Meeting, Deputy Ministers of Health or Representatives with ESBC," May 1, 1980, DLF, vol. 604, no. 5.

129 Christine Blair, "Tour Provides Sobering Look at Budworm-Damaged Forest," *Forest Times* 5, no. 3 (August 1983): 8; T.D. Smith, Lands and Forests, to R.E. Bailey, Lands and Forests, June 10, 1983, DLF, vol. 882, no. 3; "Misconceptions about Forest Industry Must Be Corrected," *Chronicle-Herald*, January 19, 1984, 40; "Funding Approved for N.S. Forestry Exhibition," *Chronicle-Herald*, January 21, 1984, 18. (The amount was $4,270, from Lands and Forests.)

130 Environmental Control Council, "Discussion Paper on Herbicide Use in Nova Scotia," n.d. [c. late 1983], DAL-EAC, box 24.9.

131 Alan Jeffers, "Streatch Will Take Over Forestry Board," *Chronicle-Herald*, March 30, 1984, 17; EAC press release, n.d., DAL-EAC, box 29.9.

132 Blair, "Tour Provides Sobering Look at Budworm-Damaged Forest," 8.

133 EAC to Charles Caccia, federal Minister of Environment, February 20, 1984, DAL-EAC, box 29.9; "Forestry Taught in Schools," *Chronicle-Herald*, December 17, 1983, 23.

134 Peter Cumming, "CAP RAP," May 2, 1984, DAL-EAC, box 24.9. "Truth in Forestry" was a pro-spray pressure group originating in Cape Breton but registered to NSFI's lawyers' firm in Halifax: *Between the Issues* 3, no. 6 (February-March 1984).

135 On ground sprays: D.L. Eldridge to G. Kerr, Minister of Environment, August 12, 1983, DLF, vol. 606, no. 8; Gerard MacLellan, Department of Environment, to D.L. Eldridge, August 19, 1983, DLF, vol. 882, no. 3; Greg Kerr to Ake Thor, NSFI, August 4, 1983, RCOF, vol. 186, no. 10. (Environment and Lands and Forests also encouraged Scott Paper to use ground spray on Christmas tree farms when aerial permits were denied by the Department of Public Health due to the nearby source of water for the Town of Wolfville: D.L. Eldridge to G. Henley, April 28, 1983, DLF, vol. 606, no. 8.) On the minister's vow: M. Haase to Premier Buchanan, July 15, 1983, DAL-EAC, box 43.5. On the end of public notice: George Moody, Minister of Environment, to Ryan Googoo, November 6, 1985, DAL-EAC, box 43.7; Letter discussing end of newspaper notification, from E.L.L. Rowe, Department of Environment, to file, January 5, 1983, DLF, vol. 606, no. 8.

136 EAC press release, August 17, 1983, DAL-EAC, box 24.7; "NDP Protest Spray Plans," *Chronicle-Herald,* August 26, 1983, 15; "NSFI Target of Anti-Spray Protestors," *Chronicle-Herald,* August 16, 1983, 21. Government had of course not stopped listening to the pulp and paper industry, and it is in that correspondence that Kerr revealed the total acreage sprayed with chemical herbicides, mostly phenoxy, in 1982 (fifteen thousand acres, both aerial and ground), and pushed for more "public education" from industry. Greg Kerr, Minister of Environment, to Ake Thor, NSFI, August 4, 1983, DLF, vol. 186, no. 10.

137 Quote from Agricultural Association of Canada president Jack Elliott, at a Department of Agriculture workshop, "Pesticides in Perspective – An Educational Seminar," April 9, 1984, quoted in *Between the Issues* 4, no. 1 (May-June 1984).

138 "Infamous Gypsy Moth Found in Alarming Numbers in Western Half of Nova Scotia," *Chronicle-Herald,* February 7, 1984, 25. The pressure to spray chemical insecticides to kill spruce budworm never really ceased either: "Cape Breton Landowners Information Update," January 1982, DAL-EAC, box 24.9.

139 Most, possibly all, of the sites at issue in the trial (among others) were sprayed with glyphosate and 2,4-D in 1984: *Between the Issues* 4, no. 1 (May-June 1984); George Moody, Minister of Environment, to Ryan Googoo, November 6, 1985, DAL-EAC, box 43.7; Paul Schneidereit, "Varying Views on Herbicide Spraying," *Chronicle-Herald,* July 21, 1984, 21.

140 Cumming, "The Stink of Defeat (draft)," 7.

141 Ibid., 10. Much the same sentiment came from Hester Lessard of the SSEPA: Murray, "Trouble in the Anti-Spray House," 7.

142 Peter Cumming, "Out of the Courts and Back to the Issue," *Between the Issues* (October 1983).

143 Cape Breton Island Wildlife Association, "Spraying: Removing Nature's Food Supply," *Chronicle-Herald,* December 15, 1983, 7.

144 David Orton's opinion was that success against biocides would require civil disobedience, and activists ought to know that "the provincial government will be on the other side of the barricades." David Orton to the Editor, *Rural Delivery* 8, no. 1 (June 1983).

145 *Q/L SSEPA News* 2, no. 2 (July-August 1983).

CHAPTER 4: TWO ENVIRONMENTALISMS

1 Lawrence Welsh, "Uranium Industry Faces Low Sales, Poor Prices as Power Demand Falls," *Globe and Mail,* March 29, 1982, B3;Bruce Little, "Shades of the Klondike in Atlantic Canada," *Atlantic Insight* 1, no. 2 (May 1979): 25; Province of Nova Scotia, Department of Mines and Energy, *Uranium in Nova Scotia: A Background Summary for the Uranium Inquiry – Nova Scotia, Report 82-7* (Halifax: Government of Nova Scotia, 1982), 3–9. Companies exploring for uranium in the province included Lacana, Gulf, and Noranda on the north shore; and Esso, Aquitaine, Shell, Eldorado, Norcen, and Saarberg on the southern mainland.

2 Ralph Torrie, "BC's Inquiry and Moratorium," *CCNR's Transitions* 3, no. 1 (May 1980); Jim Harding, *Canada's Deadly Secret: Saskatchewan Uranium and the Global Nuclear System* (Halifax: Fernwood, 2007), 28; Document on Inuit opposition to uranium mining, DAL-EAC, box 42.9; Amy Zierler, "Labrador's Great Debate: Who Wants a Uranium Mine?" *Atlantic Insight* 2, no. 4 (May 1980): 18; Saskatchewan Environmental Society and Regina Group for a Non-Nuclear Society to Susan Holtz, 1977, PANS-EAC, vol. 3434, no. 14.

Government support went as far as participation in an international price-fixing cartel involving all of Canada's uranium producers, the United Kingdom, France, South Africa, and Australia. "Uranium Cartel Probe Reports Laws Broken," *Globe and Mail*, May 27, 1981, quoted in Donna Smyth, *Subversive Elements* (Toronto: Women's Press, 1986), 116–17.

3 Ken Kelley, Sable River, to the Editor, *Rural Delivery* 4, no. 4 (September 1979); Ken Kelley, "Mining for Death," *Rural Delivery* 4, no. 6 (November 1979); EAC Board of Directors Meeting minutes, August 8, 1979, PANS-EAC, vol. 3420, no. 23; Ron and Ruth Loucks to the Editor, *Rural Delivery* 4, no. 8 (January 1980); FACT Newsletter, March 1980, DAL-EAC, box 41.3.

4 Joanne Lamey, CPAC, to Ginny Point, EAC, January 14, 1980, DAL-EAC, box 30.8.

5 Joanne Lamey, CPAC, to Ginny Point, EAC, February 13, 1980, DAL-EAC, box 30.8; *Jusun* 8, no. 2 (Summer 1980), PANS-EAC, vol. 3420, no. 24.

6 Early, "'A Grandly Subversive Time,'" 28, 36.

7 Jocelyn Rhodenizer, South Berwick Women's Institute, to EAC, September 17, 1980, DAL-EAC, box 43.2; Document on Nova Scotia Women's Institutes, January 21, 1980, PANS-EAC, vol. 3433, no. 38.

8 "Farm Women's Conference," *Rural Delivery* 5, no. 8 (January 1981); Burlington and Summerville Women's Institutes, *Hants Journal*, February 25, 1981, 5.

9 "Conference on Health Effects of Radiation, Moncton," February 20–22, 1981, DAL-EAC, box 30.10.

10 Al Kingsbury, "Uranium Moratorium Urged," *Mail-Star*, March 13, 1981, 52; Gwen Davies and Bill Johnston, "Aquitaine Mines a Rich Vein of Controversy," *Atlantic Insight* 3, no. 8 (October 1981): 16; EAC Board of Directors Meeting minutes, January 28, 1981, PANS-EAC, vol. 3420, no. 25; Burlington Women's Institute, "Brief Presented to the West Hants Municipal Council on the Subject of Uranium Mining," March 12, 1981, PANS, Royal Commission on Uranium Mining fonds, RG 44 [hereafter RCU], vol. 206, no. 28.

11 SSEPA Resolution, March 26, 1981, DAL-EAC, box 30.8; EAC Resolution, March 25, 1981, DAL- EAC, box 41.21; VOW Meeting minutes, May 4, 1981, PANS-BP, vol. 3470, no. 6.

12 VOW Atlantic Newsletter, May 1, 1981, PANS-BP, vol. 3472, no. 1; Donna Smyth, "Selling Radon Daughters: Uranium in Nova Scotia," *Canadian Forum* 61, no. 714 (December/January 1981): 6–8.

13 Al Kingsbury, "Hants Uranium Prospects Good," *Mail-Star*, April 13, 1981, 19.

14 Ralph Loomer, "Nova Scotia Can Do without Uranium Invasion," *Chronicle-Herald*, June 29, 1981, 7; VOW Atlantic Newsletter, May 1, 1981, PANS-BP, vol. 3472, no. 1.

15 Nova Scotia, *Hansard*, April 2, 1981; Davies and Johnston, "Aquitaine Mines a Rich Vein of controversy," 16; Hal Mills and Ron Loucks, "Uranium Mining Meeting Notes," April 6, 1981, DAL-EAC, box 30.10; MLA David Nantes, Select Committee on Uranium Mining, to Susan Holtz, September 3, 1981, DAL-EAC, box 44.4.

16 "New Group Joins Anti-Nuclear Drive," *Chronicle-Herald*, June 2, 1981, 22; CAPE press release, July 1, 1981, DAL-EAC, box 30.8.

17 Gillian Thomas, CAPE, to Daphne Taylor, EAC (marginal notations), May 25, 1981, DAL-EAC, box 30.8.

18 J. Brian Harley, "Maps, Knowledge, and Power," in *The Iconography of Landscape*, ed. D. Cosgrove and S. Daniels (Cambridge: Cambridge University Press, 1988), 277.

19 Clayton Campbell, "Pressure Groups Threaten Uranium Mining Operation, Conference Told," *Chronicle-Herald*, June 25, 1981, quoted in Smyth, *Subversive Elements*, 63.

20   Alexa McDonough to Ginny Point, EAC, December 18, 1981, DAL-EAC, box 30.8.

21   Muriel Siemers, "The Uranium Issue: The Harmful Effect on Agriculture," *Chronicle-Herald,* September 24, 1981, 7.

22   Press release, September 21, 1981, DAL-EAC, box 33.4; Alan Jeffers, "Issuing of Drilling Permits 'Madness,'" *Chronicle-Herald,* September 22, 1981, 2.

23   Jeffers, ibid.

24   Department of Mines and Energy, *Uranium in Nova Scotia,* 13.

25   "Saarberg Drops Plans for Uranium Exploration," *Chronicle-Herald,* September 24, 1981, 5.

26   *Chronicle-Herald,* November 6, 1981, clipping file, RCU, vol. 206, no. 28; "Medical Society of Nova Scotia General Council, Community Health Committee Report," November 20–21, 1981, RCU, vol. 201, no. 10.

27   *Chronicle-Herald,* October 26, 1981, clipping file, RCU, vol. 206, no. 28.

28   Donna Smyth, "The Public Debate Begins," *Rural Delivery* 6, no. 7 (December 1981).

29   Daphne Taylor, EAC, to Betty Peterson, December 17, 1981, DAL-EAC, box 30.8; Smyth, ibid.

30   Roy John to Fred Barrett, FACT, December 9, 1981, DAL-EAC, box 30.8.

31   Unknown to the Editor, *The Mirror,* Digby, n.d., clipping file, DAL-EAC, box 30.10.

32   Roy John to Fred Barrett, FACT, December 9, 1981, DAL-EAC, box 30.8.

33   "Hazardous Wastes in Atlantic Canada," Acadia University Conference notes, DAL-EAC, box 35.12.

34   Notice of Bertell's press conference, November 12, 1981, DAL-EAC, box 33.4; Donna Smyth, "Uranium Update," *Rural Delivery* 6, no. 8 (January 1982). At the request of some Nova Scotian activists, Bertell penned a withering response to Dalgleish in a letter to Joan Brown-Hicks at the Halifax library, December 16, 1981, DAL-EAC, box 30.10.

35   Rod Bantjes and Tanya Trussler, "Feminism and the Grass Roots: Women and Environmentalism in Nova Scotia, 1980–1983," *Canadian Review of Sociology and Anthropology* 36, no. 2 (1999): 194.

36   EAC press release, May 10, 1981, DAL-EAC, box 30.10.

37   "Health Hazards of Mineral Mining," EAC lecture (John Hartlen, Jack Garnett, Ralph Torrie), February 17, 1981, DAL-EAC, box 30.10.

38   EAC press release, May 10, 1981, DAL-EAC, box 30.10. CAPE's Gillian Thomas also objected in a letter to MLA Ron Russell, May 17, 1981, DAL-EAC, box 30.8.

39   Susan Holtz to Jack Garnett, December 20, 1980, DAL-EAC, box 30.11.

40   EAC Energy Committee Meeting minutes, March 18, 1981, DAL-EAC, box 30.11; EAC Energy Committee Meeting minutes, May 13, 1981, PANS-EAC, vol. 3420, no. 25.

41   "(EAC) Environmental Action Task Force Report," March 30, 1982, PANS-EAC, vol. 3421, no. 1; EAC Board of Directors Meeting minutes, June 24, 1981, PANS-EAC, vol. 3420, no. 25.

42   EAC Uranium Committee Meeting minutes, February 8, June 9, June 23, and July 7, 1982, DAL-EAC, box 30.11; David Orton, "Draft Resolution Regarding the Terms of Reference of the Uranium Committee, EAC," May 27, 1981, DAL-EAC, box 30.11.

43   David Orton, "What Makes an Activist? (Part 1)," *Deep Green Web,* April 2, 2011, http://deepgreenweb.blogspot.ca/2011/04/what-makes-activist-part-1.html.

44   David Orton, "Uranium Mining: Hearings into Dangers Needed," *Chronicle-Herald,* August 24, 1981, 7.

45   EAC Uranium Subcommittee minutes, May 27 and June 9, 1981, DAL-EAC, box 30.11. Orton was far from the only one to press a critique of the EAC's methods during this time.

See also Michael Clow, "A Left-Environmentalist Perspective on Canadian Industrial Strategy," paper presented at the Ecology Energy and Resources section of the Canadian Political Science Association 1981 Annual Meeting, Dalhousie University, Halifax, Nova Scotia, May 27–29, 1981; Peter Rowbottom, Cape Breton, to Susan Hotlz, March 11, 1981, DAL-EAC, box 44.3; "Moncton Conference Notes: 'Experts in Society' by Dr. Woollard," *Southern New Brunswick Nuclear News* 15 (February-March 1981); "Conference on Health Effects of Radiation, Moncton," February 20–22, 1981, DAL-EAC, box 30.10; David Underwood, Sable River, to the Editor, *Rural Delivery* 5, no. 11 (April 1981); Linda Christiansen-Ruffman, "The Ecology Action Center in the Seventies," February 1979, PANS-EAC, vol. 3420, no. 23.

46 *Chronicle-Herald,* November 6, 1981, clipping file, RCU, vol. 206, no. 28.

47 Sherri Cline to EAC, October 1, 1981, DAL-EAC, box 44.4.

48 David Orton to the head of the Halifax City Regional Library, October 1, 1981, DAL-EAC, box 30.8.

49 SSEPA press release, n.d., DAL-EAC, box 44.6 [emphasis in original].

50 Smyth, "The Public Debate Begins."

51 Susan Holtz to Hattie Perry, October 29, 1981, PANS-EAC, vol. 3421, no. 1.

52 Susan Holtz, "EAC's Position on Uranium Development and the N.S. Uranium Exploration Guidelines/Regulations," November 18, 1981, PANS-EAC, vol. 3431, no. 7, and PANS-EAC, vol. 3424, no. 12.

53 Anne Wickens to Susan Holtz, n.d., PANS-EAC, vol. 3421, no. 1.

54 Sherri Cline to Susan Holtz, January 20, 1982, PANS-EAC, vol. 3421, no. 1.

55 Anne Wickens to Susan Holtz, n.d., PANS-EAC, vol. 3421, no. 1.

56 Dorien Freve to Hattie Perry, December 8, 1981, PANS-EAC, vol. 3421, no. 1.

57 Linda Christiansen-Ruffman, "The Ecology Action Center in the Seventies," February 1979, PANS- EAC, vol. 3420, no. 23.

58 Susan Holtz to Bob Paehlke, January 14, 1981, DAL-EAC, box 44.4.

59 Bessa Ruiz to Sherri Cline, February 11, 1982, PANS-EAC, vol. 3421, no. 1. The EAC also denied its reliance on government funding, an effort undermined by its explanation in the press of the need for more of it: Sandy Smith, "Government Funds Needed to Continue EAC's Work," *Chronicle-Herald,* September 20, 1981, 5.

60 EAC news release, January 13, 1982, DAL-EAC, box 33.4; "Nuclear Technology in Nova Scotia and Canada: An Unacceptable Risk," 1982, DAL-EAC, box 37.4. Groups represented were VOW, EAC, CAPE, FACT, KASE, and Project Ploughshares.

61 Gwen Davies and Ginny Point, "Looking Back over the Past Two Years," draft, EAC Annual Report 1980–82, PANS-EAC, vol. 3420, no. 4.

62 *Toronto Star,* March 12, 1983, enclosed with letter from G.C. Eglington, Ottawa, to McCleave, May 25, 1983, RCU, vol. 204, no. 14. McCleave had inquired about possible libel action against the newspaper.

63 Order in Council #82-200, February 9, 1982, in *Report of the Nova Scotia Royal Commission of Inquiry on Uranium* (Halifax: Queen's Printer, 1985).

64 EAC Board of Directors Meeting minutes, February 24, 1982, PANS-EAC, vol. 3421, no. 1. The nine groups were: CARE, CCCC, EAC, SEPOHG, Fish or Cut Bait Collective, Recreation Directors of Nova Scotia, Taxpayers for a Safe Environment, WHEN, and the United Church – Church in Society Committee.

65 CARE press release, February 14, 1982, DAL-EAC, box 30.8.

66 EAC Brief to McCleave, January 29, 1982, marginal notations, RCU, vol. 201, no. 10.

67 EAC Board of Directors Meeting minutes, February 24, 1982, PANS-EAC, vol. 3421, no. 1.

68 Hattie Dyck, "McCleave Asks Groups' Cooperation in Inquiry," *Chronicle-Herald*, February 27, 1982; "Susan Holtz Time Allocation Sample," PANS-EAC, vol. 3421, no. 1; Martin Haase to McCleave, March 6, 1982, RCU, vol. 202, no. 5.

69 McCleave to Glenys Livingstone and Stanley Forgeron, Inquiry staff, March 18, 1982, RCU, vol. 203, no. 6.

70 Editorial, *Truro Daily News,* March 9, 1982, 4; Robert McCleave to John Conrad, Managing Editor, *Amherst Daily News,* March 9, 1982, RCU, vol. 201, no. 7; Unknown to Gillian Thomas, March 24, 1982, DAL-EAC, box 30.9.

71 Robert Whiting to McCleave, March 2, 1982, RCU, vol. 202, no. 5.

72 Judy Davis, Tatamagouche, to McCleave, March 4, 1982, RCU, vol. 201, no. 2.

73 Winston Settle to Robert McCleave, February 27, 1982, RCU, vol. 203, no. 6.

74 "Liberal MLAs Believe Uranium Inquiry Chairman Judge Robert McCleave Has Displayed a Contempt for Free Speech and They Want the Government to Remove Him from the Post," unknown publication, March 5, 1982, clipping file, DAL-EAC, box 33.3.

75 Jim Lotz to McCleave, March 8, 1982, RCU, vol. 201, no. 1.

76 McCleave to Alexa McDonough, March 17, 1982, RCU, vol. 201, no. 10.

77 McCleave to Gillian Thomas, April 10, 1982, DAL-EAC, box 30.9.

78 McCleave to Russell Logan, President, Maritime Diamond Drilling Co. Ltd., n.d., RCU, vol. 201, no. 2.

79 Ralph Loomer to Robert McCleave, February 27, 1982, RCU, vol. 201, no. 2. The Women's Health Education Network and EAC also distanced themselves from CARE: Janet Campbell (WHEN) to Robert McCleave, March 11, 1982, RCU, vol. 201, file 8; Dr. J.E. Baker (EAC) to Robert McCleave, March 4, 1982, PANS-EAC, vol. 30, no. 8.

80 For example, a new branch of the CCCC in Parrsboro: Environmental Protection in Cumberland South (EPICS) press release, n.d., DAL-EAC, box 33.4.

81 McCleave to Archbishop Hayes (Catholic), Halifax, March 23, 1982, RCU, vol. 201, no. 10; Betty Peterson, Halifax Monthly Meeting of Friends (Quaker), to McCleave, February 5, 1983, RCU, vol. 202, no. 1; McCleave to Reverend Archdeacon C.R. Elliott (Anglican), Halifax, April 10, 1982, RCU, vol. 202, no. 1; W.R. MacDonald, Clerk of Session, Saint Andrew's United Church, Wolfville, to McCleave, February 22, 1982, RCU, vol. 201, no. 2; Reverends Clint Mooney, Donald McLeod, and K.O. Robinson, to McCleave, March 8, 1982, RCU, vol. 201, no. 8; Joan Cunningham, Nova Scotia Provincial Council of the Catholic Women's League of Canada, to McCleave, n.d., RCU, vol. 201, no. 10.

82 Anne Bishop, Lismore Community Concern Committee, and Umbrella Co-operative Ltd., transcripts of Pictou hearing, hearing #16, June 15, 1982, RCU, vol. 197, nos. 5 and 6; Robert Whiting, transcripts of Chester hearing, hearing #21, July 7, 1982, RCU, vol. 198, no. 3; Jeffrey Gold, for Beverly Brett, transcripts of Baddeck hearing, hearing #31, September 8, 1982, RCU, vol. 198, no. 23; Ian Ball, transcripts of Halifax hearing, hearing #34, September 17, 1982, RCU, vol. 199, nos. 5 and 6.

83 Michael Keddy, transcripts of New Ross hearing, hearing #1, April 2, 1982, RCU, vol. 195, no. 12.

84 Norma Flynn, RESCUE, transcripts of Vaughan hearing, hearing #19, June 25, 1982, RCU, vol. 197, no. 12; Dr. C.J. Byrne, transcripts of Halifax hearing, hearing #10, May 21, 1982, RCU, vol. 196, no. 6.

85 Ron Leitold, New Germany, transcripts of Bridgewater hearing, hearing #3, April 20, 1982, RCU, vol. 195, no. 16.

86 Muriel Maybee, Lunenburg County Women's Group, transcripts of Bridgewater hearing, hearing #3, April 20, 1982, RCU, vol. 195, no. 16.

87 Erin Gore, transcripts of Chester hearing, hearing #5, April 30, 1982, RCU, vol. 195, no. 21. Bantjes and Trussler surveyed women involved in the anti-uranium movement in Nova Scotia and found a majority – 78 percent of those who could be placed – had come "from away," that is, had been born out of the province: Bantjes and Trussler, "Feminism and the Grass Roots," 192.

88 The clearest such argument came from Ross Baker, transcripts of Truro hearing, hearing #24, July 13, 1982, RCU, vol. 198, no. 9. Several female presenters also explicitly tied the legitimacy of their moral arguments to their status as mothers; for example, Cathleen Kneen, Pictou County VOW, transcripts of Pictou hearing, hearing #16, June 15, 1982, RCU, vol. 197, no. 6.

89 Torrie, "BC's Inquiry and Moratorium"; Harding, *Canada's Deadly Secret*.

90 Ernest Forbes, *The Maritime Rights Movement 1919–1927: A Study in Canadian Regionalism* (Montreal and Kingston: McGill-Queen's University Press, 1979); Margaret Conrad, "The Atlantic Revolution of the 1950s," in *Beyond Anger and Longing: Community and Development in Atlantic Canada,* ed. Berkeley Fleming (Fredericton: Acadiensis, 1988), 55–98; Jennifer Smith, "Intergovernmental Relations, Legitimacy, and the Atlantic Accords," *Constitutional Forum* 17, no. 3 (2008): 81–98.

91 Brian McVeigh, transcripts of Chester hearing, hearing #5, April 30, 1982, RCU, vol. 195, no. 21. Michael Marshall pointed out that mining companies accustomed to operating in the Canadian north, where they experienced few constraints on their activities, failed to see the difference between Nova Scotia and Canada: transcripts of Halifax hearing, hearing #10, May 21, 1982, RCU, vol. 196, no. 6.

92 Robert Finck, transcripts of Bridgewater hearing, hearing #3, April 20, 1982, RCU, vol. 195, no. 16.

93 Kenneth Seaboyer, transcripts of New Ross hearing, hearing #1, April 2, 1982, RCU, vol. 195, no. 12.

94 Muriel Maybee, Lunenburg County Women's Group, transcripts of Bridgewater hearing, hearing #3, April 20, 1982, RCU, vol. 195, no. 16.

95 AECB, transcripts of Halifax hearing, hearing #17, June 22, 1982, RCU, vol. 197, no. 7; Valerie Wilson, transcripts of Annapolis Royal hearing, hearing #20, July 6, 1982, RCU, vol. 198, no. 1.

96 Robert Bays, "Uranium Exploration and Mining: Fact and Fiction," RCU, vol. 198, no. 2; AECB, transcripts of Halifax hearing, hearing #17, June 22, 1982, RCU, vol. 197, no. 7.

97 Drs. Linda Christansen-Ruffman and Karin Flikeid, Canadian Research Institute for the Advancement of Women – Nova Scotia, transcripts of Halifax hearing, hearing #15, June 11, 1982, RCU, vol. 197, no. 4.

98 Martin Haase, transcripts of Chester hearing, hearing #5, April 30, 1982, RCU, vol. 195, no. 21.

99 Judy Davis, CARE, to the Editor, *Rural Delivery* 6, no. 12 (May 1982).

100 Robert Whiting, transcripts of Chester hearing, hearing #21, July 7, 1982, RCU, vol. 198, no. 3; tape recording of the same, RCU, Ac 673. Whiting's speech also included one of several open threats of violent civil disobedience received by the inquiry.

101 Gordon Campbell, "Our Ways Never Failed Us," music and lyrics, performed at Parrsboro, October 7, 1982, RCU, vol. 199, no. 23.

102 Susan Hower, transcripts of Liverpool hearing, hearing #4, April 27, 1982, RCU, vol. 195, no. 18.

103 Dr. William Thurlow, Digby, transcripts of Bear River hearing, hearing #6, May 6, 1982, RCU, vol. 195, no. 22; Dr. A.R. Robertson, for staff group at St Martha's Hospital and Antigonish Committee Concerned with Uranium Exploration, Antigonish, and Dr. Robert Sers, Antigonish, transcripts of Antigonish hearing, hearing #37, September 28, 1982, RCU, vol. 199, no. 11; Drs. W.L. Phillips and J.D.A. Henshaw, Valley Medical Society, transcripts of Wolfville hearing, hearing #9, May 19, 1982, RCU, vol. 196, no. 4.

104 Ralph Torrie, Ottawa, transcripts of Chester hearing, hearing #21, July 7, 1982, RCU, vol. 198, no. 3; Judy Pasternak, *Yellow Dirt: A Poisoned Land and a People Betrayed* (New York: Free Press, 2010).

105 One very good example is seen in the May family presentations in Margaree Harbour on September 7, 1982, hearing #30, which included (from Elizabeth May) criticism of the mining industry for attempting to politically influence government during the inquiry: RCU, vol. 198, no. 21.

106 Smyth, *Subversive Elements,* 233.

107 Paula Scott to MLA Ron Barkhouse, April 3, 1982, RCU, vol. 201, no. 3.

108 Donna Smyth, "Uranium Update: Trouble in the Barnyard," *Rural Delivery* 6, no. 11 (April 1982); EAC Board of Directors Meeting minutes, May 24, 1982, PANS-EAC, vol. 3421, no. 2.

109 Gillian Thomas, transcripts of Vaughan hearing, hearing #19, June 25, 1982, RCU, vol. 197, no. 12.

110 Tape recording of Chester hearing, hearing #21, July 7, 1982, RCU, Ac 673.

111 David Orton, quoted in Susan Murray, "Sour Notes in the 'Judge McCleave Waltz,'" *Atlantic Insight* 5, no. 6 (June 1983): 12–13.

112 Transcripts of Amherst hearing, hearing #42, October 7, 1982, RCU, vol. 199, no. 20.

113 Nova Scotia Federation of Labour, transcripts of Halifax hearing, hearing #22, July 9, 1982, RCU, vol. 198, no. 5.

114 Tony Seed, transcripts of Halifax hearing, hearing #38, September 29, 1982, RCU, vol. 199, no. 13.

115 McCleave to Vivian Wittenburg, May 3, 1983, RCU, vol. 203, no. 7.

116 David Orton to the Editor, *Rural Delivery* 8, no. 3 (August 1982).

117 Unknown to the Editor, *Digby Mirror,* DAL-EAC, box 30.10.

118 Atlantic Canada Chapter, Northeast Atlantic International Section, Air Pollution Control Association, *Proceedings of the Sixth Annual Technical Meeting,* September 29–30, 1982; Don MacDonald, "'Subversives Holding Up Uranium Development,'" *Chronicle-Herald,* September 3, 1982, with brief by Elizabeth May, RCU, vol. 198, no. 21.

119 Fred McMahon, "Environmental Activists' Motives Questioned," *Chronicle-Herald,* February 23, 1983, with brief by Elizabeth May, RCU, vol. 198, no. 21.

120 David Helvarg, *The War against the Greens: The 'Wise Use' Movement, the New Right, and Anti-Environmental Violence* (San Francisco: Sierra Club Books, 1994).

121 Elizabeth May complained about "a kind of McCarthyism" in a letter to Robert McCleave, February 23, 1983, RCU, vol. 203, no. 6. Marilyn Manzer did similarly in a letter to McCleave, October 1, 1982, RCU, vol. 202, no. 2; Donna Smyth, "Uranium Update: Can It!" *Rural Delivery* 7, no. 5 (October 1982); Dirk van Loon, Editorial, *Rural Delivery* 7, no. 5 (October 1982).

122 Ginny Point, transcripts of Halifax hearing, hearing #15, June 11, 1982, RCU, vol. 197, no. 4.

123 EAC press release, November 18, 1982, DAL-EAC, box 33.4.

124 Dean Whalen (CARE) to Robert McCleave, March 4, 1982, RCU, vol. 203, no. 6; CARE brief, June 15, 1982, RCU, vol. 203, no. 6.

125 CARE brief, June 15, 1982, RCU, vol. 203, no. 6; "CARE presentation to the NS Uranium Inquiry," June 15, 1982, DAL-EAC, box 30.8.

126 "Dean Whalen – Sherri Cline Incident at Pictou," RCU, vol. 203, no. 6; McCleave to Dean Whalen, June 16, 1982, DAL-EAC, box 30.9.

127 Tony Law, Scotsburn, to Robert McCleave, June 22, 1982, RCU, vol. 202, no. 7.

128 Stanley Forgeron, inquiry secretary, to Fred Popowich, assistant librarian, Pictou-Antigonish Regional Library, November 17, 1982, RCU, vol. 203, no. 3. The librarian was told that CARE had never submitted a written brief.

129 "Dean Whalen – Sherri Cline Incident at Pictou," RCU, vol. 203, no. 6.

130 Don Rushton to the Editor, *Rural Delivery* 7, no. 2 (July 1982).

131 EAC Board of Directors Meeting minutes, June 23, 1982, PANS-EAC, vol. 3421, no. 2.

132 Multiple letters, RCU, vol. 200, no. 9; Gwenyth Phillips (KASE) to Robert McCleave, February 26, 1983, RCU, vol. 202, no. 4; Gillian Thomas, Bill Zimmerman, and George Gore, the Western Group Drafting Committee, to the Editor, *Rural Delivery* 7, no. 8 (January 1983). The four were Ruth Conrad, Ron Leitold, Elizabeth May, and Martin Haase.

133 Sherri Cline (CARE), Gail Fresia (CCCC), Don Rushton (CCCC), and David Orton (SEPOHG), to the Editor, *Rural Delivery* 7, no. 7 (December 1982) [emphasis in original].

134 Gillian Thomas (CAPE), Bill Zimmerman (SSEPA), and George Gore (CAUM), the "Western Group Drafting Committee," to the Editor, *Rural Delivery* 7, no. 8 (January 1983).

135 McCleave to participants, February 18, 1983, DAL-EAC, box 30.8.

136 Uranium Commission press release, n.d., RCU, vol. 203, no. 6; McCleave to all stage 1 participants, February 18, 1983, DAL-EAC, box 30.8.

137 Subpoena to Charles Lapp, RCU, vol. 203, no. 6. Lapp later sent a bill to McCleave's office for $905.30 to cover his lawyer's fee: RCU, vol. 203, no. 6.

138 Transcript, March 4, 1983, RCU, vol. 200, no. 10; McCleave to David Chipman, President of the Nova Scotia Barristers' Society, April 6, 1983, RCU, vol. 210, no. 10.

139 Transcript, March 4, 1983, RCU, vol. 200, no. 10; McCleave to Don Rushton, March 7, 1983, RCU, vol. 203, no. 6.

140 Transcript, March 4, 1983, RCU, vol. 200, no. 10.

141 *Truro Daily News,* March 14, 1983, 4; Transcript of CBC Radio Noon, March 7, 1983, RCU, vol. 203, no. 6.

142 *Truro Daily News,* March 14, 1983, 4; Nova Scotia House of Assembly Debates and Proceedings, March 7, 1983, RCU, vol. 204, no. 13.

143 "Public Screening of: Uranium the Nova Scotia Experience – the 30 minute slide-tape show subpoenaed by Judge McCleave," poster, RCU, vol. 203, no. 6. Donna Smyth's account of the whole episode in *Rural Delivery* also came with a small drawing of a redacted kangaroo, added by the publisher: Donna Smyth, "Uranium Update: Beyond Uranium," *Rural Delivery* 7, no. 11 (April 1983).

144 Transcript, March 18, 1983, RCU, vol. 200, no. 11. McCleave admitted to requiring medical advice to handle the pressure, in a letter to E.L.L. Rowe, Deputy Minister of Environment, May 3, 1983, RCU, vol. 201, no. 10.

145 Transcript, March 18, 1983, RCU, vol. 200, no. 11; Don Rushton, "So Long, Stage II: McCleave Gets Set to Ride Off into the Sunset," *New Maritimes* 2, no. 6 (March 1984): 10–11. Smyth estimated twenty protesters, Rushton thirty.

146 Donna Smyth, "Uranium Update: To Be Continued...," *Rural Delivery* 7, no. 12 (May 1983).

147 Jim Vibert, "How Will 'Examine' Opposition Charges," *Chronicle-Herald*, n.d., clipping file, RCU, vol. 202, no. 10; Attorney General press statement, March 22, 1983, DAL-EAC, box 30.8; Deputy Attorney General to McCleave, March 22, 1983, RCU, vol. 204, no. 4.

148 Robert McCleave to Clive Schaefer, May 6, 1983, RCU, vol. 203, file 7.

149 Susan Holtz to Harry How, Attorney General, March 9, 1983, DAL-EAC, box 43.6; Smyth, "Uranium Update: To Be Continued."

150 Ralph Loomer to Robert McCleave, March 10, 1983, vol. 202, no. 2. Stephanie May also wrote to reassure McCleave that the May family was still "singing your praises": Letter from Stephanie May to McCleave, July 7, 1983, RCU, vol. 203, no. 7.

151 Hal Mills, co-chair, EAC Uranium Committee, to Robert McCleave (copy open letter to Premier Buchanan), c.c. to the Attorney General, March 21, 1983, RCU, vol. 203, no. 4. Also printed in *Between the Issues* 3, no. 2 (May-June 1983).

152 EAC Board·of Directors Meeting minutes, March 23, 1983, PANS-EAC, vol. 3421, no. 3.

153 Sherri Cline to Susan Holtz, March 28, 1983, DAL-EAC, box 30.8.

154 McCleave to participants, February 18, 1983, DAL-EAC, box 30.8; Rushton, "So Long Stage II," 11.

155 Rushton, ibid.; Sherri Cline to the Editor, *Rural Delivery* 7, no. 12 (May 1983).

156 Smyth, "Uranium Update: Beyond Uranium."

157 *Q/L SSEPA News* 1, no. 12 (May 1983).

158 *Report of the Nova Scotia Royal Commission on Uranium Mining.*

159 EAC Uranium Committee minutes, April 10, 1985, PANS-EAC, vol. 3421, no. 5; Lyndon Watkins, "Anti-Uranium Winners Plan Picnic," *Mail-Star,* March 20, 1985, quoted in Smyth, *Subversive Elements,* 262–63.

160 *Report of the Nova Scotia Royal Commission on Uranium Mining;* "Position Paper," RCU, vol. 195, no. 3.

161 EAC Uranium Committee minutes, April 10, 1985, PANS-EAC, vol. 3421, no. 5; Watkins, "Anti-Uranium Winners Plan Picnic."

162 EAC Uranium Committee minutes, ibid.

163 McCleave to Roy John, National Uranium Tailings Program, April 12, 1984, RCU, vol. 203, no. 7; Martin Haase to McCleave, February 3, 1984, RCU, vol. 203, no. 3.

164 Michael Doyle, "Use of Word 'Parade' Is Defamatory: Dr. Yaffe," *Chronicle-Herald,* January 18, 1985, quoted in Smyth, *Subversive Elements,* 257; Gillian Thomas to the Editor, *Rural Delivery* 8, no. 4 (September 1983).

165 *Arts Magazine,* n.d., clipping file, PANS-BP, vol. 3470, no. 6; "Civil Jury Rules Dr. Smyth Did Not Defame Dr. Yaffe," quoted in Smyth, *Subversive Elements,* 258.

166 *Report of the Nova Scotia Royal Commission on Uranium Mining;* EAC Board of Directors Meeting minutes, July 17, 1985, PANS-EAC, vol. 3421, no. 5.

CHAPTER 5: WATERMELONS AND MARKET GREENS

1 The value of Nova Scotia as a lens through which to view Canadian and North American environmentalism in general is particularly great in view of the persistence of this rural

vitality: while much of the rest of the country continued in rapid urbanization throughout the 1980s, Nova Scotia's proportion of rural population remained large and consistent throughout the late decades of the twentieth century, a population from which new rural activists appeared. Nationally, the percentage of rural population fell from 24 to 19 percent from 1981 to 2011; in Nova Scotia it fell only slightly, from 45 to 43 percent. New Brunswick and Prince Edward Island shared similarly high proportions of rural residents. Statistics Canada, "Population, Urban and Rural, by Province and Territory," http://www.statcan. gc.ca/tables-tableaux/sum-som/l01/cst01/demo62d-eng.htm.

2 Barbara Clark, Wallace, Cumberland Resists Unhealthful Development (CRUD), to the Editor, *Rural Delivery* 5, no. 11 (April 1981); Harry Thurston, "The C.R.U.D. Hits the Fan in Cumberland County," *Atlantic Insight* 3, no. 6 (July 1981): 21–22; Chris Wood, "The Toxic Time Bomb," *Atlantic Insight* 3, no. 7 (August/September 1981): 84, 87–88, 91.

3 Civil disobedience in this case included dumping twenty kilograms of nails on the road to the site, among other actions. Kevin Cox, "Power but No Glory in Point Aconi," *Globe and Mail*, March 16, 1991, D2; Campbell Morrison, "Appeal Judges Reject Aconi Foes' Arguments," *Daily News*, June 7, 1991, 3; Susan LeBlanc, "Trial Begins for Greenpeace Activists," *Mail-Star*, December 14, 1990, D20; Alan Jeffers, "C.B.'s Future Black Like Coal," *Chronicle-Herald*, December 6, 1990, D8; Patricia Lynn Hutchinson, "Committee Concerned Over Effects of Proposed Point Aconi Project," *Chronicle-Herald*, June 26, 1990, D8.

4 Maude Barlow and Elizabeth May, *Frederick Street: Life and Death on Canada's Love Canal* (Toronto: HarperCollins, 2000), 55.

5 Ibid., 75; G.L. Trider and O.C. Vaidya, *An Assessment of Liquid Effluent Streams at Sydney Steel Corporation* (Ottawa: Environment Canada, Environmental Protection Service, Atlantic Region, 1980).

6 Bruno Marcocchio to the Editor, *Cape Breton Post*, February 7, 2004, http://www. safecleanup.com; Glenn Hanam to the Editor, *Cape Breton Post*, March 6, 2004, http:// www.safecleanup.com. Much the same process was applied to the Point Aconi controversy: Randy Jones, "Citizen's Groups Want to Be Taken Seriously," *Mail-Star*, March 3, 1993, D5.

7 Dr. Beth MacCormick and Leon Dubinsky, to EAC, n.d., DAL-EAC, box 45.11.

8 Shepard Krech, *The Ecological Indian: Myth and History* (New York: W.W. Norton, 1999).

9 "The Battle of Kelly's Mountain," 1989, Acadia University Esther Clark Wright Archives, Kings Environment Group fonds [hereafter KEG], file 74; Hornborg, "Environmentalism, Ethnicity and Sacred Places."

The business of quarrying gravel for the US market moved on to Digby County soon after the Kelly's Mountain failure, and spent many years attempting to find a foothold there: "Society for the Preservation of the Eastern Head," August 13, 1990, KEG, file 81.

10 EAC to "Friends," March 8, 1984, DAL-EAC, box 29.6; "Plan 'B': The Administrative Law Route," n.d., DAL-EAC, box 24.9.

11 "Grant Application to Public Awareness Program for Science and Technology" (rejected), May 14, 1984, DAL-EAC, box 37.10; "Grant Application to Public Awareness Program for Science and Technology" (rejected), October 15, 1985, DAL-EAC, box 37.10; "Report on FOE Pesticides Lobby," 1983, DAL-EAC, box 37.8. EAC also pursued more consultation with the province: memo, 1985, PANS-EAC, vol. 3433, no. 27.

12 Clipping file, PANS-BP, vol. 3469, no. 8; David Israelson, *Toronto Star*, January 10, 1987, clipping file, PANS-EAC, vol. 3433, no. 29.

13 Ralph Surette, "Fear of Spraying," *Atlantic Insight* 5, no. 7 (July 1983): 32. Forester and author Ralph Johnson, for example, had his history of the forests of Nova Scotia edited by government printers to remove anti-clearcutting sections. Johnson to T.C. De Fayer, February 7, 1985, Public Archives of Nova Scotia, Ralph S. Johnson fonds, vol. 2863, no. 40, cited in Paul Webster, "Pining for Trees: The History of Dissent against Forest Destruction in Nova Scotia 1749–1991" (MA thesis, Dalhousie University, 1991).

14 *Q/L SSEPA News* 2, no. 3 (September/October 1983).

15 *Chronicle-Herald,* August 31, 1983, 2.

16 *Q/L SSEPA News* 2, no. 3 (September/October 1983).

17 Duncan MacLellan, "A Study of Selected New Brunswick, Nova Scotia, Regional, and National Forestry Sector Interest Groups," report for the Council of Maritime Premiers, n.d., DAL-EAC, box 46.13.

18 David Orton, "Deep Ecology and the Green Movement," 1986–87, Greenweb, http://home.ca.inter.net/~greenweb/DE&Green_Movement.html.

19 Diana Cole, "National ENGO Meeting in Ottawa, 1983," *Q/L SSEPA News* 2, no. 1 (June 1983).

20 Presentation by Nova Scotia Department of Environment, Halifax hearing, January 27, 1983, RCOF, vol. 158b, no. 3; "EAC Response to the NS Pest Control Products Act," October 1985, DAL- EAC, box 41.15.

21 David Orton, "Informed Consent or Informed Rejection of Pesticide Use: A Concept for Environmental Action," *Philosophy and Social Action* 16, no. 4 (October/December 1990), KEG, file 61.

22 Charlie Restino, CAP, to Premier Buchanan, May 26, 1988, KEG, file 61.

23 Jerry White, Sprayers of Dioxin, to Neil Livingston, September 10, 1984, DAL-EAC, box 24.9; Sherri Cline and Judy Davis, to Neil Livingston, October 15, 1984, DAL-EAC, box 24.9.

24 Farley Mowat, "Grass Roots Crusader: Elizabeth May and the Budworm Battle," in *Rescue the Earth; Conversations with the Green Crusaders* (Toronto: McLelland and Stewart, 1990), 188–205; *Between the Issues* 4, no. 2 (July/August 1984).

25 Quoted in David Orton, "Problems Facing the Green Movement in Canada and Nova Scotia – Greenweb Bulletin #17," *Greenweb*, January 1990, http://home.ca.inter.net/~greenweb/%20Problems_Green_Movement.pdf, accessed Summer 2013.

26 Ibid.; Webster, "Pining for Trees," 209.

27 "II. Energy Conservation – Economic Aspects," CCNR briefs, June 3, 1980, PANS-EAC, vol. 3422, no. 2; "A Soft Energy Path for Canada," *Alternatives* 12, no. 1 (Fall 1984); "2025: Soft Energy Futures for Canada – 1988 Update," DAL-EAC, box 12.8.

28 Susan Holtz, report on Environment Canada's stakeholder group – State of the Environment Advisory Group, May 1986, DAL-EAC, box 32.16; Deborah Jones, "Energy Conservation Saving Money in Atlantic Canada," *Atlantic Insight* 6, no. 11 (November 1984): 19–21; Susan Holtz, "Energy Policy from an Environmental Perspective: The Core Elements," September 1987, DAL-EAC, box 15.15.

29 Susan Holtz, "The Philosophers Confer," *Between the Issues* 3, no. 6 (February/March 1984).

30 "Proposal for an Atlantic Environmental Newsletter" to Environment Canada by EAC, February 12, 1981, DAL-EAC, box 44.3.

31 EAC Board of Directors Meeting minutes, November 5, 1988, PANS-EAC, vol. 3421, no. 6.

32 Susan Holtz to "environmentalists," October 7, 1980, PANS-EAC, vol. 3434, no. 9; Susan Holtz, "Report on 1987-88 Activities of Ecology Action Center Senior Researcher Susan

Holtz," April 30, 1988, PANS-EAC, vol. 3421, no. 6; Annual Report 1987–88, April 30, 1988, PANS-EAC, vol. 3421, no. 6.

33 EAC Annual Report 1987–88, April 30, 1988, PANS-EAC, vol. 3421, no. 6.

34 EAC Board of Directors Meeting minutes, February 25, 1981, PANS-EAC, vol. 3420, no. 25. Membership supplied $10,000 to $11,000, less than a third of the centre's total funds, in 1986, for example, declining to only about $8,000 the following year. "EAC Unaudited Financial Statements for the Year Ended March 31, 1986," DAL-EAC, box 23.19; "EAC Unaudited Financial Statements for the Year Ended March 31, 1987," DAL-EAC, box 23.19.

35 EAC Board of Directors Meeting minutes, December 4, 1985, PANS-EAC, vol. 3421, no. 5.

36 EAC Board of Directors Meeting minutes, multiple dates, 1985, PANS-EAC, vol. 3421, no. 3.

37 EAC Board of Directors Meeting minutes, May 15, 1985, PANS-EAC, vol. 3421, no. 5; EAC Board of Directors Meeting minutes, March 25, 1981, PANS-EAC, vol. 3420, no. 25; Lois Corbett, "Co-Director's Report," April 21, 1990, PANS-EAC, vol. 3421, no. 8.

38 EAC Board of Directors Meeting minutes, June 13, 1988, PANS-EAC, vol. 3421, no. 6.

39 David Orton, "Problems Facing the Green Movement in Canada and Nova Scotia – Greenweb Bulletin #17," Greenweb, http://home.ca.inter.net/~greenweb/%20Problems_Green_Movement.pdf, accessed Summer 2013.

40 EAC press release, October 9, 1986, DAL-EAC, box 38.15; "Application for Approval – Resource Management and Pollution Control Division, NSPC," 1990, KEG, file 66.

41 Ian Sherman to the Editor, Scotia Sun, n.d., RCOF, vol. 191, file 1 [emphasis in original].

42 Michael Clow, "A Left-Environmentalist Perspective on Canadian Industrial Strategy," paper presented at the Canadian Political Science Association 1981 Annual Meeting, May 27–29, 1981, DAL-EAC, box 44.4. An earlier example of socialist ecological thought in Canada was the editorial position of the radical leftist journal Our Generation, which insisted on the common opposition to "a system of natural and human exploitation and domination." Our Generation 7, no. 1 (January-February 1970): 4.

43 Charlie Restino, article clipping, 1987, DAL-EAC, box 29.9.

44 David Orton, "Discussion Paper: The Green Movement and Our Place in It – Position of the North Shore Environmental Web," 1988, Greenweb, http://home.ca.inter.net/~greenweb/NSEW_Position_on_Green_Movement.pdf.

45 Orton, "Informed Consent or Informed Rejection of Pesticide Use"; Patrick Curry, Ecological Ethics: An Introduction (Cambridge: Polity, 2006), 84–88.

46 "Gathering of the Greens," August 3–5, 1990, PANS-BP, vol. 3476, no. 12; "NSEN," 1990, KEG, file 66.

47 Holtz, "The Philosophers Confer."

48 David Orton, "The Greens: An Introduction," in Toward a New Maritimes: A Selection from Ten Years of New Maritimes, ed. Scott Milsom and Ian McKay (Charlottetown: Ragweed Press, 1992 [1990]), 281–85.

49 David Orton, "The North Shore Environmental Web," n.d., PANS-EAC, vol. 3423, no. 14; Letter, Elizabeth May to "Susans," n.d., DAL-EAC, box 44.1; David Orton, "Forestry Herbicide Use: A Hazard to Our Environment," 1988, Greenweb, http://home.ca.inter.net/~greenweb/Forestry_Herbicide_Use.pdf; Q/L SSEPA News 2, no. 1 (June 1983).

50 "Building a Green Nova Scotia," NSEN submission to Nova Scotia Roundtable on Environment and Economy, 1991, DAL-EAC, box 19.4; "AEN Meeting: General Footage, May 11–13, 1990," video, DAL-EAC, box 5.53.

51 "International Uranium Congress," June 15, 1988, PANS-EAC, vol. 3424, no. 28.

52 The three-part relationship finds echoes in, for example, Jennifer Read, "'Let Us Heed the Voice of Youth': Laundry Detergents, Phosphates, and the Emergence of the Environmental Movement in Ontario," *Journal of the Canadian Historical Association* 7, no. 1 (1996): 227–50; Jane Barr, "The Origins and Emergence of Quebec's Environmental Movement: 1970–1985" (MA thesis, McGill University, 1995); Frank Zelko, "Making Greenpeace: The Development of Direct Action Environmentalism in British Columbia," *BC Studies* 142/143 (Summer 2004): 197–239; Ryan O'Connor, *The First Green Wave: Pollution Probe and the Origins of Environmental Activism in Ontario* (Vancouver: UBC Press, 2014); Van Huizen, "Flooding the Border"; and John-Henry Harter, "Environmental Justice for Whom? Class, New Social Movements, and the Environment: A Case Study of Greenpeace Canada, 1971–2000," *Labour/Le Travail* 54 (Fall 2004): 83–119.

53 Dominique Clément, *Canada's Rights Revolution* (Vancouver: UBC Press, 2008), 204. The US comparison may be made with Paul Sutter, *Driven Wild: How the Fight against Automobiles Launched the Modern Wilderness Movement* (Seattle: University of Washington Press, 2002).

54 Hornborg, "Environmentalism, Ethnicity, and Sacred Places," 259.

55 Ibid., 263.

56 Marie Vandergraaf, transcripts of New Ross hearing, hearing #1, April 2, 1982, RCU, vol. 195, no. 12.

57 As remarked by Rod Bantjes (and in Chapter 4), this is not the story often told of a female-dominated movement: Bantjes and Trussler, "Feminism and the Grass Roots," 183. For similar findings in places outside Nova Scotia, see S. Cable, "Women's Social Movement Involvement: The Role of Structural Availability in Recruitment and Participation Processes," *Sociological Quarterly* 33, no. 1 (1992): 35–50. The mythology, however, has had a strong grip on the movement itself, as seen in Elizabeth May's statement that "women are essentially *different* from men ... operate more from a left-brained intuitive thought process. We are biologically and spiritually connected to the cosmos ... by nature, much more *selfless* than men." May, "Gaia Women," in Farley Mowat, ed., *Rescue the Earth! Conversations with the Green Crusaders* (Toronto: McClelland and Stewart, 1990), 249.

58 May, *Budworm Battles,* 116; May, "Gaia Women."

Bibliography

PRIMARY SOURCES

Archives

Acadia University Esther Clark Wright Archives
Harrison Flint Lewis fonds, accession 2006.020-LEW
Kings Environment Group fonds, accession 1996–001-KEG

Dalhousie University Archives and Special Collections
Dalhousie University Institute of Public Affairs/Henson College fonds, UA-26
Ecology Action Centre fonds, MS-11-13
Movement for Citizens Voice and Action fonds, MS-11-1

Personal Papers
Brian Gifford papers, in the possession of Brian Gifford, Halifax, Nova Scotia
Rudy Haase papers, in the possession of Rudy Haase, Chester, Nova Scotia

Public Archives of Nova Scotia (PANS)
Department of Lands and Forests fonds, MG20
Ecology Action Centre fonds, MG20
Man and Resources Program fonds, MG20
McInnes fonds, RG44
Nova Scotia Royal Commission on Forestry fonds, RG44
Betty Peterson fonds, MG1
Gerald Regan fonds, RG100
Royal Commission on Uranium Mining fonds, RG44
South Shore Environmental Protection Association fonds, MG20
Universalist Unitarian Church fonds, MG4

Interviews

Bishop, Roy, January 16, 2012, via telephone
Cameron, Silver Donald, November 1, 2011, Halifax, Nova Scotia
Gifford, Brian, February 22, 2013, Halifax, Nova Scotia
Haase, Martin Rudy, October 9, 2011, Chester, Nova Scotia
Ruffman, Alan, February 21, 2012, Halifax, Nova Scotia

Periodicals

4th Estate (Halifax)
Atlantic Insight
Between the Issues (Halifax)
Cape Breton Post
Chronicle-Herald (Halifax)
Daily News (Halifax)
Dartmouth Free Press
Evening News (New Glasgow)
Forest Times (Halifax)
Globe and Mail (Toronto)
Halifax Field Naturalists Newsletter
Hants Journal
Mail-Star (Halifax)
Montreal Gazette
Montreal Star
Mysterious East (Fredericton)
Nuclear Reaction (New Brunswick)
Queens/Lunenburg SSEPA News
Rural Delivery (Liverpool)
Truro Daily News

Government Reports

Department of Lands and Forests. *Nova Scotia Forest Inventory: Cape Breton Island Subdivision 1970.* Halifax: Lands and Forests, 1970.

Government of Nova Scotia. *Supplement to the Public Accounts of the Province of Nova Scotia for the Year Ended March 31, 1977.* Halifax: Queen's Printer, 1978.

McInnes, Russell. *Report of the Royal Commission into the Nova Scotia Light and Power Company Ltd. Gold River Hydro Development.* Halifax: Government of Nova Scotia, 1961.

Province of Nova Scotia. *Annual Report: Environmental Control Council: For the Year Ending Dec. 31 1974.* Department of Environment Library, reference number 354.33.

Province of Nova Scotia, Department of Mines and Energy. *Uranium in Nova Scotia: A Background Summary for the Uranium Inquiry – Nova Scotia, Report 82–7.* Halifax: Government of Nova Scotia, 1982.

Report of the Nova Scotia Royal Commission on Uranium Mining. Halifax: Queen's Printer, 1985.

Report of the Task Force Operation Oil (Clean-up of the Arrow Oil Spill in Chedabucto Bay) to the Minister of Transport. Ottawa: Information Canada, 1970.

Rust Associates. *A Review of the Boat Harbour Waste Treatment Facilities for Nova Scotia Water Resources Commission*. Montreal: Rust Associates, 1970.

Science Council of Canada. *Canada as a Conserver Society: Resource Uncertainties and the Need for New Technologies*. Report No. 27. Ottawa: SCC, 1977.

–. *Natural Resource Policy Issues in Canada*. Report No.19. Ottawa: SCC, 1973.

Statistics Canada. *Census Divisions and Subdivisions, Population, Occupied Private Dwellings, Private Households and Census and Economic Families in Private Households, Selected Social and Economic Characteristics, Nova Scotia*. Toronto: Statistics Canada, 1983. http://archive.org/details/1981959851983engfra.

–. "Population, Urban and Rural, by Province and Territory." http://www.statcan.gc.ca/tables-tableaux/sum-som/l01/cst01/demo62d-eng.htm.

Trider, G.L., and O.C. Vaidya. *An Assessment of Liquid Effluent Streams at Sydney Steel Corporation*. Ottawa: Environment Canada, Environmental Protection Service, Atlantic Region, 1980.

Other Primary Sources

Atlantic Canada Chapter, Northeast Atlantic International Section, Air Pollution Control Association. *Proceedings of the Sixth Annual Technical Meeting*. September 29–30, 1982.

Bedford Basin Pollution Committee. *Report of the Bedford Basin Pollution Committee of the Council of the Bedford Service Commission*. Bedford: Bedford Service Commission, 1970.

Bott, Robert, David Brooks, and John Robinson. *Life after Oil*. Edmonton: Hurtig, 1983.

Chanclor, William, and Pat Murphy. "Robert Whiting: What One Man Can Do." *Axiom* 2, no. 4 (May 1976): 6–9, 21.

Clow, Michael. "A Left-Environmentalist Perspective on Canadian Industrial Strategy." Paper presented at the Ecology Energy and Resources section of the Canadian Political Science Association 1981 Annual Meeting, Dalhousie University, Halifax, Nova Scotia, May 27–29, 1981.

Editorial. *Our Generation* 7, no. 1 (January-February 1970): 4.

Edwards, Gordon. "Nuclear Wastes: What, Me Worry?" 1978. http://www.ccnr.org/me_worry.html.

Folster, David. "Double Trouble – Power Bubble." *Maclean's*, October 6, 1980, 38–39.

Heritage Trust of Nova Scotia. *Annual Report 1970–1971*. Halifax: The Trust, 1971.

Holtz, Susan. *2025: Soft Energy Futures for Canada*. Vol. 3, *A Soft Energy Path for Nova Scotia*. Ottawa: Energy, Mines and Resources, 1983.

Laski, Heather. "A Costly Fight in Cape Breton." *Maclean's*, May 9, 1983, 20.

Lovins, Amory, and Hunter Lovins. "Introduction." In *Life after Oil*, by Robert Bott, David Brooks, and John Robinson. Edmonton: Hurtig, 1983.

May, Elizabeth. *Budworm Battles*. Halifax: Four East, 1982.

–. "A Case History of Citizen Action Victory." *PEI Environeer* 6, no.3 (1978): 23.

"Moncton Conference Notes: 'Experts in Society' by Dr Woollard." *Southern New Brunswick Nuclear News* 15 (February-March 1981).

Rushton, Don. "So Long, Stage II: McCleave Gets Set to Ride Off into the Sunset." *New Maritimes* 2, no. 6 (March 1984): 10–11.

Smyth, Donna. "Selling Radon Daughters: Uranium in Nova Scotia." *Canadian Forum* 61, no. 714 (December/January 1981): 6–8.

–. *Subversive Elements.* Toronto: Women's Press, 1986.

"Special Report: A Soft Energy Path for Canada." *Alternatives* 12 (Fall 1984): 1.

Torrie, Ralph. "BC's Inquiry and Moratorium." *CCNR's Transitions* 3, no. 1 (May 1980): 1.

Secondary Sources

AECL. *Canada Enters the Nuclear Age.* Montreal: McGill-Queen's University Press, 1997.

Almeida, Paul, and Linda Brewster Stearns. "Political Opportunities and Local Grassroots Environmental Movements: The Case of Minamata." *Social Problems* 45, no. 1 (February 1998): 37–60. http://dx.doi.org/10.2307/3097142.

Arsenault, Chris. *Blowback: A Canadian History of Agent Orange and the War at Home.* Halifax: Fernwood, 2009.

Ashforth, Adam. "Reckoning Schemes of Legitimation: On Commissions of Inquiry as Power/Knowledge Forms." *Journal of Historical Sociology* 3, no. 1 (March 1990): 1–22. http://dx.doi.org/10.1111/j.1467-6443.1990.tb00143.x.

Bantjes, Rod, and Tanya Trussler. "Feminism and the Grass Roots: Women and Environmentalism in Nova Scotia, 1980–1983." *Canadian Review of Sociology and Anthropology* 36, no. 2 (1999): 179–98. http://dx.doi.org/10.1111/j.1755-618X.1999.tb01274.x.

Barlow, Maude, and Elizabeth May. *Frederick Street: Life and Death on Canada's Love Canal.* Toronto: HarperCollins, 2000.

Barr, Jane. "The Origins and Emergence of Quebec's Environmental Movement: 1970–1985." MA thesis, McGill University, 1995.

Blum, Elizabeth. *Love Canal Revisited: Race, Class, and Gender in Environmental Activism.* Lawrence: University Press of Kansas, 2008.

Bothwell, Robert. *Nucleus: The History of Atomic Energy of Canada Limited.* Toronto: University of Toronto Press, 1988.

Cable, S. "Women's Social Movement Involvement: The Role of Structural Availability in Recruitment and Participation Processes." *Sociological Quarterly* 33, no. 1 (1992): 35–50. http://dx.doi.org/10.1111/j.1533-8525.1992.tb00362.x.

Cameron, Silver Donald. *The Education of Everett Richardson: The Nova Scotia Fishermen's Strike 1970–71.* Toronto: McLelland and Stewart, 1977.

Campbell, Claire, ed. *A Century of Parks Canada, 1911–2011.* Calgary: University of Calgary, 2011.

Carson, Rachel. *Silent Spring.* New York: Fawcett Crest, 1962.

Clément, Dominique. *Canada's Rights Revolution.* Vancouver: UBC Press, 2008.

Conrad, Margaret. "The Atlantic Revolution of the 1950s." In *Beyond Anger and Longing: Community and Development in Atlantic Canada,* ed. Berkeley Fleming, 55–98. Fredericton: Acadiensis, 1988.

Crossley, Nick. *Making Sense of Social Movements.* Buckingham, UK: Open University Press, 2002.

Curry, Patrick. *Ecological Ethics: An Introduction.* Cambridge: Polity, 2006.

De Marchi, Bruna. "Seveso: From Pollution to Regulation." *International Journal of Environment and Pollution* 7, no. 4 (September 1997): 526–37.

Dobson, Andrew. *Green Political Thought.* London: Routledge, 2000 (original work published in 1990).

Doern, Bruce, and Thomas Conway. *The Greening of Canada: Federal Institutions and Decisions*. Toronto: University of Toronto Press, 1994.

Early, Francis. "'A Grandly Subversive Time': The Halifax Branch of the Voice of Women in the 1960s." In *Mothers of the Municipality*, ed. Judith Fingard and Janet Guildford, 253–80. Toronto: University of Toronto Press, 2005.

Edwards, Gordon. "Canada's Nuclear Industry and the Myth of the Peaceful Atom." In *Canada and the Nuclear Arms Race*, ed. Ernie Regehr and Simon Rosenblum, 122–70. Toronto: James Lorimer, 1983.

Egbers, Adrian. "Going Nuclear: The Origins of New Brunswick's Nuclear Industry, 1950–1983." MA thesis, Dalhousie University, 2008.

Environment Canada. Emergencies Science and Technology Division. "Bunker C Fuel Oil (Irving Whale)." Ottawa: n.d. http://www.etc-cte.ec.gc.ca/databases/Oilproperties.

Evans, Sterling. *The Green Republic: A Conservation History of Costa Rica*. Austin: University of Texas Press, 1999.

Evenden, Matthew. *Fish versus Power: An Environmental History of the Fraser River*. Cambridge: Cambridge University Press, 2004. http://dx.doi.org/10.1017/CBO9780511512032.

Forbes, Ernest. *The Maritime Rights Movement 1919–1927: A Study in Canadian Regionalism*. Montreal and Kingston: McGill-Queen's University Press, 1979.

Froese-Stoddard, Alison. "Ship Harbour National Park: The Breakdown between National Agendas and Local Interests." Unpublished manuscript (2011–12). Adapted to Alison Froese-Stoddard, "A Conservation 'Could Have Been': Ship Harbour National Park," NiCHE Canada, *The Otter* blog, http://niche-canada.org/2012/08/02/a-conservation -could-have-been-ship-harbour-national-park/.

Giddens, Anthony. *The Consequences of Modernity*. Stanford, CA: Stanford University Press, 1990.

Gottlieb, Robert. *Forcing the Spring: The Transformation of the American Environmental Movement*. Washington, DC: Island Press, 1993.

Guha, Ramachandra. *Environmentalism: A Global History*. New York: Longman, 2000.

–. *How Much Should a Person Consume? Environmentalism in India and the United States*. Los Angeles: University of California Press, 2006.

–. "Radical American Environmentalism and Wilderness Preservation: A Third World Critique." *Environmental Ethics* 11, no. 1 (1989): 71–83. http://dx.doi.org/10.5840/enviro ethics198911123.

–. *The Unquiet Woods: Ecological Change and Peasant Resistance in the Himalaya*. 2nd ed. Oxford: Oxford University Press, 1989.

Guha, Ramachandra, and Juan Martinez-Alier. *Varieties of Environmentalism: Essays North and South*. London: Earthscan, 1997.

Habermas, Jürgen. "New Social Movements." *Telos* 1981, no. 49 (1981): 33–37. http://dx. doi.org/10.3817/0981049033.

Haq, Gary, and Alistair Paul. *Environmentalism since 1945*. London: Routledge, 2012.

Hardin, Garret. "The Tragedy of the Commons." *Science* 162, no. 3859 (December 13, 1968): 1243–48. http://dx.doi.org/10.1126/science.162.3859.1243.

Harding, Jim. *Canada's Deadly Secret: Saskatchewan Uranium and the Global Nuclear System*. Halifax: Fernwood, 2007.

Harley, J. Brian. "Maps, Knowledge, and Power." In *The Iconography of Landscape*, ed. D. Cosgrove and S. Daniels, 277–312. Cambridge: Cambridge University Press, 1988.

Harter, John-Henry. "Environmental Justice for Whom? Class, New Social Movements, and the Environment: A Case Study of Greenpeace Canada, 1971–2000." *Labour/Le Travail* 54 (Fall 2004): 83–119. http://dx.doi.org/10.2307/25149506.

Hays, Samuel. *Beauty, Health, and Permanence: Environmental Politics in the United States, 1955–1985.* Cambridge: Cambridge University Press, 1987. http://dx.doi.org/10.1017/CBO9780511664106.

Helvarg, David. *The War against the Greens: The 'Wise Use' Movement, the New Right, and Anti-Environmental Violence.* San Francisco: Sierra Club Books, 1994.

Herrington, William, and George Rounsefell. "Restoration of the Atlantic Salmon in New England." *Transactions of the American Fisheries Society* 70, no. 1 (1941): 123–27. http://dx.doi.org/10.1577/1548-8659(1940)70[123:ROTASI]2.0.CO;2.

Hornborg, Alf. "Environmentalism, Ethnicity and Sacred Places: Reflections on Modernity, Discourse and Power." *Canadian Review of Sociology and Anthropology* 31, no. 3 (1994): 245–67. http://dx.doi.org/10.1111/j.1755-618X.1994.tb00948.x.

–. "Undermining Modernity: Protecting Landscapes and Meanings among the Mi'kmaq of Nova Scotia." In *Political Ecology across Spaces, Scales, and Social Groups,* ed. Susan Paulson and Lisa Gezon, 196–216. New Brunswick, NJ: Rutgers University Press, 2004.

Hutchison, George, and Dick Wallace. *Grassy Narrows.* Scarborough, ON: Van Nostrand Reinhold, 1977.

Huxley, Aldous. *Do What You Will.* London: Chatto and Windus, 1956 (original work published in 1929).

Inglehart, Ronald. *The Silent Revolution: Changing Values and Political Styles among Western Publics.* Princeton, NJ: Princeton University Press, 1977.

Kenny, James, and Andrew Secord. "Engineering Modernity: Hydroelectric Development in New Brunswick, 1945–1970." *Acadiensis* (Fredericton) 39, no. 1 (Winter/Spring 2010): 3–26.

Kinkela, David. *DDT and the American Century.* Chapel Hill: University of North Carolina Press, 2011.

Krech, Shepard. *The Ecological Indian: Myth and History.* New York: W.W. Norton, 1999.

Kuhn, Thomas. *The Structure of Scientific Revolutions.* Chicago: University of Chicago Press, 1962.

Latour, Bruno. *We Have Never Been Modern.* Cambridge, MA: Harvard University Press, 1993 (original work published in 1991).

Loo, Tina. "People in the Way: Modernity, Society, and Environment on the Arrow Lakes." *BC Studies* 142/143 (Summer/Autumn 2004): 161–96.

–. *States of Nature: Conserving Canada's Wildlife in the Twentieth Century.* Vancouver: UBC Press, 2006.

MacEachern, Alan. *The Institute of Man and Resources: An Environmental Fable.* Charlottetown: Island Studies Press, 2003.

–. *Natural Selections: National Parks in Atlantic Canada, 1935–1970.* Montreal and Kingston: McGill-Queen's University Press, 2001.

Martinez-Alier, Juan. *Ecological Economics: Energy, Environment, and Society.* Oxford: Basil Blackwell, 1990.

–. *The Environmentalism of the Poor: A Study of Ecological Conflicts and Valuation.* Northhampton, UK: Edward Elgar, 2002. http://dx.doi.org/10.4337/9781843765486.

Martini, Edwin. *Agent Orange: History, Science, and the Politics of Uncertainty.* Boston: University of Massachusetts Press, 2012.

May, Elizabeth. "Gaia Women." In *Rescue the Earth! Conversations with the Green Crusaders,* ed. Farley Mowat, 247–65. Toronto: McClelland and Stewart, 1990.

McLaughlin, Mark. "Green Shoots: Aerial Insecticide Spraying and the Growth of Environmental Consciousness in New Brunswick, 1952–1973." *Acadiensis* (Fredericton) 40, no. 1 (Winter/Spring 2011): 3–23.

Meadows, Donella, Dennis Meadows, Jørgen Randers, and William Behrens III. *The Limits to Growth.* New York: Universe, 1972.

Mersey Tobeatic Research Institute. "Mersey Messages – Old Lake Rossignol." March 10, 2009. http://www.merseytobeatic.ca/pdfs/Mersey%20Messages/Mersey%20Messages%20March%2010%202009.pdf.

Mowat, Farley. *Rescue the Earth; Conversations with the Green Crusaders.* Toronto: McLelland and Stewart, 1990.

Naess, Arne. *The Ecology of Wisdom: Writings by Arne Naess.* Berkeley: Counterpoint, 2008.

Nelson, Jennifer. *Razing Africville: A Geography of Racism.* Toronto: University of Toronto Press, 2008.

O'Connor, Ryan. *The First Green Wave: Pollution Probe and the Origins of Environmental Activism in Ontario.* Vancouver: UBC Press, 2014.

Orton, David. "The Greens: An Introduction." In *Toward a New Maritimes: A Selection from Ten Years of New Maritimes,* ed. Scott Milsom and Ian McKay, 281–85. Charlottetown: Ragweed Press, 1992 (original work published 1990).

Parra, Francisco. *Oil Politics: A Modern History of Petroleum.* London: I.B. Tauris, 2004.

Pasternak, Judy. *Yellow Dirt: A Poisoned Land and a People Betrayed.* New York: Free Press, 2010.

Pepper, David. *Modern Environmentalism.* London: Routledge, 1996. http://dx.doi.org/10.4324/9780203412244.

Rangarajan, Mahesh. *Fencing the Forest: Conservation and Ecological Change in India's Central Provinces 1860–1914.* Delhi: Oxford University Press, 1996.

Read, Jennifer. "'Let Us Heed the Voice of Youth': Laundry Detergents, Phosphates, and the Emergence of the Environmental Movement in Ontario." *Journal of the Canadian Historical Association* 7, no. 1 (1996): 227–50. http://dx.doi.org/10.7202/031109ar.

Robinson, Danielle. "Modernism at a Crossroad: The Spadina Expressway Controversy in Toronto, Ontario ca. 1960–1971." *Canadian Historical Review* 92, no. 2 (June 2011): 295–322.

Rootes, Christopher, ed. *Environmental Movements: Local, National, and Global.* Portland, OR: Frank Cass, 1999.

Sandberg, L. Anders. "Forest Policy in Nova Scotia: The Big Lease, Cape Breton Island, 1899–1960." *Acadiensis* (Fredericton) 20, no. 2 (Spring 1991): 105–28.

Savoie, Donald. *Regional Economic Development: Canada's Search for Solutions.* Toronto: University of Toronto, 1992.

Savoie, Donald, and John Chenier. "The State and Development: The Politics of Regional Development Policy." In *Still Living Together: Recent Trends and Future Directions in Canadian Regional Development,* ed. William Coffey and Mario Polese, 407–22. Montreal: Institute for Research on Public Policy, 1998.

Schumacher, E.F. *Small Is Beautiful.* London: Blond and Briggs, 1973.

Scott, James C. *Seeing Like a State: How Certain Schemes to Improve the Human Condition Have Failed.* New Haven, CT: Yale University Press, 1998.

Smith, Jennifer. "Intergovernmental Relations, Legitimacy, and the Atlantic Accords." *Constitutional Forum* 17, no. 3 (2008): 81–98.

Sutter, Paul. *Driven Wild: How the Fight against Automobiles Launched the Modern Wilderness Movement.* Seattle: University of Washington Press, 2002.

Thomas, P. "The Kouchibouguac National Park Controversy: Over a Decade Strong." *Park News* 17, no. 1 (1981): 11–13.

Thompson, E.P. *Customs in Common.* London: Merlin Press, 1991.

Thurston, Harry. *The Sea among the Rocks.* East Lawrencetown, NS: Pottersfield Press, 2002.

Van Huizen, Philip. "Flooding the Border: Development, Politics, and Environmental Controversy in the Canadian-U.S. Skagit Valley." PhD dissertation, University of British Columbia, 2013.

Vandermeulen, J.H., and D.E. Buckley. "The Kurdistan Oil Spill of March 16–17, 1979: Activities and Observations of the Bedford Institute of Oceanography Response Team." Canadian Technical Report of Hydrography and Ocean Sciences No. 35. Ottawa, January 1985. http://www.dfo-mpo.gc.ca/Library/90618.pdf.

Webster, Paul. "Pining for Trees: The History of Dissent against Forest Destruction in Nova Scotia 1749–1991." MA thesis, Dalhousie University, 1991.

Worster, Donald. *Nature's Economy.* Cambridge: Cambridge University Press, 1998.

Wright, Miriam. *A Fishery for Modern Times: The State and Industrialization of the Newfoundland Fishery, 1934–1968.* Don Mills, ON: Oxford, 2001.

Zelko, Frank. "Making Greenpeace: The Development of Direct Action Environmentalism in British Columbia." *BC Studies* 142/143 (Summer 2004): 197–239.

Index

NATURE | HISTORY | SOCIETY

GENERAL EDITOR: GRAEME WYNN